A DATED TYPE-SERIES
OF LONDON MEDIEVAL POTTERY

PART 4: SURREY WHITEWARES

A DATED TYPE-SERIES
OF LONDON MEDIEVAL POTTERY

PART 4: SURREY WHITEWARES

Jaqueline Pearce and Alan Vince,
with Anne Jenner, Michael Cowell and Jeremy Haslam

Published by the London & Middlesex
Archaeological Society

First published 1988

Typeset and printed by BAS Printers Limited,
Over Wallop, Hampshire

Design and production: Melissa Denny of
Diptych

Cover transparency: Louise Woodman

ISBN 0 903290 34 0

**The Society is grateful to English
Heritage for a grant towards the
publication of this special paper**

CONTENTS

INTRODUCTION

ABSTRACT

White-firing, sandy earthenwares were one of the main types of pottery used in London from the middle of the 13th century until the 16th century. They came from a number of sources in Surrey and along the Surrey-Hampshire border and can be divided into four classes based on fabric, manufacturing techniques and typology. Three of these classes appear to come from geographically distinct areas, and are termed Kingston-type ware, Coarse Border ware and Cheam whiteware. The fourth ware is commonly, but incorrectly, termed 'Tudor Green' ware, and appears to have been a minor product of all three industries. A type-series of forms and decoration for all four wares is published here, based on material found in the City of London. Evidence for the date-range and frequency of these types is presented, and the implications of these data for the origins and relationships of the industries are discussed.

This book is the fourth in a series which, when complete, will form a dated corpus of medieval pottery found in the City of London. Excavations carried out since 1973 by the Department of Urban Archaeology (DUA) have produced considerable quantities of pottery, mainly in the form of sherds. A significant number of assemblages come from contexts for which an absolute date can be given. Collections made by the museums serving London and by interested individuals during the late 19th and early 20th centuries have accumulated what is undoubtedly the largest collection of substantially complete medieval pots in this country, if not in Europe. The majority of these vessels are now housed in the Museum of London reserve collection, and a smaller number in the British Museum, with material in the possession of other museums in London and the Home Counties providing many valuable additions to these collections. Most of the complete pots were found in wells, cellars and pit fills in the course of construction work, often in associa-

tion with other, fragmentary vessels. However, records of the context and circumstances of discovery were seldom made. Careful study of both fragmentary, excavated pottery and of the complete vessels has allowed the two forms of evidence to be combined and to complement each other. One provides data on the frequency of the types and their period of use in London; the other gives an extensive type-series and information on manufacturing methods and decorative schemes.

In the late medieval period Surrey whitewares accounted for up to two-thirds of all the pottery used in London. Because of the difficulties in distinguishing the products of the various kilns (see Appendices 4 and 5) and because of the essential similarities of the industries, many aspects of these wares are here discussed together. The central section of the book, the type-series, is arranged in four parts, one for each of the three main industries – Kingston-type ware, Coarse Border ware, Cheam whiteware – and one for the more problematic 'Tudor Green' ware. Within each section the pottery is illustrated and described by class, form and type of vessel. Summary statistics showing the relative frequency of Surrey whitewares in selected groups of pottery are given in Appendix 6, but a more complete record is kept in the Museum of London computer.

A study of medieval Surrey whitewares, which included an extensive type-series, was undertaken by Jeremy Haslam during 1971-4, as part of a research fellowship in the history of ceramics granted by the West Surrey College of Art and Design (Farnham). It was not possible at that time to construct a chronological framework, since the various sources producing Surrey whitewares had not been clearly defined, and the large pottery-rich revetment dumps behind the Thames waterfront in London had yet to be discovered. However, analysis of recently excavated material has now made it possible to extend the scope of Haslam's original work, and many of his drawings are included in the present work.

I SURREY WHITEWARES

The history of the classification of Surrey whitewares has been outlined by Clive Orton in the preliminary report on the pottery from Trig Lane and need not be repeated here (Orton 1982a, 94-7). The threefold classification which he proposed has been adopted here, with the addition of 'Tudor Green' ware, as the foundation of the present study. The earliest Surrey whitewares from London are dated *c.*1250 and are similar in fabric to pottery from a late medieval kiln at 70-72 Eden Street, Kingston upon Thames (TQ 1816 6920; Hinton 1980). They were therefore termed *Kingston-type ware*, although no archaeological evidence was known from Kingston for production as early as the mid-13th century. The term has been retained in this book, in spite of the more recent discovery of a group of whiteware wasters at 5-15 Bankside, SE1 (TQ 3236 8045), which are indistinguishable in form and fabric from the Kingston products (Dennis and Hinton 1983). No kilns producing such pottery have been found in Southwark.

Later Surrey whitewares have been separated into two main groups – those from Cheam and those from the Surrey-Hampshire border. The term *Farnborough Hill ware*, used by Orton for the second group, is thought to be too specific for the products of an industry whose kilns are known not only at Farnborough Hill, but also at Farnham and possibly at Ash (see Fig 3). We have therefore used the term *Coarse Border ware*, to differentiate it from *Border ware*, Orton's term for the products of the same region in the 17th and 18th centuries (Orton and Pearce 1984, 35). The term *Cheam whiteware* is used to refer to vessels from London which are identical in fabric and form to those from the kilns known at Cheam (Marshall 1924; Orton 1982b). Strictly speaking, since it cannot be proved that other centres were not also producing identical vessels, *Cheam-type whiteware* would be a more accurate name. However, the former term is well established in the literature, and to amend it might give the false impression that there is some reason to doubt that the London finds were made in the Cheam kilns.

The terminology, sources and date of '*Tudor Green*' ware have been discussed at length (for example, Holling 1977; Moorhouse 1979). However, although the name given to the ware is now seen to be misleading, it is probably too late to introduce a new terminology without causing further confusion. The term '*Tudor Green*' ware is used here to denote thin-walled, glazed vessels made in a white fabric without obvious visible inclusions. Vessels similar in form to 'Tudor Green' types, but whose fabrics are identical to Kingston-type ware or Coarse Border ware, are here treated as examples of those wares.

The abbreviations used in the Museum of London archive are given on page 173.

METHODS OF MANUFACTURE

With the exception of handmade forms, such as dripping dishes, all the Surrey whitewares from each of the main sources were thrown on a fast wheel. This is clearly shown by the parallel, horizontal throwing-marks which can be seen inside nearly all vessels, and, unless removed by subsequent treatment, outside as well. Some whiteware vessels also have closely-set ripples, or stretch-marks, spiralling up the body from the base. Experiments carried out by Anne Jenner have shown that such marks are produced during throwing on a fast wheel, by twisting the pot relative to the wheelhead. Certain forms are particularly susceptible to such stretching; for example, baluster jugs are almost invariably twisted where the clay was squeezed in to form the waisted base, after the vessel had become too tall or narrow for the potter to reach inside with his hand. Completely closed pots, such as money-boxes and urinals, also regularly show the same sort of ripples resulting from the twisting of the clay on the wheel.

With few exceptions, all the rim forms known in each of the Surrey whiteware industries could have been made using very simple finger positions. Certain Cheam whiteware forms were probably 'turned' after throwing, to trim the rim to the desired shape. Otherwise, there is no evidence that formers of metal, wood or bone were used, either when throwing the body, or in shaping the rim and base.

Evidence for the way in which pots were removed from the wheel is frequently obscured by subsequent treatment of the base, particularly by knife-trimming. However, a number of small, undecorated Kingston-type ware forms were clearly cut from the wheel by drawing a taut length of wire or gut straight across under the base. Cheam whiteware jugs are invariably flat-based and were seldom knife-trimmed. Many show that a looped wire was drawn under the base, leaving a distinctive fan-shaped mark in the clay.

The bases of most Kingston-type and Coarse Border ware jugs were relatively thick when thrown, and were then pared down with a knife to a thickness that was better suited to a safer and more even firing. Knife-trimming was also used to decorative effect on certain baluster jugs to produce a vertically facetted waist. However, on most Kingston-type and Coarse Border ware vessels, the process was carried out quickly and with little attention to the external appearance of the finished pot. Little trimming, if any, was necessary on Cheam whiteware jugs and other forms, although some appear to have been lightly shaved while being turned slowly on a wheel. The only form of base decoration of any importance is thumbing, which is described in detail below (see p. 34). Thumbed bases are common on Kingston-type ware and Coarse Border ware jugs, but are virtually unknown in Cheam whiteware.

Despite close examination there is no convincing evidence for the methods used to make Surrey whiteware jug handles, ie whether they were thrown or rolled. The methods used to attach the handles are varied and are described individually below in relation to the various forms. They appear to vary both within an industry and between industries, and can be a good indication of the 'school' of potting in which their makers were trained.

The various decorative techniques used on Surrey whiteware vessels are described in detail for each of the main industries. The greatest variety is found in Kingston-type ware, and the least in Cheam whiteware. A few early Kingston-type ware vessels were more or less completely coated with a white slip which was slightly lighter in colour than the body. Slip was also applied to Kingston-type ware jugs as a form of plastic decoration. The light-firing slip, which has here been termed 'white' slip, usually appears the same colour as the body, although it often lacks the sand inclusions characteristic of the body-clay. An iron-rich 'red' slip was also used, and seems likely to have gained its colour from iron naturally present in the clay, rather than from the added hammerscale which was occasionally used to achieve a similar effect. Experimental reproduction of slip decoration such as that found on early Kingston-type ware has shown that the clay was applied when it had a butter-like consistency (we are grateful to Suzanne Lang for this information). Red slip was also used to decorate certain Coarse Border ware and Cheam whiteware jug forms. Although it was noticeably thinner when applied, since it could be painted onto the body, it is similar in appearance to that used on the Kingston-type vessels. Clay was also used in a much stiffer state to make the applied features on Kingston-type and Coarse Border ware anthropomorphic jugs, and on Coarse Border ware and 'Tudor Green' lobed cups to make human figures, animals and plants.

Decoration consisting of simple impressed or incised lines, commonly made with a comb, is found in all the Surrey whiteware industries, and particularly in early Coarse Border ware, sometimes in combination with other forms of decoration, sometimes on its own. Stamped decoration is found in Kingston-type ware and Coarse Border ware, but not in Cheam whiteware. Three different types of stamp were used. Individual stamps, usually simple ring-and-dot patterns, were commonly applied to added pads or strips of thick slip, but were also used directly on the body, for example to represent eyes. These stamps are found mainly on early Kingston-type ware. A number of more elaborate, moulded and applied stamps are known on Coarse Border ware jugs. Roller stamps were also used on early Kingston-type ware jugs, almost always over applied strips, but are not a feature of Coarse Border ware decoration, in which applied strips were either pinched or nicked. Finally, large, carefully moulded stamps were used to decorate raised bosses on the bodies of certain Kingston-type ware jugs. A few of these stamps, which may have been made from metal or hardwood, display considerable skill in their design and execution. Some of the decorative methods used by the Surrey whiteware potters are almost entirely restricted to a single industry. However, on their own, they cannot be regarded as a foolproof means of identification, especially since, after the 13th century, a large proportion of vessels made in all the industries simply have a mottled green glaze, and no other decoration.

Both a clear lead glaze, which appears yellow-brown over the 'white' clay, and a mottled green glaze, coloured by copper, were used by the Surrey whiteware potters. There is no evidence for splash-glazing or dipping. The glaze was therefore probably painted onto the pot. This is suggested by the fact that the potters were able to control which parts of the pot were glazed. Many late 14th- and 15th-century Coarse Border ware and Cheam whiteware jugs were simply glazed in a 'bib', or over the upper half of the body only. Earlier vessels have a more complete cover of glaze, although it was probably applied in the same manner. In common with other medieval jugs from London, Surrey whiteware jugs and cooking pots appear consistently to have been fired in an inverted position. Since glaze often ran during firing, it could easily have settled in a pool inside the vessels if they had been fired upright, so there would be an obvious practical advantage to stacking pots upside down. Bowls and other flatwares appear to have been fired on their sides, or as they most conveniently fitted into the firing-stack.

FABRICS

Surrey whiteware fabrics from London have been examined in three ways: under a binocular microscope; in thin-section, looking at both qualitative characteristics and grain-size distributions; and using Neutron Activation Analysis (see Appendices 4-5; see also Fig 1). These methods confirm that three main groups can be isolated, corresponding to Kingston-type ware, Cheam whiteware and Coarse Border ware. However, there are considerable variations within each group, and it is not possible to assign every sherd of Surrey whiteware to a group on the basis of fabric alone without taking into account form and decoration.

1. Kingston-type ware

Colour: surfaces are varying shades of buff (Munsell 7.5YR 8/2, 10YR 8/2, 8/4, 7/1, 2.5Y 9/2, 8/2, 7.5YR 8/4). Cores and margins are either the same, pale grey (N 9/0) or pale pink (7.5YR 9/2). The fabric is hard, has a rough feel, and a fine texture (see Fig 1a).

Inclusions: abundant, well-sorted quartz <0.5mm, rounded and sub-angular, iron-stained, rose, clear, milky and grey. Sparse to moderate red and black iron-rich compound <0.5mm. The degree of abundance of quartz and iron-rich compound varies – some examples are finer than others. Sparse angular white flint, and sparse limestone. Abundant flecks of mica <0.1mm (see below).

Glaze: crazed, and varies from thin and often pitted to thick and glossy. Varying shades of green, sometimes mottled (5Y 5/6, 10YR 6/4, 6/6, 5/4, 5/6), dark green (2.5GY 4/2, 5/6, 6/6), or occasionally brown (10YR 4/4). Iron-rich compound often causes red or brown streaks in or under the glaze. Inclusions in the fabric are usually visible through the glaze.

2. Coarse Border ware

Colour: core and/or margins are usually either beige or buff (10YR 9/2, 8/2, 9/4) or reduced (N8/0, 9/0) with oxidised margins (10YR 9/2, 2.5Y 9/2). Surfaces are either oxidised or reduced – greyish brown (2.5Y 8/2, 7/2), pinkish brown (7.5YR 8/4), orange brown (7.5YR 8/6, 7/6), or the more typical buff (2.5Y 8.2). The fabric is hard, with a rough to harsh feel, and has an irregular, coarse texture (see Fig 1b).

Inclusions: abundant, ill-sorted quartz, rounded and subangular <1.0mm. Iron-stained to varying degrees – staining along the cracks is very clear in some grains; others are an overall rose colour. Moderate clear/transparent grains, and sparse grey and white grains. Sparse to moderate red iron-rich compound <0.8mm. Sparse angular black or white flint, and abundant flecks of mica <0.1mm, but usually much smaller and therefore not a notable characteristic under the binocular microscope.

Glaze: the finish varies from thick and glossy to thin and pitted. Crazed. The colour varies from light to dark green and is sometimes mottled (5GY 3/2, 2.5GY 5/4, 4/4, 7/4, 7/6).

1a

1b

1c

1d

3. Cheam whiteware

Colour: varying shades of buff (2.5Y 8/2, 10YR 8/4, 9/4, 7/4). Cores and/or margins either oxidised (7.5YR 8/4, 2.5Y 9/2) or reduced (2.5Y 8/2). The fabric is hard, has a rough feel, and a fine texture (see Fig 1c).

Inclusions: very similar to Kingston-type ware, but slightly finer matrix. Abundant iron-stained, clear, grey and milky quartz <0.25mm. Sparse to moderate red and black iron-rich compound <0.5mm. Sparse angular white flint. Abundant flecks of mica <0.1mm.

Glaze: crazed and varies from thick and glossy to thin and pitted. Bubbling also occurs in the glaze. Varying shades of green, often mottled – dark

1. Details of the fabric of (a) Kingston-type ware; (b) Coarse Border ware; (c) Cheam whiteware; (d) 'Tudor Green' ware, showing differences in texture and appearance.

green (7.5GY 4/4, 3/2), light green (10Y 6/6) or yellow (2.5Y 9/6, 8/8, 7/8).

4. 'Tudor Green' ware

Colour: surfaces, cores and margins usually the same colour – either buff (10YR 8/2, 9/2, 9/1, 2.5Y 8/2) or pale grey (N 9/0). The fabric is soft to hard, with a smooth feel, and has a fine texture (see Fig 1d).

Inclusions: rounded and subangular very fine-textured quartz, iron-stained, white, milky and grey in colour – moderate to abundant, but not visible to the naked eye, and only with difficulty detected under the binocular microscope. Moderate red and black iron-rich compound <0.5mm. Sparse limestone.

Glaze: crazed, usually well covered and fairly thick and even. Varying shades of green, often mottled (2.5GY 6/8, 6/6, 5/6, 5GY 5/6, 7.5GY 4/4). Often dark mottling on pale, yellowish green (7.5Y 7/4).

SOURCES

Surrey whitewares were made from a white-firing clay containing angular quartz of fine silt and sand grade, and tempered with varying quantities of rounded quartz sand. Variations in texture between handle and body fabrics, and between the body and the slip used in decoration, indicate that, when it was dug, the clay probably contained varying quantities of angular quartz silt and fine sand, and white mica, but no rounded quartz. Although these inclusions are rare in, or absent from the London Clay which forms the basis of the Thames Basin clay lands, they are typical of the Reading Beds. White-firing potting clays have been obtained from the Reading Beds at various times – in the London region, they were used in the early Roman period at Brockley Hill and Radlett, on the Hertfordshire–Middlesex border; and, in the post-medieval period, Farnham, in Surrey, was the centre of a thriving pottery industry (Holling 1971). Kingston upon Thames was known as a centre for pottery production from the mid-13th century onwards – waster deposits have been excavated at two whiteware kiln sites, at Eden Street, and at the Knapp-Drewett site in Union Street. A dump of wasters from Bankside in Southwark included vessels identical in fabric to the Kingston material (see Appendix 4). Since none of these sites lies on the Reading Beds, it is most likely that the clay was brought by cart or by boat to the various kilns. The advantages of production close to a major navigable river must have been sufficient to encourage the carriage of raw clay, despite the fact that the clay would loose an appreciable amount of its weight on firing. It is quite probable therefore, that other, as yet undiscovered, kiln sites, which could have been situated just as far from the clay source, were also in operation at the same time. Both Cheam and the Surrey-

Hampshire border potteries of Farnham, Farnborough Hill and Ash lie close to the Reading Beds, and it may be that they were located so as to reduce the distance that the raw clay had to be carried.

DISTRIBUTION

Surrey whiteware pottery fabrics contain few distinctive inclusions, and cannot be positively identified by eye. Only sherds which combine the appropriate fabric characteristics with a distinctive form or decoration can therefore be used to plot the distribution of the different wares. In the late 13th and early 14th centuries these distinctive types include Kingston-type ware metal copy jugs, and jugs with applied decoration or stamped bosses. Coarse Border ware combed jugs can also be dated to this period, but no systematic search has been made for them as a specific type in museum collections. Although museums in north Hampshire, Berkshire, Hertfordshire, Surrey and Kent have been visited, the number of findspots is very low (see Figs 2-4). There are too few 'negative' sites (ie whose pottery assemblages definitely contained no Surrey whitewares) to prove that Kingston-type ware was not traded up-river or overland into south Buckinghamshire or west Surrey. Nevertheless, the present pattern suggests that the main market for late 13th- to early 14th-century Kingston-type ware was London itself (Fig 2).

In the later 14th century, distinctive Surrey whiteware products included Kingston-type ware baluster jugs, small rounded and biconical jugs, lobed and plain cups of the type produced at the Knapp-Drewett site in Kingston, and Cheam whiteware biconical jugs. These types are even more rare in museum collections in the Home Counties than those of the preceding period, but this is due partly to the general scarcity of later 14th-century pottery from the region just outside London. The distribution of Cheam whiteware has, however, been plotted by Orton (see Fig 4; Orton 1982b, Fig 26), and appears to have been centred on London and its immediate environs, providing an interesting comparison with Kingston-type ware (for further discussion of the distribution of Cheam whiteware see Orton 1982b, M40-1).

There is little typological variation in Coarse Border ware products from the mid-14th century to the mid-15th century. The main distinctive fea-

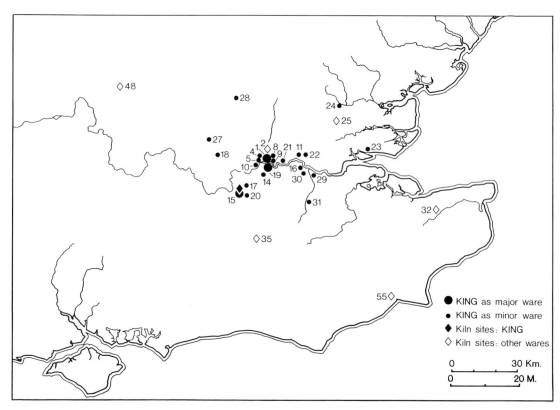

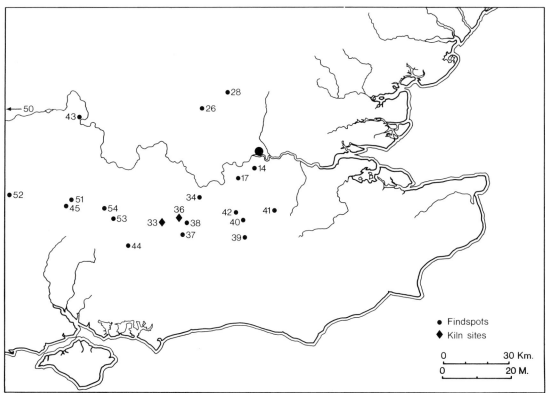

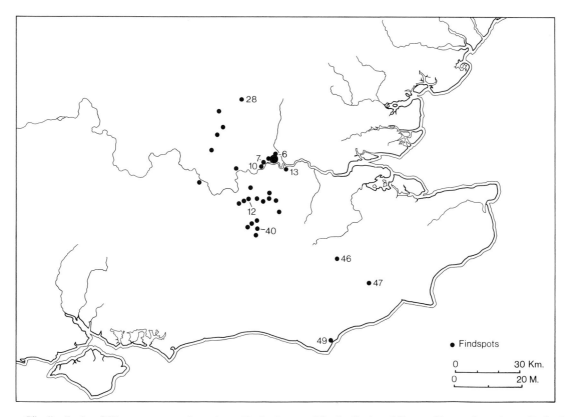

2. The distribution of Kingston-type ware in south-east England (for key see Appendix 2).

4. The distribution of Cheam whiteware in south-east England (for key see Appendix 2).

3. The distribution of Coarse Border ware in south-east England (for key see Appendix 2).

ture is the presence of lid-seated rims on cooking pots, bowls and cisterns, which is not found in London until the early 15th century (see below). It is, therefore, possible to show that certain vessels are of 15th-century date, although none can be attributed with any confidence to the 14th century. The area of distribution of late 14th- to early 15th-century Coarse Border ware (see Fig 3) is much larger than that of any other earlier or contemporaneous Surrey whitewares, and covers much of the Thames Basin, Berkshire and Hampshire as far south as Winchester, although not, apparently, as far as the south coast, since it is rare in, or absent from, Southampton.

DATING

Handmade Early Surrey coarseware vessels, mainly cooking pots, made in a white-firing clay which was tempered with a coarse quartz sand, were used in London from the middle of the 11th to the middle of the 12th century (Vince and Jenner forthcoming; Vince 1985, 37). There is little difficulty in distinguishing large fragments of these vessels from those of high medieval Surrey whitewares, although small sherds might be difficult to identify. Their use is separated from that of later Surrey whitewares in London by a period of about a century, during which time the majority of the pottery used in the capital was of local origin.

The latest datable assemblages from London to contain no Surrey whitewares (ie predating their introduction) were found at Billingsgate Lorry Park (period XI) and Seal House (Waterfront III. For the distribution of Surrey whitewares in London see Figs 5–8). The former assemblage contained a short-cross penny of early 13th-century date (1205 or later), and the Seal House group was dated by dendrochronology to c.1210. The earliest groups to include Surrey whitewares date to the middle of the century. These came from Billingsgate Lorry Park (period XII), in a

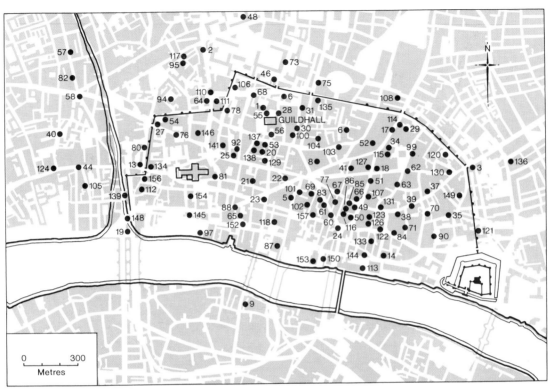

5. *Above: Finds of Kingston-type ware in the City of London.*
(For key see Appendix 3).

6. *Below: Finds of Coarse Border ware in the City of London.*
(For key see Appendix 3).

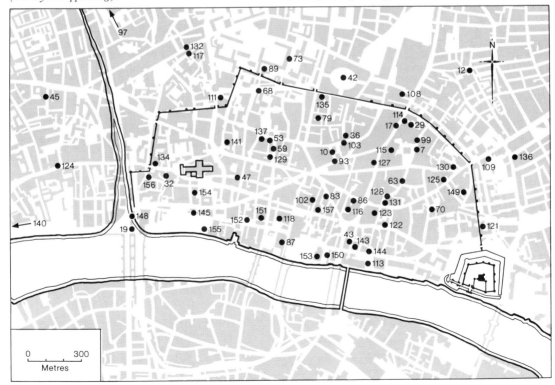

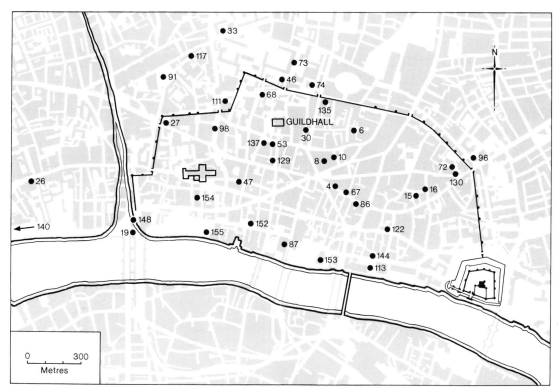

7. *Above: Finds of Cheam whiteware in the City of London.
(For key see Appendix 3).*

8. *Below: Finds of 'Tudor Green' ware in the City of London.
(For key see Appendix 3).*

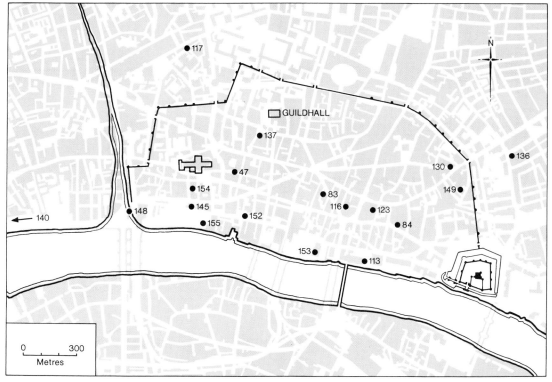

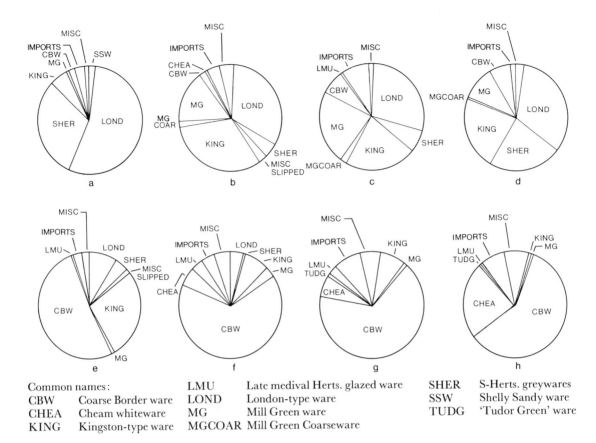

Common names:

CBW	Coarse Border ware	LMU	Late medival Herts. glazed ware	SHER	S-Herts. greywares
CHEA	Cheam whiteware	LOND	London-type ware	SSW	Shelly Sandy ware
KING	Kingston-type ware	MG	Mill Green ware	TUDG	'Tudor Green' ware
		MGCOAR	Mill Green Coarseware		

9. *The relative frequency by rim percentage (eves) of Surrey whitewares and other pottery in mid-13th- to mid-15th-century assemblages in London: a) mid-13th-century (Seal House and Billingsgate); b) late 13th century (Trig Lane); c) c.1270 (Swan Lane); d) early 14th century (Ludgate Hill); e) mid-14th century (Trig Lane); f) c.1360 (Trig Lane); g) c.1380 (Trig Lane); h) early to mid-15th century (Trig Lane).*

deposit dated *c.*1250 by an assemblage of short-cross and long-cross pennies (Vince 1985, Fig 37), and from Seal House Waterfront IV, which is dated solely by its relationship to Waterfront III and is therefore estimated to be between 20 and 40 years later than *c.*1210. Both assemblages contain a small percentage of Kingston-type ware, mainly jugs with applied decoration and either green or polychrome glaze. The Billingsgate group also contains sherds of Coarse Border ware jugs with combed decoration. They show that Surrey whitewares were coming into use in London during the second quarter of the 13th century.

Before long, Kingston-type ware had gained a substantial market in London. At Trig Lane, the Group 2 and Group 3 revetment dumps, dated *c.*1270 and *c.*1290 respectively, contain considerable quantities of Kingston-type ware, and small quantities of Coarse Border ware (see Appendix 6 for the quantified data from this and other sites and Fig 9 for the relative frequencies of Surrey whitewares from London). A large deposit from Swan Lane, dated *c.*1270–80 by coins and pilgrim souvenirs, also contains a high proportion of

Kingston-type ware, as does the previous waterfront dump from this site. This latter group contains a long-cross penny and must therefore be dated between 1250 (from the coin) and 1280 (since it is earlier than the succeeding dump). A date of *c.*1260 seems most likely. Although it was recovered during a watching brief and was not independently dated, this group shows that the Kingston-type industry must have been growing rapidly. This corresponds closely with the first documentary evidence for potters in Kingston upon Thames supplying sites in the London area (Hinton 1980, 382). The range of forms and decorative styles represented in this material is wider than in the mid-13th-century groups, although this may be due entirely to the increase in sample size. Two distinctive decorative styles, which can be dated to this period by their inclusion in this Swan Lane group, are stamped bosses and metal copy baluster jugs.

A very large collection of Surrey whitewares was recovered in 1982 from the filling of the City ditch at Ludgate. This material was shown to have been deposited later than 1302 and before c.1340 by a combination of numismatic and documentary evidence (Vince 1985, 89). Unlike the waterfront assemblages described above, the Ludgate pottery consisted of large fragments of vessels amongst which was an unusual two-handled storage jar (Fig 102) and several jugs. Other groups datable to the early 14th century are rare in London, but it would appear from existing evidence that there was little development in the range of forms or decoration from the late 13th century, and that Surrey whitewares held a comparable share in the pottery market.

By the middle of the 14th century, to judge by the assemblage from Trig Lane Group 7, Surrey whitewares were the commonest types of pottery in the City, and, within this group, Coarse Border ware was almost twice as common as Kingston-type ware. This major change was accompanied by a change in typology in both industries. In Kingston-type ware polychrome glazing and applied decoration are rare, and may be residual, while stamped boss decoration reached the peak of its popularity. Combed decoration was no longer used on Coarse Border ware, and the large rounded jug or cistern is the commonest form, followed by cooking pots and bowls. It is unfortunate that the Trig Lane Group 7 assemblage is dated only by its stratigraphic position – it must be earlier than the succeeding waterfront, Group 10, which is dated c.1360 by dendrochronology, and later than the Group 3 revetment. The date of c.1340 assigned to the assemblage by the excavator is therefore an educated guess, confirmed by the relative depth of accumulated foreshore deposits separating the revetment from Group 3 on the one hand, and Group 10 on the other (Milne and Milne 1982). Further mid-14th-century asemblages have been found at the Custom House site, Groups C1 and C2 (Thorn 1975), the Public Cleansing Depot, Dowgate, and at the East Watergate (Baynard's Castle). However, detailed examination of these groups has not yet been carried out, and they are only broadly datable.

The late 14th-century sequence is demonstrated by a series of revetment dumps dated by dendrochronology. Trig Lane Group 10 is dated c.1360, and Group 11 c.1380, while a group from Swan Lane is dated later than 1394, but earlier than the succeeding foreshore and waterfront of c.1430. There is a steady increase in the proportion of Coarse Border ware present in these assemblages, although there is no discernible typological development. All three groups contain Kingston-type ware, but as a progressively smaller proportion of the total assemblage. This late Kingston-type ware is rarely decorated, except for wheel-applied incised bands, and stamped bosses of the 'wheat-ear' pattern. Rounded jugs with strap handles were first used in London at this time. Cheam whiteware is also found for the first time, in the Trig Lane Group 10 assemblage, and is present in increasing quantities in the succeeding groups, although no typological progression is apparent during this period. The only other type of Surrey whiteware found in these late 14th-century groups is the untempered fineware, which was used for lobed and plain cups. These vessels are regularly found in assemblages by the end of the 14th century, but are present only as occasional sherds throughout the late 13th to 14th century sequence. Unfortunately, their earlier occurrence is too sparse, and the sherds too small for any forms to be reconstructed with confidence. Moreover, it is impossible to be certain that they belong to the assemblages in which they were found, since a small number of post-medieval intrusive sherds is to be expected in most groups.

The latest medieval phase in the City about which we have information is dated to the early to mid-15th century. A foreshore and overlying revetment dump from Swan Lane can be coin-dated to c.1413–30, since of the 12 coins recovered, four belong to the reign of Henry V, whose issues are relatively uncommon, and none to the reign of Henry VI. A small group from the south-east angle tower of Baynard's Castle can probably be dated to c.1428, and the huge assemblage from Trig Lane Group 15 can be dated to the middle of the 15th century. It has been given a tentative dendochronological date of 1440 or later, and contained a coin possibly from the reign of Henry VI (minted 1427–30), and two early 15th-century French *jettons*, dated by Stuart Rigold to c.1430. All these groups reveal the same pattern; Surrey whiteware pottery was still as common as it was in the late 14th century, but the proportion of Cheam whiteware had increased at the expense of Kingston-type ware, which is found in negligible quantities. New forms are found in both Cheam whiteware (barrel-shaped jugs and pipkins) and in Coarse Border ware (the lid-seated or 'bifid' rim on cooking pots and bowls).

There is little direct evidence for the late 15th-century pottery of London. Deposition along the waterfront had ceased, and pit groups from inland sites rarely contain independently datable artefacts. An exception is a group from East-cheap, which contained fragments of Raeren stoneware drinking jugs, a large quantity of Surrey whitewares and few red earthenwares other than late London-type ware. This absence of red earthenwares decorated with white slip suggests a deposition date in the late 15th century, rather than in the 16th century. The Surrey whitewares are tentatively identified as Cheam whiteware. A few pit groups from the City contain predominantly unglazed red earthenwares, some of which have white slip decoration, together with Raeren stoneware. From the absence of Frechen stone-wares, a date in the first half of the 16th century is suggested for these groups. The small quantities of Surrey whitewares found show that Coarse Border ware had ceased to be used in London by this time, but that Cheam whitewares, or possibly fine wares from the Surrey-Hampshire border, were available. However, it would be rash to chart the end of the Surrey whiteware industries on such flimsy evidence.

II DESCRIPTION AND TYPE-SERIES

The four main groups of Surrey whitewares, as defined on p. 7, are each described here by *class* of vessel, ie major categories based largely on function or supposed usage, such as 'jug' or 'cooking pot'. This classification also holds good for vessels such as 'bowls' and 'dishes' whose original function may now be uncertain, or which may have had several different purposes. Classes are divided into *forms* sharing those characteristics of shape and treatment which enable one to be distinguished from another, ie 'baluster jug' or 'rounded jug'. Forms may finally be divided into *types* such as 'cylindrical-necked baluster jug' or 'large rounded jug', ie sharing those features which allow them to be classified as a particular form, but differentiated by variations in the basic shape and in ranges of size.

Jugs, as the commonest and most varied class of Surrey whitewares, are described in detail in terms of form, rim, base and handle form and decoration. The capacities of complete vessels were measured to the nearest 10ml, using dry rice.

1. KINGSTON-TYPE WARE

Jugs

Form

A number of different forms of jug were made in Kingston-type ware, some of which may be further sub-divided into different types. However, only a limited number of types can be reliably identified from sherds, notably metal copy, rilled and narrow-necked baluster jugs. Generally speaking, positive identification of forms or types from small fragments is impossible, or at best dubious, when the diagnostic features are insufficiently distinctive. This could present problems with dating Kingston-type jugs, were it not for the existence of other dating factors which enable a chronological framework to be constructed. Perhaps the most useful and reliable of these is body decoration, which can be divided into a number of easily recognisable types (see pp. 35-45). Jug sherds with plastic decoration, for example, are found in the City in contexts dated to the mid- to late 13th century, but are not represented at all in the Kingston and Bankside waste dumps, which are dated late in the life of the industry (Hinton 1980; McCracken, Nenk and Vince forthcoming; Dennis and Hinton 1983). Bossed decoration is found at all these sites, but only infrequently in comparison to material from London; and simple combed or grooved decoration, or undecorated forms, seem to be characteristic of this later stage of production in the mid- to late 14th century. Strap handles appear to be a late introduction on the basis of their presence in the Eden Street and Knapp-Drewett kiln material and of their absence from contexts dated to the 13th century in London. The combined evidence from the Kingston and Bankside waste dumps, the excavated material from London, and the complete vessels in the museum collections to which it can be related, has been used to construct the chronological framework for the main Kingston-type jug forms (see Fig 41).

1. Baluster

Baluster jugs may be recognised by their rounded, ovoid or pear-shaped body, constricted at the lower end, and then flaring out again at the base. Some vessels have only a slight constriction, and others a very pronounced waisted profile. Most types, but not all, have a distinct shoulder and approximately parallel-sided neck. The overall height is always at least twice the maximum girth. Six different types of baluster jug have been identified.

a) Large (Figs 48-51): This type of jug is both larger and more substantially built than other vessels of baluster form. The body is consequently rather elongated or oval in shape. The neck is slightly flared, often with a bridge spout. Handles are thick and heavy, with applied 'ears' and a squashed oval or strap section. Vessels of this form are all highly decorated, and may have polychrome glazing. Anthropomorphic decoration can only rarely be associated with jugs of large baluster form (Fig 51; see also Thorn 1978, Fig 51; Thorn and Thorn 1972a). Large baluster jugs are greater than 5000ml in capacity. However, since no complete examples were examined, no upper limits for the range, or individual measurements can be given. They are dated to the mid-13th century.

b) *Cylindrical-necked* (Figs 10-11; 52-55; 56, No 27): This type is in certain respects comparable with the large baluster form described above. Size is an important distinguishing factor (see below). The neck is typically more or less straight sided, or very slightly flared, and is frequently cordonned or grooved, or both. However, jugs can sometimes be tentatively assigned to this type even when the neck is incomplete, on the basis of body shape, size and type of decoration (eg Fig 53, Nos 13, 16). Some vessels have a pinched and pulled pouring lip, but bridge spouts are not associated with this type. The base is normally, but not invariably, well splayed. Cylindrical-necked baluster jugs appear to have been made throughout the life of the Kingston-type industry, although the type can be dated principally to the late 13th and 14th centuries.

The mid-13th-century jug may have a biconical body, with polychrome plastic decoration (Fig 52, Nos 9-11). This can be compared with early 13th-century London-type ware copies of Rouen and north French jugs (Pearce *et al.* 1985, Figs 25-34). Later jugs may be decorated with stamped bosses, or wheel-applied grooves and combed bands (Figs 53-55; 56, No 27). The overall measured capacity range of complete jugs is 1060-4570ml, although the majority of vessels fall in the range of 2000-3000ml.

c) *Metal copy* (Figs 12; 56, Nos 28-32; 57-59): This type was inspired by the form of contemporaneous metal vessels (eg Lewis 1978, 34, Fig 41), and typically has a long, straight-sided neck with a grooved collar rim, a rounded body and a well-defined, restricted and flared base, emphasised by vertical knife-trimming. The base is commonly recessed by means of a distinctive process which is otherwise associated only with tall baluster types (Figs 60-62). The handle is most characteristic of sub-rectangular section, terminating on the body in a definite 'tail', and

is decorated with incised vertical lines and stabbing. This form of handle is restricted to metal copy jugs, although some vessels of this form may instead have a rod handle (Fig 56, No 31). The jug may be plain, or decorated with horizontal bands of combing or grooves around the neck and body; applied 'scales' or pellets; or stamped bosses. A bichrome effect was obtained in certain examples by the application of a clear, lead glaze to the rim and the inside of the neck, contrasting with green glaze on the body. The jugs illustrated in Fig 56, Nos 30-32 are incomplete, but are included with the metal copy baluster jugs on the basis of handle form, and decoration. In shape, however, they have affinities with narrow-necked baluster jugs and may instead be decorated versions of this type. Capacities range from 1010 to 2810ml. There is no evidence for the presence of metal copy baluster jugs in London until the late 13th century.

The vessels illustrated in Fig 59, Nos 47-8, although possessing the characteristics of metal copy baluster jugs, are better termed 'ewers'. They are distinguished by a narrow neck with a pronounced tubular spout with zoomorphic features (Fig 18c).

d) *Tulip-necked* (Fig 60): This is a particularly tall type of baluster jug. The neck is bulbous with an inturned rim, and curves gently into the body, whose shape it mirrors. The resulting profile is smoothly rounded and elegant. The base commonly has a sharp vertical bevel, and may be slightly recessed, although a small number of thumbed bases also survive (eg Nos 51-2). The shoulder is cordonned, and the handle is of rod form, often with a finger and thumb impression on either side at the top. The type is always undecorated, and closely parallels the well-known tulip-necked baluster jugs which dominated London-type ware assemblages dating from the late 13th and early 14th centuries (Pearce *et al.* 1985, Fig 37). Only one of the jugs examined is complete (No 49), and has a capacity of 1950ml. They can be dated to the late 14th century.

e) *Rilled* (Fig 61, Nos 55-56): This type differs from the baluster types described above in having no shoulder, or any clear division between neck and body. The pear-shaped body simply tapers to the rim, which may have a pulled and pinched lip. The upper part of the body, from just below the rim and sometimes as far as the maximum girth, is rilled by means of continuous combing while the jug was still on the wheel. The base is

10. Kingston-type ware : highly decorated cylindrical-necked baluster jug with polychrome glazing (height 324mm).

11. Kingston-type ware: highly decorated cylindrical-necked baluster jug with polychrome glazing (height 344mm).

12. Kingston-type ware : metal copy baluster jug with bichrome glazing (height 336mm).

13. Kingston-type ware: highly decorated anthropomorphic conical jug with polychrome glazing (height 256mm).

constricted and flared, with a vertical bevel, and the waist is knife-trimmed with vertical strokes. The capacity of the only complete vessel examined was measured at 2310ml. Rilled baluster jugs are dated to the 14th century.

f) Narrow-necked (Figs 61, Nos 57-61; 62): This type is related to rilled baluster jugs in shape, but may be distinguished from them by the absence of rilling and by the rim diameter, which is much smaller than that of the base. The base is recessed and externally bevelled, and may be thumbed, but in all other respects the two types are similar. They are also comparable in date, although none were identified among the Eden Street or Knapp-Drewett kiln material (Hinton 1980; McCracken, Nenk and Vince forthcoming). Measured capacities fall in the range of 720-1820ml.

2. Conical

(Figs 13; 63-65; 66, No 80)

Conical jugs are more or less straight-sided, with only a slight shoulder or none at all. Some vessels have an almost pear-shaped profile as a result of knife-trimming just above the base (eg Fig 63, No 69). The rim diameter is generally less than that of the base, which may be slightly convex in appearance, and is often thumbed. The form is found in mid- to late 13th-century contexts, with the addition of applied 'ears' on the handle, bridge spout and plastic decoration, sometimes polychrome. Anthropomorphic conical jugs are rare, but not unknown (Figs 13; 63, No 65). This highly decorated style is succeeded typologically by stamped boss decoration (Fig 63, Nos 68-9). Conical jugs are, however, predominantly late 14th-century in date, at which period they are undecorated, except for a number of raised, horizontal bands at intervals around the body. The handle is usually of strap section and deeply stabbed, and the rim may have a pinched and pulled lip. The base is generally thumbed. The jug illustrated in Fig 63, No 67, is badly warped and poorly made, and is tentatively classified as a conical jug on the basis of its tall, approximately straight-sided, unwaisted shape, which appears to be closer to the conical form than to the baluster. A limited capacity range of 1950-2250ml was measured.

3. Pear-shaped

(Figs 14-16; 66, Nos 81-85; 67-69)

Jugs of this form have no distinct shoulder, with

14. Kingston-type ware: pear-shaped jug with sgraffito *decoration and green glaze (height 248mm).*

the upper part of the body resembling the conical jug in appearance. The maximum girth is low on the body of the jug, and the profile generally curves gently inwards from this point to the base. Bases are commonly thumbed, and several complete jugs have a bridge spout. An unusual carinated jug (Figs 14; 66, No 81), which is really halfway between pear-shaped and conical forms in shape, is decorated with vertical combing, and recalls Mill Green ware both in form and decoration (Pearce *et al.* 1982, Fig 5, No 7). Pear-shaped jugs are predominantly a mid-13th-century form and so are commonly highly decorated. Their production continued into the late 14th century, at which date they were either plain, or decorated with simple horizontal combing or grooving. Capacities range from 2130-3150ml.

A distinct variation on the form of the pear-shaped jug is represented by the tall, waisted jugs illustrated in Figs 68, Nos 95-96 and 69. This form is not common and can be recognised by a more or less pronounced constriction of the body at the point where the lower end of the handle is attached. The shape of the body otherwise

15. Kingston-type ware : highly decorated pear-shaped jug with clear glaze (height 364mm).

16. Kingston-type ware : highly decorated pear-shaped jug with green glaze (height 308mm).

approximates to the description of the pear-shaped form given above. They may be highly decorated, or plain, or have stamped bosses. The jug illustrated in Fig 68, No 96 was made in two sections, joined together at the waist. It is not certain whether any other Kingston-type jugs were made in this fashion.

4. Squat

(Fig 70)

Squat jugs are similar to rounded jugs in appearance (see below), with a distinct shoulder and short, more or less straight-sided neck. The body curves without any constriction into the base, which is generally convex in shape and thumbed. The height and maximum girth are approximately equal, so that their shape is more squat than rounded, although the distinction between the two forms is by no means always clear. Squat jugs may be decorated simply with horizontal combing or grooves, or with applied 'scales' or pellets, or stamped bosses. None were recognised among the Eden Street or Knapp-Drewett kiln material, and the type may be dated in London to the late 13th and 14th centuries. Measured capacities range widely from 820-5730ml.

5. Rounded

(Figs 71-77)

This form has a rounded or globular body with a distinct shoulder and neck, and is therefore related in shape to the squat jug. Although the two forms may be difficult to distinguish when fragmentary, complete rounded jugs tend to be greater in height than in girth. Bases may be convex or flat. They are often thumbed, and this can give them a slightly flared and recessed appearance, recalling the profile of the baluster form (eg Fig 71, No 110). The earliest occurrence of rounded jugs in London can be dated to the mid-13th century, and the form remained in circulation throughout the 14th century.

One almost complete polychrome, highly decorated rounded jug in the Museum of London reserve collection (Fig 71, No 109) has a bridge spout modelled in the form of a ram's head. A number of similar heads, also found in London, most probably come from jugs of this form (Figs 25d-f; 71, Nos 107-8). Plastic, zoomorphic body decoration is found on the polychrome jug illustrated in Fig 71, No 110. However, decoration of rounded jugs more commonly takes the form of stamped bosses (Fig 72), or applied pellets or 'scales' (Fig 73, Nos 117-120). The latter is a feature of rounded jugs apparently inspired by metal prototypes, and may be compared with metal copy baluster jugs (Figs 56, Nos 30-2; 57, Nos 33-6), although they differ from this type in having an elongated pouring lip. Mid- to late 14th-century rounded jugs are undecorated, except for simple cordons, grooves or combed horizontal bands around the neck and body (Figs 73, Nos 121-3; 74-77). This type was found in the Eden Street kiln waste (Hinton 1980, Fig 2, No 6). A large number of sparsely glazed rounded jugs, with pinched and pulled pouring lips and broad, stabbed strap handles (cf Fig 77, Nos 140-42) were found at the Knapp-Drewett site (McCracken, Nenk and Vince forthcoming). Capacities range from 1780 to 4600ml, with the majority of vessels holding between 2040 and 2970ml.

6. Large rounded/squat

(Fig 78)

A small number of very substantial, but incomplete jugs found in London may be either squat or rounded in form. It was not possible to reconstruct a complete profile from any surviving fragments. All appear to date from the later life of the industry.

7. Small rounded

(Figs 79-81; 82, No 181)

Small rounded jugs have the same basic shape as the rounded form, but are distinguished from them by their capacity. They are almost invariably undecorated, or simply have combed or incised horizontal bands. Handles are characteristically of rod section, and bases may be flat or slightly convex, but are only rarely thumbed. Larger examples may have a pinched and pulled pouring lip. One remarkable small rounded jug, now in the Museum of London reserve collection, is decorated with applied anthropomorphic features (Fig 82, No 181; Spencer 1969, 388-90). Capacities fall within two ranges: 385-550ml and 750-1400ml. Small rounded jugs as a type can be dated to the 14th century.

8. Biconical

(Figs 82, Nos 182-92; 83, Nos 193-7)

Biconical jugs, comparable in form with Cheam

whiteware biconical jugs (Fig 122, Nos 543-51; Orton 1982b, Fig 17, Nos 24-30), are in many respects similar to small rounded jugs – a number of vessels could be accommodated in either class (eg Fig 82, No 182). However, biconical jugs as defined here tend to be taller in relation to their girth than small rounded jugs – their height may be more than twice their maximum girth. The neck is straight-sided, and long and narrow in relation to the body, with no pouring lip. The most characteristic feature of this form is the carination at the mid-point of the body, which gives it a biconical profile. All vessels have a simple rod handle, and most are completely undecorated – a few jugs have one or two bands of combing or cordons. Measured capacities fall mostly within the range of 360-430ml, although a few larger jugs bring the upper limit to 1020ml. The type can be dated to the late 14th century.

9. Miniature

(Figs 17; 83, Nos 198-210; 84; 85, Nos 221-2, 225)

Miniature versions of conical, pear-shaped, rounded and baluster jugs were made in Kingston-type ware. They are all wheelthrown, with rod handles, and some have a pinched pouring lip. Three of the illustrated miniature jugs appear to copy the form of London-type ware drinking jugs (Fig 83, Nos 198-9, 206; see Pearce *et al.* 1985, Figs 64-6). A large number of surviving miniature baluster jugs are made in anthropomorphic or, less commonly, zoomorphic form (Fig 84). The capacities of miniature jugs, which are in the range of 30 to 180ml, distinguish them from their larger counterparts.

Rim form

Most Kingston-type ware jug forms may have any one of a number of different rim forms. There are a few notable exceptions: for example, narrownecked baluster jugs, easily recognisable by their rim and neck diameter, have a 'beaded' rim, thickened and rounded externally (Figs 61, Nos 57-61; 62). Tulip-necked baluster jugs may be identified by the bulbous neck and simple inturned rim, with internal bevel (Fig 60). Metal copy baluster jugs have a distinctive form of collar rim, externally thickened, with a wide vertical bevel (Figs 57-59). This may be emphasised by undercutting, and is almost invariably finished with a single, central groove.

17. *Kingston-type ware: miniature zoomorphic baluster jug (height 128mm).*

Collar rims of less distinctive type are found on other jug forms. Rounded jugs with animal-headed spouts (Fig 71, Nos 107-9), and certain large anthropomorphic jugs (eg Fig 85, Nos 227-9) have a collar which was simply produced by pushing the clay outwards just below the rim. On other forms, notably conical, pear-shaped, squat and rounded jugs, such a collar might be made more pronounced by the addition of a cordon or more definite carination (eg Figs 63, No 68; 65, No 75; 70, No 100). However, this rim form is not common.

The commonest form of rim, which is found on jugs of all types apart from those already mentioned, is plain with a flattened top. This was made simply by pressing the clay downwards with the thumb when finishing the rim. The angle and degree of pressure produced slight variations in appearance so that the rim may be slightly thickened at the top, and internally or externally bevelled. For example, large baluster jugs have internally bevelled rims (Figs 48-51), whereas externally bevelled rims of triangular section are common on small rounded jugs (eg Fig 79, Nos 151, 154-5), although they are also found on other forms. The rims of a number of cylindrical-necked baluster and rounded jugs are thickened both internally and externally to such an extent as to give them a 'hammer-head' appearance, distinctly undercut (eg Figs 53, No 17; 56, No 27; 75, Nos 133, 136). More complex rims were sometimes made on decorated vessels such as cylindrical-necked baluster jugs by the addition of rilling or closely-spaced grooving on the neck, extending almost to the top of the rim (Fig 52, No 10).

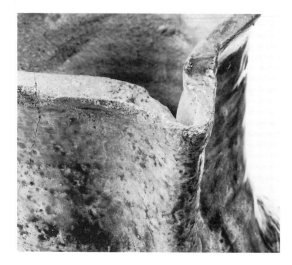

Spouts and lips

A small number of Kingston-type jug forms appear to have been made with no spout or pouring lip of any kind. These include narrow-necked, tulip-necked and most metal copy baluster jugs. A sample of over thirty-five complete, or nearly complete, small rounded jugs from the British Museum and Museum of London reserve collections was examined. Only four, all at the larger end of the range, definitely have a pouring lip; of the rest, very nearly all definitely have no spout or lip. No evidence was found for any form of lip on biconical jugs. The majority of undecorated rounded jugs also have no special provision for pouring. All other forms may, or may not, have a spout or lip.

The commonest form of pouring lip is both pulled and pinched, and is found on bossed and stamped, and undecorated jugs of most types (eg Figs 74, Nos 125-6; 77). It was made by pulling the rim outwards slightly with the forefinger, and pinching in the clay on either side with the thumb and middle finger. A distinctive form of pulled and pinched lip is associated with rounded jugs decorated with applied 'scales' or pellets (Figs 18a; 73, Nos 117-20). This type of lip, which appears to have been derived from metal prototypes, is also found on a few cylindrical-necked and metal copy baluster jugs (Fig 55, Nos 23-25). The wall of the vessel was pulled out with the finger, or with a long tool, from the rim to at least halfway down the neck, and sometimes as far as the shoulder. The sides of this lip were gently squeezed or smoothed inwards and pinched in at the rim. The resulting lip is generally V-shaped and quite narrow.

The simplest form of pouring lip is pinched

18. Kingston-type ware: details of jug spouts and pouring lips.

only, and is limited to undecorated miniature jugs whose rim diameter is far too small for both pulling and pinching to have been practicable (Fig 83, No 208).

Bridge spouts are restricted to early decorated jug forms, and in particular to large baluster jugs, pear-shaped and conical jugs (Figs 48, No 2; 49, No 3; 50, Nos 4-5; 63, No 66; 67, Nos 86-7; 68, No 96). A hole, roughly circular, sub-rectangular or triangular in shape, was cut in the wall of the jug just below the rim, leaving a bridge of clay across the top and the rim itself unaltered (Fig 18b). A semi-tubular, handmade spout was attached to the neck of the jug, the clay of which was carefully smoothed over the join. Since the spout was likely to project above the rim, it was commonly cut down to the level of the bridge in a semi-circular shape, or smoothed back onto the rim. The finished spout could then be included in the overall decorative scheme.

A small pear-shaped jug in the Museum of London reserve collection (Fig 66, No 83) has a bridge spout of so called 'parrot-beak' type, comparable with those common to Saintonge ware jugs (eg Platt and Coleman-Smith 1975, Figs 184, 185). This form of spout has not, however, been identified on any other Kingston-type jugs from London.

A noteworthy adaptation of the bridge spout may be seen in the face-spouts of anthropomorphic and zoomorphic jugs. All surviving examples of the latter take the form of a modelled ram's head whose nostrils act as the outlet for the contents of the jug (Figs 25d-f; 71, Nos 107-9). Human heads are also adapted in this way, although the illustrated face-spouts differ in principle. For example, one type (Fig 85, No 227) retains the bridge of clay at the rim, although none of the facial features are pierced through the clay to allow pouring; instead the liquid would have been poured over the forehead. The jug illustrated in Fig 86, No 231, however, has no bridge; the rim was cut away behind an applied face whose chin takes the form of a tubular spout grasped by hands extended from the body of the jug. The other illustrated examples make use of the mouth for pouring. Both the ewers in the Museum of London reserve collection (Figs 18c; 59, Nos 47-8) have a tubular spout attached to the rim over a bridge, decorated with incised animal features.

Apart from their use on the ewers described above, tubular spouts are rare in Kingston-type ware, and only two examples are noted here, both

atypical. The first, on an extremely small miniature jug (Fig 83, No 210), is simply a tube of clay pushed roughly through the shoulder of the jug from outside, and left protruding some way into the interior. The size of the vessel obviously precluded any attempt to trim the spout at this point. The other example, again incomplete, is now detached from the original vessel and takes the form of a human figure, probably female, as suggested by the details of dress (Fig 86, No 238). The head is missing, but the arms were realistically modelled and applied to the front of the spout.

Handle form

The methods by which handles were attached to Kingston-type ware jugs varied according to the size of the vessel, or, more particularly, the diameter of the rim. A few variations can be related to specific types, and these will be discussed in more detail below (see also Pearce 1984, 21-3). However, as a general rule, the handle was

19. Kingston-type ware: (a); detail of jug rim and upper handle attachment; (b) detail of jug interior showing lower handle attachment.

not just pressed or luted onto the body of the jug at both ends, but was more firmly secured at least at one end by some kind of disruption of the vessel wall. This is best demonstrated at the lower end of the handle where it meets the body, rather than at the rim or neck, because no retouching of the join subsequently covered those parts of the inside of the jug that could not clearly be seen by the user. The rim/neck join, however, was generally, but not always, well disguised (Fig 19a). In some cases, the handle was simply pushed onto the wall of the jug and the join well smoothed over on the outside, leaving the throwing-marks inside the neck only slightly disturbed. More frequently, the upper part of the handle was fixed to the jug by the same method as the lower end. However, inside the neck, the clay of the handle itself, where it had broken through the wall, was smoothed over the join, or extra clay was added to cover it.

Many jugs were too small, or had too long a neck to allow the potter's hand to work inside the thrown vessel. In such cases, the lower end of the handle was most commonly secured by being pressed into and partly through a hole or slit cut in the wall of the pot (Fig 19b). Often the clay removed from the body in the process remained stuck to the wall immediately below. One method was to cut a neat, circular hole and carefully insert the handle. Alternatively, the vessel wall might be stabbed from outside, with a pointed tool or a knife, depending on the size of the handle (Pearce 1984, Fig 7). The complete rilled baluster jug illustrated in Fig 61, No 55 has two knife slashes in the body, forming an inverted 'V'-shape. Inside, the jug was generally left untouched, but outside the clay of the handle was smoothed into the body. Where the angle between the inside of the handle and the body was very acute, extra clay was added and smoothed around the join.

A different method was used to attach handles to larger jugs. The lower end of the handle, and possibly the upper, was pressed onto the body of the jug, and the wall was pushed into it from inside with the thumb or fingers (Pearce 1984, Fig 9). Broad strap handles, for example, were made more secure by pushing two or three fingers into the end of the handle through a horizontal knife-gash.

There are a few interesting variations on these techniques. For example, the handle of the pear-shaped jug illustrated in Fig 68, No 92 was simply luted onto the body of the vessel, which is extremely unusual for a jug of this size: the only other vessels for which this method was adopted are some of the smallest miniature jugs, whose overall shape would have been seriously endangered by any stabbing or cutting (eg Fig 83, Nos 204-6). The baluster jug illustrated in Fig 60, No 51 is another anomaly. Its handle was made of red-firing clay, pushed through the body from outside, although the jug itself was made from the characteristic white-firing Kingston-type clay (for an analysis of the fabrics see Appendix 5).

Perhaps the most distinctive form of Kingston-type ware jug handle belongs to the metal copy baluster jug (Figs 56, Nos 28-32; 57-59; see also Pearce 1984, Fig 10). These handles have a sub-rectangular section, and were fixed at the rim by the usual means (see above). However, the lower end of the handle was formed into a 'tail', whose sides terminate in a point. This was laid over and pressed into a hole cut in the jug wall. However, it was not pushed through the hole, and was therefore left standing out slightly from the side of the jug. Extra clay was then applied around the join and smoothed into the body. This form of handle, even on undecorated metal copy baluster jugs, was almost invariably decorated with two incised vertical lines which meet in a point at the bottom. Between them a single vertical row of stabbed holes was made, either with a pointed tool of round or square section, or with the thumb- or fingernail. However, although this form of handle is unique to metal copy jugs, some examples of this type of jug have a handle of rod section, which does not terminate in a tail, but simply has a single thumb-impression at the base (eg Fig 56, Nos 30-32). Such handles are, nevertheless, often decorated in the manner described above.

The commonest type of handle at all periods of manufacture has a rod section. It may be found on baluster jugs of all types, on pear-shaped, squat, rounded, conical and miniature jugs, and was invariably applied to small rounded and biconical jugs. Handles of oval or sub-rectangular section are less common, but can be found on most types of jug, in particular large baluster and conical jugs of mid-13th- to early 14th-century date, pear-shaped, squat and rounded jugs. Decoration, when it occurs, almost always takes the form simply of one to four vertical incised lines running the length of the handle, and sometimes containing one or more rows of round or square stab-marks (eg Figs 48, No 1; 64, No 73). Stabbed handles are also found without incised lines

(Fig 65, No 76). Stabbing presumably served not only as decoration, but also ensured the correct firing of what was probably the thickest part of the jug. During the earlier phases of production, in the 13th century, handles often had two 'ears' of clay added to the top of the rim/neck join, in imitation ultimately of early 13th-century northern French models, and probably more directly of contemporary London-type ware jugs (eg Figs 48-52; Pearce *et al.* 1985, Fig 25). During the late 13th and 14th centuries, this feature became less common, and was replaced by a single thumb and finger impression on either side of the handle, rather than on the top (eg Figs 54, No 22; 75, Nos 133, 136). A very unusual handle, with a sub-rectangular section, is illustrated in Fig 86, No 237. It is incomplete, and cannot be linked with any particular form of jug. The decoration, however, is so far unparalleled in Kingston-type ware, and consists of a human face modelled on the upper surface near the rim/neck join. In common with anthropomorphic jugs (see pp. 38-42), the nose is made separately, and the mouth, eyes and beard are incised.

A single thumb impression at the base of the handle/body join is a common feature of jugs which were too small to allow the potter to put pressure on the lower join from inside, for instance on small rounded and biconical jugs. The impression may be very clear, deliberate and almost circular (eg Figs 52, No 9; 70, No 102; 73, Nos 118-19), or may have been made by drawing the thumb downwards in a single movement, making a much longer impression, often with a definite groove left by the nail (Fig 82, No 182). It is also found on larger jugs and probably served to make the handle more secure. The small squat jug illustrated in Fig 70, No 104 is unusual in having four small finger impressions radiating from the lower handle attachment.

Strap handles are generally a late 14th-century form, and are found on cylindrical-necked baluster, squat, conical and rounded jugs. The last two can be paralleled by material from the Eden Street kiln waste (Hinton 1980, Fig 2, Nos 6, 7). The broader strap handles often have a slightly grooved upper surface, and may have three or four light finger impressions at the handle/body join. In common with other handle forms described above, functional decoration consists of one or more vertical incised lines and rows of stab-marks. A few of the squat and conical jugs examined have two lightly impressed 'ears' on the top of the handle (Figs 65, Nos 75-76; 70,

No 100). This is a feature common to Mill Green ware vessels of the same form (eg Pearce *et al.* 1982, Figs 4, No 4; 11, Nos 26, 27).

Base form

The bases of only a few Kingston-type ware jugs are treated in such a way as to be distinctive of that type alone. For example, recessed bases are found on a small proportion of cylindrical-necked baluster and pear-shaped jugs (eg Figs 52, Nos 9-10; 66, No 82). The base was first smoothed or trimmed with a knife, but was not cut out to form the recess; rather, the clay of the base-angle was pulled down around the circumference. This process left very faint finger- and thumb-marks around the outside, although the inside of the recess remained relatively smooth in appearance.

Metal copy baluster jugs have a distinctive form of recessed base, made in a different mannner from that described above (Figs 57, Nos 37-8; 58, Nos 40-1; 59, Nos 44-5). This type of base is also found on the majority of tulip-necked baluster jugs, and on rilled and narrow-necked baluster jugs (Figs 60-62). The jug was thrown with a widely splayed foot which gave a very acute base-angle. Once the jug had been removed from the wheel, the flat underside of the base was smoothed or trimmed. While the clay was still quite soft, the edge of the base was smoothed around the circumference with the thumb and fingers, forming a bevel. This had the effect of pushing the clay downwards to make a narrow, folded recess all round the base. The clay might also overlap the top edge of the bevel in places. Another noteworthy, but not exclusive, feature of metal copy and other baluster jugs with a similar base form, is the use of knife-trimming to accentuate the 'waist' between the body and the base. Long, vertical knife-strokes may extend from the base-angle up to the maximum girth, giving a facetted appearance (eg Fig 56, No 27). A similar form of vertical knife-trimming may be seen on London-type ware early baluster jugs (Pearce *et al.* 1985, Fig 24, Nos 49, 50). The unusual white-slipped jug illustrated in Fig 59, No 44, shows that the bevel/recess was made first, after the underside of the base had been trimmed. The vessel was then slipped, and finally the lower part of the jug was trimmed in vertical facets, removing the slip. Although the majority of metal copy and related baluster jugs were trimmed vertically, a few were trimmed in the same way as the majority of other jugs (see below).

Thumbed bases are found on most Kingston-type jug forms, and particularly cylindrical-necked baluster, pear-shaped, conical, squat, and rounded jugs. Other types which may have a thumbed base include small rounded and large baluster jugs, and, rarely, metal copy baluster jugs. Bases treated in this way were often slightly recessed as the clay at the circumference was pulled down by the process of thumbing, either at intervals, or all the way round. 'Sagging' bases were also thumbed in the same manner, but because of their convex profile, any recessing was less marked. 'Sagging' or convex bases without thumbing are not so common, and are mainly restricted to small rounded jugs (Fig 80, Nos 161, 163-4, 166, 169). In such instances, when the jug is small and narrow-mouthed, or when there is only slight convexity, a sagging profile was generally produced by knife-trimming. The bases of larger vessels, however, were often pushed out by hand from inside the jug after removal from the wheel, as indicated by internal dents and impressions. They were then trimmed externally as necessary (eg Fig 76, Nos 138-9).

Various different patterns of thumbing were used with very little discernible relationship to any particular form. After knife-trimming, thumb impressions were made, often in a continuous line around the base, either overlapping, touching, or separate, but closely-spaced. Alternatively, they may be grouped together in various combinations at fairly regular intervals around the base; groups of anything from two to seven, but commonly of three or four impressions, are found on any one pot, and each group may contain a different number of impressions (eg Figs 58, No 43; 63; see also Fig 20a).

Flat and undecorated, ie unthumbed, bases are a common feature of biconical jugs (Figs 82; 83, Nos 193-7), and small rounded jugs (Fig 81, Nos 176-9). Some flat bases are also slightly indented at the centre. This form of base is uncommon in other jug types.

Jugs were probably removed from the wheel by pulling a taut length of fine wire or catgut in a single motion under the base, occasionally leaving fine scratch-marks in the clay. Smaller jugs were more commonly removed in this way than larger ones, although the tell-tale marks may subsequently have been obscured by knife-trimming or smoothing. If a vessel was trimmed while the clay was still fairly soft, as indicated by the presence of finger-dents around the edge of the base, then evidence for the process is almost

20. Kingston-type ware: details of jug bases, showing thumb impressions inside (a); and (b) kiln scars.

imperceptible, since the tool skimmed smoothly across the clay and tended not to drag inclusions along with it. However, jugs were also trimmed when in a leather-hard state, and this is far more obvious, since inclusions were caught by the blade and dragged across the base.

The distinctive vertical knife-trimming associated with metal copy baluster jugs has already been described (see p. 33). The usual pattern of trimming the lower part of the body of a jug was in series of short horizontal or oblique, overlapping strokes. The trimmed zone sometimes extended as far as the maximum girth, but more often covered only a few centimetres. This would generally be adequate to achieve the desired effect of reducing the thickness of the base at its circumference, and to ensure successful firing. In rare instances the trimming was rather overenthusiastically carried out; for example, on the jug illustrated in Fig 53, No 17, the trimming tool cut deeply into the clay underneath the base in an arc, making it over-thin and so weakening it. The clay consequently cracked around this weakness during firing, and glaze seeped into the fissure, partially filling it. The vessel is almost, but not quite, unusable. The small rounded jug illustrated in Fig 79, No 152 has also suffered, although not so severely, from over-trimming, since the base has been cut off at a distinct angle from the horizontal.

'Makers' Marks'

Two nearly complete Kingston-type jugs found in London have what appear to be non-decorative marks or symbols incised on the body after firing. Both jugs are otherwise undecorated; one is conical (Fig 65, No 76), and the other pear-shaped (Fig 68, No 93). In both cases the symbol is the same and is found on the shoulder, opposite the handle. It takes the form of an arrow made with three knife-strokes, pointing vertically towards the rim. The arrow symbol can be closely paralleled by a non-decorative mark on a Mill Green ware conical jug now in the Museum of London (Pearce *et al.* 1982, Fig 4, No 4). It has been suggested that this example represents a personal mark, or identifies part of an order placed with the potter (*ibid.*, 287-9). Marks interpreted as trade-marks, or as recording batches or consignments of pots, are also known in London-type ware (Pearce *et al.* 1985, Figs 36, No 119; 38, No 129), and the Kingston-type ware marks were probably made for a similar purpose.

The only other example of an intentional non-decorative mark illustrated here is part of a symbol incised underneath the base of a jug whose form cannot now be identified (Fig 88, No 253). It is obviously different from those described above, but since it is incomplete, it is uncertain whether it can be similarly interpreted.

Decoration

1. Highly decorated style

Highly decorated jugs generally have an overall lead glaze, coloured green by the addition of copper. Polychrome jugs are less common, but are not made in any of the other decorative styles identified in Kingston-type ware – the body of the jug was clear-glazed, and copper or red slip was used to add emphasis to the design by colouring certain features (Figs 10-11; 13). Highly decorated jugs with a clear glaze alone are rare, and only two complete examples are illustrated here (Figs 15; 66, Nos 83-4).

Plastic decoration was built up from strips and bands of clay, which was generally the same in composition as that used to make the body of the jug, but without the quartz sand temper. It is consequently much finer than the body, but fired to the same colour. Decorative strips of a 'buttery' consistency, and therefore not strictly 'slip', were applied by being squeezed onto the body of the pot between the thumb and fingers. This generally gave them a triangular section, but could also spread the finer clay on either side, so that it merged into the neighbouring decoration. Differential shrinkage during firing occasionally caused sections of the strips to flake away from the jug (eg Fig 48, No 1). Decorative strips were also made from somewhat coarser clay, which may be whiter or redder than the body, or identical in colour.

Large baluster and pear-shaped jugs, including the waisted examples, are the types which most commonly have plastic decoration. The only other types which may be highly decorated are cylindrical-necked baluster, conical and rounded jugs.

Very simple designs consisting of regularly-spaced vertical applied strips are quite common in London-type ware (eg Pearce *et al.* 1985, Fig 33), but rare in Kingston-type ware (Figs 49; 50, No 4; 66, Nos 82-3). The majority of highly decorated jugs have rather more complex patterns of applied strips, which may be combined with other applied motifs, stamps and polychrome glazing. Decorative schemes may be built up from clay strips applied in three or four zones from the rim to just above the base, and in various combinations of diagonal, vertical and undulating lines, chevrons, conjoined lozenges and lens shapes (Figs 48; 52, No 9; 63, Nos 65, 67; 66, Nos 84-5; 87, Nos 239, 244-45).

Greater complexity of design results from the introduction of other elements into schemes such as those outlined above. These include floral motifs (Figs 50, No 5; 52, No 10; 87, No 243) and small groups or lines of single, overlapping 'scales' or pellets of 'buttery' clay (Figs 50, Nos 5, 7; 51; 71, No 109). On some jugs these appear to be intended to represent clusters of grapes, leaves or other fruit (Figs 52, No 11; 63, No 66; 67, No 87). Ring-and-dot stamps on little applied 'blobs' of clay (Figs 21-23) commonly form a part of design

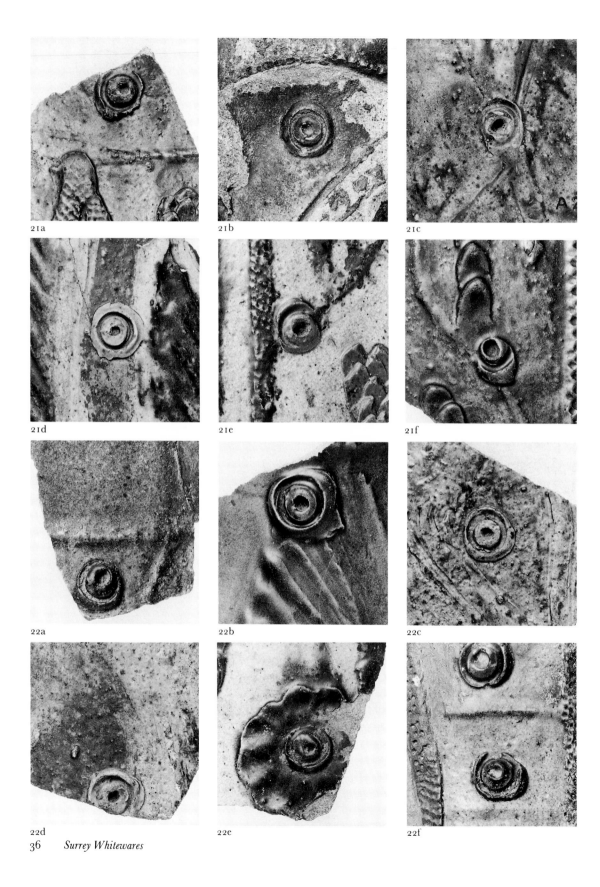

21a

21b

21c

21d

21e

21f

22a

22b

22c

22d

22e

22f

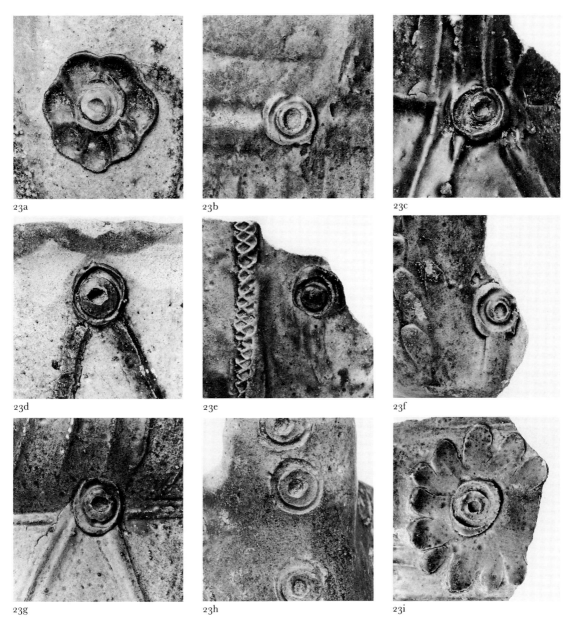

23a	23b	23c
23d	23e	23f
23g	23h	23i

21–3. Kingston-type ware : details of ring-and-dot stamps from miscellaneous jugs.

schemes of this sort, and are also used with simpler combinations of applied strips. The jug illustrated in Fig 87, No 248 is decorated with ring-and-dot stamps on applied red clay 'blobs', combined with lines of ring-and-dot stamps made directly in the clay of the jug in vertical lines down the centre and each side of the bridge spout. Strips of clay may also be roller-stamped, but the only pattern that seems to have been used at all frequently con-

sists of a close grid of crossed diagonals (Figs 50, No 7; 52, Nos 10-11; 66, No 82; 87, Nos 240, 242, 246). Both roller-stamps and other stamps used by the Kingston potters lack the variety displayed by London-type ware (Pearce *et al.* 1985, Pl 7-12). One of the most complex and unusual schemes of decoration illustrated here is found on a green-glazed pear-shaped jug (Figs 16; 67, No 87) and consists of two tiers of vines with central stalks, and both straight and curling tendrils bearing clusters of grapes and plain applied discs of clay. The most unusual element of this decoration is a series of large bosses around the waisted centre of the body, pushed out from inside, and squeezed externally into sub-rectangular shapes. Only one other example of this form of boss has been identified to date, and probably comes from a jug decorated in an equally elaborate fashion (Fig 88, No 252).

Polychrome glazing might be found with any of the decorative schemes described above. Copper was generally painted onto the applied strips to colour them green, especially when plant decoration was intended. Red-firing clay or slip was commonly used for the ring-and-dot stamps, and for groups of 'scales' representing grapes and flower motifs (Fig 52, Nos 10-11). Thin red slip was also smeared onto the body of the pot in areas defined by white strips (eg Figs 63, No 65; 71, Nos 109-110).

A unique highly decorated, polychrome rounded jug is illustrated in Fig 71, No 110 (see also Rackham 1972, Pl B). The chief element in the decoration is a series of three large lozenge-shaped panels, each containing a single rampant animal, probably imaginary, against a background of red slip. Ring-and-dot stamps are used to represent the eyes, and on the body, as well as lines of thumb- or finger-nail nicks, which may indicate fur or scales. The treatment of the animals' bodies can be compared with that of a small group of mid-13th-century London-type ware jugs decorated with applied birds (Pearce *et al.* 1985, Figs 43; 57, Nos 227, 229). The decoration can also be closely paralleled in a northern French jug found at Alsted in Surrey, in a context dated *c.* 1250-70 (Ketteringham 1976, Fig 30).

All the elements of the Kingston-type highly decorated style, from its simplest manifestation to the most elaborate, may be found in the north French style and highly decorated London-type ware from the early to mid-13th-century (Pearce *et al.* 1985, Figs 33-4, 39-44, 50-55, 87). The origins of these styles were in northern France, and were adapted by the London-type ware potters to suit their own tastes and those of their customers. It is likely that the mid-13th-century Kingston-type vessels were directly inspired both by the French originals and by the London products, to which, stylistically, they bear a very close resemblance.

2. Anthropomorphic and zoomorphic decoration
The commonest form of anthropomorphic decoration on Kingston-type ware jugs consists of

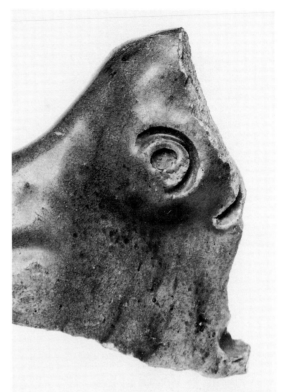

24a

24b

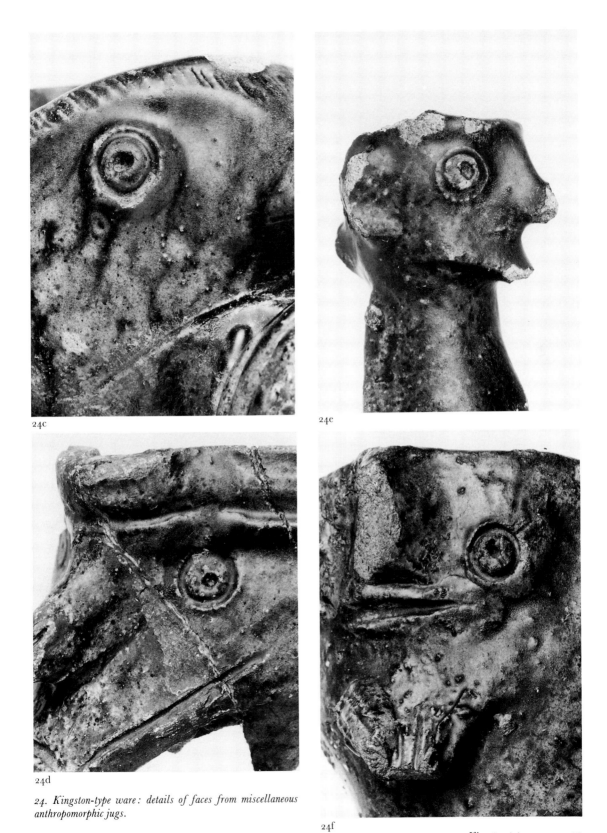

24c

24e

24d

24. Kingston-type ware: details of faces from miscellaneous anthropomorphic jugs.

24f

a modelled human face built up on the rim opposite the handle (Figs 24; 25a-c). The body of the jug represents the body of the figure, with applied arms and hands and sometimes items of dress. Unfortunately, the head and fragments of the rim are often the only parts which survive, so that very few complete jug profiles can be reconstructed. Forms known to have anthropomorphic decoration include cylindrical-necked baluster, pear-shaped, conical and small rounded jugs (Figs 51; 52, No 12; 63, No 65; 69, No 99; 82, No 181). Nearly all are highly decorated, some have polychrome glazing (eg Figs 13; 63, No 65), and a few have stamped bosses (Fig 69, No 99). A range of miniature anthropomorphic jugs was also made in Kingston-type ware (Figs 84; 85, Nos 221-2, 225). They are invariably green-glazed, but otherwise undecorated, and can be compared with the Mill Green series (Pearce *et al.* 1982, Fig 9, Pl IV). Fragments of anthropomorphic jugs, datable to the late 14th century, were also found in Kingston, at Eden Street (Hinton 1980, Fig 3, Nos 28-32).

Bridge-spouts made in the form of a human face are illustrated in Figs 51; 85, Nos 227, 229; 86, No 230 (see also Thorn 1978, Fig 51). The contents of the jug were poured either through the

25b

25a

25c

25d

25e

25f

25. Kingston-type ware: details of faces from miscellaneous anthropomorphic jugs (a-c); animal-head spouts from rounded jugs (d-f).

mouth, or over the forehead. Only two other specific adaptations of applied faces to facilitate pouring are illustrated here: Fig 63, No 65, which has a pulled and pinched pouring lip; and Fig 86, No 231, which has a head whose chin extends into a tubular spout held between two hands.

Kingston-type ware anthropomorphic jugs share certain characteristics with the comparable range of London-type ware jugs. However, whereas London-type ware anthropomorphic jugs display a degree of similarity in the facial features, both in appearance and in method of application (Pearce *et al.* 1985, Fig 56, Nos 211-13), the more numerous surviving Kingston-type faces are quite varied. The entire face may be made separately from the same clay as that used for the body, and applied to the rim of the jug, often extending above it (eg Fig 84, Nos 211, 214, 216). Alternatively, the more prominent features, such as nose, chin and ears, were simply applied to the rim, which was often slightly distorted in the process, and was pushed out to give emphasis to the shape of the face (eg Figs 52, No 12; 63, No 65). Many of the faces appear to be those of men, with a beard represented by various patterns of incised lines (eg Figs 63, No 65; 82, No 181). Incised lines were also used to indicate the mouth and eyebrows, and occasionally the nostrils. Eyes were mostly shown by ring-and-dot stamps, made directly onto the face, or on applied blobs of clay (Figs 24; 25). Beardless faces may be of either sex, but women can only be identified by the addition of details of dress and hairstyle; for example, on the head illustrated in Fig 86, No 232, incised lines were used to represent the barbette and fillet characteristic of ladies' head-wear in the 13th and 14th centuries (Cunnington and Cunnington 1969, 50, 52, Fig 17).

Four anthropomorphic jugs in the Museum of London reserve collection have crowned and bearded faces stamped from the same mould, with only the ears formed separately (Fig 84, Nos 212-3). The modelling of the features is extremely fine, and in marked contrast to the majority of Kingston-type face jugs. The presence of a crown suggests that the model was a king, although it is impossible to be more precise in identification. A remarkably similar moulded head, with a crown, beard and flowing hair was found in the Eden Street kiln material at Kingston, applied to the neck of a large, incomplete jug (Hinton 1980, Fig 3, No 28).

The majority of Kingston-type face jugs have applied arms modelled in the round from the same type of clay as was used for the body (Figs 84, Nos 211-12, 214-18; 85, Nos 225-27). They were attached, appropriately, to the shoulder of the jug, and have hands which may be folded in various unlikely positions – clasped together, crossed or made to grasp at the chin. The fingers were generally represented by incised lines, and were not always limited to four in number. Occasionally, the hands were more carefully modelled (Fig 86, Nos 231, 233-5, 238). Two of the jugs under discussion have additional details of dress in the form of an applied brooch, positioned on the 'chest', between the arms. The jug illustrated in Fig 82, No 181 has been classified as Dunning's Type II (Dunning 1969, 388-9; Spencer 1969), and has a lozenge-shaped brooch with a pin and four settings. The other vessel (not illustrated here), whose face is that of a woman with barbette and fillet headdress, has a simple annular brooch with pin (Thorn 1978, Fig 51).

Jugs with faces formed on the body, as found in London-type ware (Pearce *et al.* 1985, Fig 56, Nos 211-213), are extremely rare in Kingston-type ware. The only example illustrated (Fig 86, No 236) differs in appearance from the faces described above, and has a prominent applied nose with large nostrils, and heavy, incised eyebrows and eyes. Even more unusual, in fact so far unique, is the representation of a human face on the upper part of a jug handle, which unfortunately cannot be related to any recognised vessel form (Fig 86, No 237; see p.33); and the large tubular spout with incised indications of women's dress (Fig 86, No 238).

Far less variety is shown by jugs with zoomorphic decoration, which principally takes the

form of applied animal-head spouts on highly decorated, polychrome rounded jugs (Figs 25d-f; 71, Nos 107-9). The spouts can be identified as rams by the addition of two curled horns. The entire head was modelled separately and attached to the neck of the jug in the same way as a bridge spout, over a hole cut just below the rim. The eyes are ring-and-dot stamps, the mouth a long incised line each side of the muzzle, and the nostrils have been neatly pushed through the end of the snout with a pointed tool or stick to allow liquid to be poured. A large number of these heads, all remarkably similar in appearance, are housed in the Museum of London reserve collection.

A green-glazed, undecorated miniature baluster jug with zoomorphic features is illustrated in Fig 84, No 219 (see also Fig 17). The animal head, applied at the rim, opposite the handle, is incomplete, and does not actually form a spout, so that in this case liquid would have to be poured over the head, between the horns.

3. Stamped bosses

Stamped boss decoration is associated in particular with green-glazed cylindrical-necked baluster and rounded jugs (Figs 53-54; 72). Other forms which may be decorated in this manner include metal copy baluster, conical, pear-shaped and squat jugs (Figs 56, Nos 28-9; 63, Nos 68-9; 69, No 99; 70, No 100; 88, Nos 249-51).

At least fourteen different motifs and rather more individual stamps are illustrated here (see Figs 26-8a-c; 89-93). Various groupings of finger impressions are visible inside the jug, behind the stamps, since it would have been necessary for the potter to support the wall of the pot while making the stamped impression. However, the prevention of cracking was not the only reason for this internal support of the stamped area; the bossed effect achieved when the stamp was pushed out from

26. Kingston-type ware: and stamped bosses in the form of a shield (a) and fleur-de-lys (b-c).

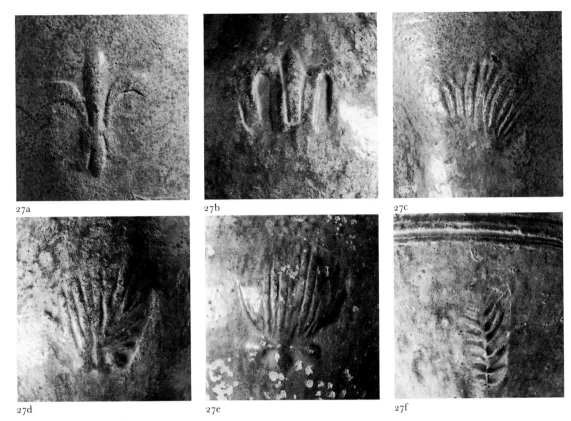

27a 27b 27c

27d 27e 27f

27. *Kingston-type ware: details of stamped bosses from miscellaneous jugs, in the form of* fleur-de-lys *(a-b), shells (c-e) and 'wheatear' (f).*

inside the jug was obviously intentional. The shape and size of the stamp necessitated different degrees of support and the use of up to four fingers, and sometimes the thumb as well (eg Fig 53, Nos 13, 16).

The range of stamps used on Kingston-type vessels from London includes several which cannot be paralleled at either of the Kingston kiln sites, or Bankside. Perhaps the commonest of these are stamps of a shield containing three chevrons (Figs 26a; 89, Nos 254-59; Thorn and Thorn 1972), *fleur-de-lys* (Figs 26b-c; 27a-b; 89, Nos 260-61; 90) and scallop shells (Figs 27c-e; 91). However, mid- to late 14th-century jugs are commonly decorated with bosses of so called 'wheatear' or 'fernleaf' pattern (Fig 93), and these are known at Kingston, in both the Eden Street and the Knapp-Drewett kiln material (Hinton 1980, 382, Fig 4; McCracken, Nenk and Vince forthcoming, Figs 2, Nos 14-16; 4, Nos 31-3). They were supported and bossed with single long finger impressions inside the jug. The shape of *fleur-de-lys* stamps required a different grouping comprising one long finger impression and two or three smaller fingertip impressions, or four to five small impressions. The shield stamp was usually bossed with three

long, rather indistinct, finger impressions. The shell stamps may be quite large and prominently bossed, and appear to have no consistent orientation. Other, less common, stamps found in London include small rosettes (Figs 69, No 99; 92, Nos 282, 285), crosses (Fig 92, No 283), 'raspberry' motifs (Fig 92, No 284) and heraldic devices (Figs 28a; 92, Nos 280-81). The stamp illustrated in Fig 92, No 279 consists of three crosses, the central one dominant, and may represent the Crucifixion. Fig 92, Nos 277-78 are also worthy of comment – each shows a pair of birds, placed back-to-back, but with their necks craning towards each other. They are separated by a tree or plant, and the whole stamp is contained within an oval surround. This figure may be paralleled in London-type ware, on a large jug decorated with pairs of applied confronted birds placed either side of a tree (Pearce *et al.* 1985, Fig 57, No 229). It is also a common motif on contemporary decorated floor tiles (Eames 1980, Nos 1958-1992).

Stamped bosses were generally placed in two or three horizontal zones around the body of the jug. These zones may be separated or highlighted by cordons or grooves. Most of the stamps may be used on their own (eg Fig 63, No 68), but may also be combined with zones of one or more different stamps (Fig 53, Nos 13, 16), or alternate with them in the same zone (Fig 53, Nos 14-15). 'Wheat-ear' bosses were invariably unaccompanied by another stamp, and may be spaced at regular intervals in one or more horizontal rows (Fig 54, No 19), or stamped rather more at random around the body of the jug (Fig 54, No 18).

A rounded jug now in the Museum of London reserve collection has an exceptional form of stamped and bossed decoration (Fig 72, No 116). A single row of regularly-spaced 'blobs' of fairly coarse, red-fired clay, deeply stamped with a star-shaped device, runs around the shoulder of the jug, each slightly pushed out from inside (Fig 28b).

4. Pellet decoration

This type of decoration is found on green-glazed metal copy and cylindrical-necked baluster, squat and rounded jugs (Figs 56, Nos 30-32; 57, Nos 33-36; 70, Nos 101-03; 73, Nos 117-120). The idea is fairly simple, and was used with little variation. The body of the jug was covered with closely-spaced rows of 'scales' or pellets of untempered, fine clay. Each pellet was applied with the thumb or finger while the clay was in a 'buttery' state, leaving a pointed or rounded tongue standing out slightly from the body at its upper end, and smoothed down onto the jug at

28. Kingston-type ware: details of various stamp-impressions from miscellaneous jugs.

the lower. The jug may be densely covered with pellets from the shoulder to just below the maximum girth (Fig 56, Nos 30-32), or have only three or four rows of pellets, rather more widely-spaced vertically (Fig 73, Nos 117, 120).

Applied pellet decoration, both on its own and combined with other elements, can be closely paralleled with late 12th- and 13th-century London-type ware green-glazed jugs (e.g. Pearce *et al.* 1985, Figs 24, No 50; 53, Nos 191, 193, 198).

5. Grooved decoration

The simplest form of decoration found on Kingston-type ware jugs of most forms was that applied to the vessel while it was still on the wheel. This consists of horizontal grooves made either with a pointed tool or with a comb. Such decoration may be limited to a single band of combing, or to one or two grooves on the neck, shoulder, or body. Small rounded jugs are commonly treated in this manner (Figs 79-81). Larger vessels may have several bands of combing (eg Figs 58, No 42; 59, Nos 44-45, 47), or a zone of continuous combing, similar in appearance to the decoration of rilled baluster jugs. (eg Fig 54, No 22).

Very rarely, sherds of Kingston-type jugs are found with combed decoration in patterns that do not conform to the strictly horizontal 'schemes' described above. The most substantial example illustrated here is the unusual, carinated pear-shaped jug (Figs 14; 66, No 81). Wavy vertical lines, contained within straight verticals made with a four-pronged comb, are placed around the body in a zone stretching from just below the rim to the carination. This form of decoration is common to Mill Green ware, in which it is applied to jugs of similar form (Pearce *et al.* 1982, Fig 5, No 7). The only other illustrated jug carrying non-horizontal combed decoration is of large rounded/squat form, and has curved and wavy vertical incised lines between plain strips of applied clay (Fig 78, No 144).

Cooking vessels

Complete, or nearly complete, Kingston-type cooking vessels of any form are poorly represented in the reserve collections of both the Museum of London and the British Museum. The bulk of the material available for study comes from recent excavations, principally in the form of sherds. Consequently, it is seldom possible to reconstruct complete vessel profiles. Since the majority of Kingston-type ware cooking vessels – such as cooking pots, pipkins and cauldrons – appear to differ only in detail, confident ascription of body sherds to any one of these forms cannot be made without the presence of diagnostic features. Frequently the most that can be said is that such sherds belong to a vessel used for cooking. Furthermore, Kingston-type ware cooking vessels show far less typological variation than, for example, London-type ware (Pearce *et al.* 1985, Figs 67-9). Therefore, the dates at which certain forms first came into use in London can only be suggested. It is also, for the reasons outlined above, difficult to calculate the relative frequencies of the different forms. As far as can be determined, cooking pots appear to be commoner than other forms used in the kitchen (see Appendix 6).

1. Cooking pots

(Fig 94)

Only two complete Kingston-type ware cooking pots are illustrated in this book (Nos 296-7). Body sherds from excavations show that the globular shape of these vessels was common to all Kingston-type cooking pots.

Rims may be simply everted, with an internal bevel (Nos 296, 301-2), or an almost vertical external bevel (No 300). In all these examples the neck of the cooking pot flares outwards to the rim from a constriction at the shoulder. More frequently, a short, approximately straight-sided

neck separates the body from the the rim, which may be externally thickened and internally bevelled (Nos 298, 303, 304), or flat-topped (Nos 297, 305-10). Some cooking pots with a flat-topped rim have either no neck at all, or only a very short neck, in which case the shape of the complete vessel would probably be closer to that of a jar (Nos 305, 309).

Surviving cooking pot bases and base sherds are either flat or have a slightly convex profile (Nos 296-7). The lower part of the body may be knife-trimmed up to 30mm or more from the base angle, and No 297 shows clear signs of having been over-zealously trimmed underneath the base, so that the blade of the trimming-tool cut deeply into the clay in a wide arc. This pot was also damaged during handling – the rim is dented in two places – probably when the vessel was picked up. This weakened the body, which has cracked from these points. The vessel was, nevertheless, fired and appears to have been used since there are indications of its having been heated in cooking.

Sparse patches, spots and dribbles of green glaze are found on the external surface of most cooking pots, although some have no glaze at all. Inside the cooking pot there may be a spread of glaze over the base; No 297, for example, clearly shows how the liquid glaze ran during firing. The only form of decoration to be recognised on any of the Kingston-type cooking pots from London consists of roughly applied vertical, thumbed strips extending from the shoulder down the outside of the body (No 310).

Kingston-type ware cooking pots are found in London in late 13th- to mid-14th-century assemblages. The small quantities present in late 14th-century groups probably reflect a general decline in the use of Kingston-type ware in favour of products from other industries (see Fig 9; Appendix 6).

2. Pipkins

(Fig 95, Nos 311-17)

A much larger number of complete pipkins has survived than any other form of Kingston-type cooking vessel. Although smaller they closely resemble cooking pots in shape. However, they can be distinguished from this form by the presence of a handle. The body is globular or biconical, and the neck flares from a constriction at the shoulder. In variety of rim forms, pipkins may again be compared with cooking pots, but commonly have a pinched pouring lip, approximately at 90° from the handle. One unusual example (No 317) appears to have been specially made for left-handed pouring, unless the handle was wrongly positioned by mistake.

Handles are all of strap form, attached to the shoulder of the vessel, at an angle of about 45° to the rim. They were pushed through the body from the outside – a technique used with certain forms of jug (see p.32). Extra pads or strips of clay were then wrapped around the join and smoothed into the body (eg No 317). Handles often have a shallow groove on the upper, and sometimes the lower surface. Two or three thumb or finger indentations at the base of the handle ensured a more secure attachment to the body (Nos 314, 316-17). The base may be flat, slightly indented, or slightly sagging in profile, and was knife trimmed, both underneath and around the lower part of the body. A spread of green glaze was applied inside the base, as with cooking pots (see above). The occasional spots and patches of glaze on the outside of the vessel were probably accidental. Most pipkins were placed directly over heat in use, as shown by heavy sooting and blackening of the base and sides. No 317 was caked with soot, not only over the entire exterior, but also on both sides of the handle and just inside the rim.

Pipkins can be dated in London to the 13th and 14th centuries, and were also found in Kingston at the Eden Street site (Hinton 1980, Fig 3, No. 21).

3. Tripod pipkins

(Fig 95, Nos 318-19)

Tripod pipkins differ from pipkins principally in the addition of three feet or legs. Consequently, vessels which can be positively identified are very few, since body sherds might well be interpreted as belonging to either cooking pots or pipkins. The legs of both the illustrated examples are incomplete, although the thickness and length of the stubs suggests that they might have been longer and more substantial than the short feet of London-type ware tripod pipkins (Pearce *et al.* 1985, Fig 68, Nos 361-2). In this respect, they bear a close resemblance to cauldrons (see below). There is no evidence that the surviving vessels had any form of pouring lip.

No tripod pipkins were recorded at Eden Street, or Bankside, and sherds from London excavations are very rare.

4. Cauldrons

(Fig 96, Nos 320-23)

Kingston-type cauldrons are closely related in form both to cooking pots and tripod pipkins. The body is globular in shape, with three long legs and two handles. The neck is flared, and the rim is generally internally bevelled (cf. certain cooking pot forms, eg Fig 94, Nos 296-304). Two diametrically opposed, angled loop handles of rod or squared section were applied at the neck and shoulder. The methods of application differ – for example, one of the handles of No 321 had broken away from the neck in such a way as to show clearly how it was applied. A circular hole was pushed through the neck from outside, and the end of the handle pressed into it. Small pads or lumps of clay were then smoothed around the join both outside and inside. The lower part of the handle is missing. However, the one surviving cauldron fragment whose handles are complete shows an interesting contrast in method of attachment (No 320). The lower end of the handle was pressed onto the outside of the body, while the potter pushed his thumb or finger into the stump from inside the vesel. Both methods of attachment are known to have been used with jug handles (see p.32).

Bases have a convex profile, with three long, heavy, broad legs attached at the base angle. Only one complete cauldron leg is illustrated (No 322). It is both broader and heavier than other surviving tripod pipkin legs, and has a wide central groove on the outer surface.

Kingston-type ware cauldrons can be dated in London to the late 13th and early 14th centuries, but form only a small proportion of Kingston-type assemblages during this period (see Appendix 6). This may be a reflection of the difficulty in recognising the form from body sherds alone. No cauldrons were identified among the kiln waste from Kingston (Hinton 1980), or from Bankside (Dennis and Hinton 1983).

5. Dripping dishes

(Fig 96, Nos 324-30)

No complete Kingston-type dripping dishes have been found in London, but surviving fragments show that they were built up by hand from slabs of clay. It is difficult to reconstruct the shapes of complete vessels, although it seems probable, on the basis of excavated sherds, that they were shallow dishes of oval or D-shaped plan. Rims are rounded (No 330), bevelled internally (Nos 324-5), externally thickened (No 327), or almost flanged in appearance (No 329). Bases are flat, and the sides heavily knife-trimmed, which can give a distinctly angled profile (No 324). The base sherd illustrated by No 328 must have come from an exceptionally narrow dripping dish, no more than 50mm wide across the bottom.

The evidence of other contemporaneous wares, such as London-type ware (Pearce *et al.* 1985, Figs 70-71) suggests that Kingston-type dripping dishes had at least one handle and a pouring lip. The very nature of the form, designed as it was to collect the juices from spit-roasted joints, would have made both necessary, in order to handle the dish when hot, and to pour off the accumulated gravy. However, excavated handles are extremely rare, although pinched and pulled pouring lips are more common (Nos 327, 330). The vessel illustrated in No 329 is unusual in that its walls were thickened by the addition of a layer of clay inside the dish. Dripping dishes are normally glazed inside, and heavily sooted and blackened outside.

6. Frying pans

(Figs 96, Nos 331-33; 97, No 334)

The term 'frying pan', when applied to medieval pottery, is based on a comparison with modern forms and need not imply a similar method of cooking, although all the vessels examined are sooted and blackened around the base. It is often difficult to distinguish Kingston-type frying pans from dripping dishes. The chief difference between the two seems to be that frying pans are wheelthrown and circular in plan, and that dripping dishes are hand-made in more irregular shapes. Frying pan rims are externally thickened or flanged, and no pouring lips can be definitely associated with the form. Two different types of handle are known: one is of solid strap form (Fig 96, Nos 331, 333), fixed over the rim in an horizontal or angled position; the other is a short, tubular form (Fig 97, No 334), which can be paralleled at Eden Street (Hinton 1980, Fig 3, No 19). The latter type was probably intended to act as a socket for a wooden handle, which would make it easier to hold when hot. Frying pans are normally glazed only on the inside surface, and are heavily knife-trimmed.

Bowls and dishes

Bowls

(Figs 97, Nos 335-42; 98, Nos 343-47)

The distinction between bowls and dishes is generally based on relative dimensions and is inevitably rather arbitrary. Very few complete profiles are known in Kingston-type ware, and many vessels do not fit easily into either category. Since the openware forms under discussion here are closely related in terms of function, they are best considered together under one heading, and are therefore termed 'bowls'.

Bowl rims are commonly thickened externally, often to such a degree as to give a flange, bevelled internally (Fig 97, No 341) or externally (Fig 97, No 336). Thickening of the rim flange internally produces a 'hammer-head' form (Fig 97, No 338). Bases which can be related to these forms show heavy knife-trimming. This tends to give complete vessels a slightly convex profile, with a flat or sagging base (Figs 97, Nos 340, 341; 98, Nos 343-45, 347). There may be a thin spread of green glaze inside the base, with dribbles and spots both inside and out. The way in which the glaze has run shows that many bowls were inverted in the kiln. Decoration is rare – the only example illustrated here is a large bowl with vertical, thumbed, applied strips of clay (Fig 97, No 336). Many vessels are poorly finished, and blackened and encrusted with soot around the base and sides, and so must have been used in the kitchen (Figs 97, Nos 336, 342; 98, Nos 343, 346).

The bowl illustrated in Fig 98, No 343, is unusual in having a pinched and pulled pouring lip. Another unusual bowl (No 345) has a handle of oval section, attached just over the rim at a slight angle from the horizontal, and Fig 97, No 335 is part of a bowl that appears to have been oval in plan. It was glazed both inside and out, which is very uncommon, and was probably intended to be used for serving food.

Kingston-type ware bowls were in use in London from the mid- to late 14th century, and were found among both the Eden Street and Bankside kiln waste (Hinton 1980, Fig 3, Nos 22-24; Dennis and Hinton 1983, Fig 3, Nos 14-17).

Small dishes or 'saucers'

(Fig 98, Nos 348-66)

These are comparable in form and probably in function with the London-type ware small dish or 'saucer' (Pearce *et al* 1985, Fig 72, Nos 392-6; pp.125-6), and with the less common Coarse Border ware form (Fig 118, Nos 510-13). They can be recognised as distinct from bowls, as described above, by their small size.

Kingston-type 'saucers' are remarkably uniform in size. They are either straight-sided, resembling an inverted, truncated cone, or have a slightly convex profile, accentuated by knife-trimming. Rims are rounded (Nos 349-54), bevelled and sometimes thickened externally (Nos 355-61), flat-topped (Nos 364-5), or hooked (No 366). Bases are flat and unaltered after removal from the wheel (Nos 349, 359), or slightly indented (Nos 355-8). They may have been wiped across by hand, causing the clay of the base angle to spread onto the sides in places. Sagging bases are rare (No 351). Some 'saucers' are knife-trimmed (Nos 351, 366), but not all, and many display a lack of finish suggestive of mass-production. This is borne out by distorted and dented rims and walls, lumps of clay stuck to the body, kiln scars and 'bubbled' glaze. All the small dishes examined have a spread of green glaze inside the base. Several are sooted on the outside, as if used to heat or keep small quantities of food warm. This is not inconsistent with their function, being similar to that suggested for London-type ware 'saucers', ie to hold sauces or condiments at table.

Condiment dishes

(Fig 99, Nos 367–72)

Condiment dishes, made specially to hold seasonings for use at the table, take various shapes in Kingston-type ware. Only two handmade condiment dishes are illustrated here. The one complete vessel (No 369) is sub-rectangular in shape, with rounded ends, and almost vertical, knife-trimmed sides. The base is flat, and the whole dish was built up by hand from slabs of clay. Two internal partitons across its width form three separate compartments. A fairly thick, patchy, dark green glaze covers both internal and external surfaces. The other handmade condiment dish (No 368) is incomplete, with only one internal dividing slab remaining, but may have been of similar form. The rim is rounded, the sides heavily knife-trimmed, and the dish is glazed inside, with only a few spots outside. The form is also known in London-type ware (Pearce *et al*. 1985, Fig 72, No 398).

Wheelthrown condiment dishes are all different in shape. The simplest (No 367) is a small circular dish of 'saucer' form, with a single partition across the diameter, made from a flattened slab of clay. It is glazed inside, but not outside. This form can also be paralleled in London-type ware (*ibid.*, Fig 72, No 399). A smaller, almost vertical-sided dish (No 372) has a broad basket handle of strap form, decorated with an incised central line and small diagonal slashes on either side. It is glazed both inside and out, and originally formed half of a double condiment dish. The companion dish was probably identical, and the two were simply luted together.

The two other illustrated condiment dishes might be termed 'closed' forms, since their rim diameter is less than that of the base. No 370 was made as a single condiment dish, and was decorated with horizontal grooves applied while it was still on the wheel. A simple anthropomorphic mask was applied just below the rim, over the grooving. It is shaped like an inverted pear with three finger-tip indentations in which two stabbed eyes and an incised mouth were made. The lower part of the body and the flat base were knife-trimmed, and the dish was glazed both inside and out. The other closed form (No 371) was originally part of a double condiment (cf. No 372). The surviving half is complete, and retains the central bridge of clay which connected the two. This is decorated across the top with a line of finger-nail indentations. The dish has a carinated shoulder, an upright, rounded rim, and knife-trimmed base and sides. It was glazed internally.

Kingston-type ware condiment dishes were introduced into London in the mid-14th century, at about the same date as small dishes or 'saucers'. None were found among the various kiln dumps.

Other forms

Money-boxes

(Fig 99, Nos 373-83)

Kingston-type ware money-boxes are completely closed in form, with a knife-cut slit to take coins. They were made in a variety of shapes, the commonest of which is rounded or globular with a pointed top, resembling a bishop's mitre (Nos 373-79). A few money-boxes are more bottle-shaped, and elaborately finished at the top, with a moulded knop (Nos 380-83). All known vessels are wheelthrown, with a flat or slightly indented base. They were rarely knife-trimmed.

The majority of money-boxes have vertical coin-slits. Experiments carried out by Anne Jenner have shown that is necessary to make the coin slit twice the width required to allow for shrinkage during firing. All surviving money-boxes appear to have been broken around the coin-slit, either before or after deposition, probably in order to extract the contents. A sparse, patchy green glaze was applied externally, and decoration is virtually unknown. No money-boxes were found in the Kingston or Bankside material.

Aquamaniles

(Fig 100, Nos 384-86)

Aquamaniles are rare in Kingston-type ware, and all identifiable fragments from London to date are illustrated in this book. The more substantial examples both represent animals, and at least one had a rider. Unusually, the animal in question appears to be a cow, with a bell hanging around its neck (No 384). Its body was thrown as a cylinder, and its head and chest, and the body of the rider were hand-moulded and luted onto the main body section. Curled horns, made from small pieces of rolled clay, were attached to the head, and one must have fallen off during, or just before, firing, leaving the area beneath partially coated with glaze. Strips of applied clay were also used to make the legs and feet of the rider, and the chain and bell around the animal's neck. A rectangular piece of clay, with incised decoration, was added immediately behind the rider to represent a saddle. The cow's chain, forelock and mouth were also incised, and ring-and-dot stamps were used for the eyes. The nostrils were deeply stabbed, and a circular hole was pushed through the centre of the snout to allow for pouring. The whole vessel was covered with a dark green glaze.

The other illustrated animal aquamanile (No 386) is also incomplete – all that remains is the front half of the animal's body including the chest, neck and front legs. The end of what was probably a handle was pushed through the wheelthrown section, at the back of the neck. Applied strips of clay run down the neck from the head, and may represent reins. If so, then the complete aquamanile probably carried a rider.

The sherd illustrated in Fig 100, No 385 may also have come from an aquamanile, as suggested by the unusual thickness of the handmade wall,

and the vertical orientation. A well-modelled circular brooch, with its pin, was made from red clay and luted onto the white-fired body of the vessel. White-firing clay was also used for the seven settings around the ring of the brooch.

Drinking horn

(Figs 29; 100, No 387)

A very unusual vessel in the Museum of London reserve collection is probably best described as a drinking horn (see also Cherry 1985, 11, Fig 2). It is so far without parallel, and consists of a wheelthrown cup with a rounded base, to which a wheelthrown cylinder of clay has been attached. A large hole was cut in the side of the cup, and the end of the cylinder smoothed into it. Four small feet were added to the bottom of the horn, and the front of the cup was decorated with a bearded human face, whose appearance is comparable with those of the Kingston-type anthropomorphic jugs (Figs 84-86). The nose, beard and eyebrows were modelled separately, the eyes were stabbed, and the beard and mouth incised. A male human figure, holding his enlarged penis, sits astride the vessel, behind a small rod handle, fixed from the rim of the cup to the cylinder. However, his body and the end of the cylinder are missing, so it is impossible to reconstruct the original appearance of the complete vessel. The cup is covered with a dark green glaze both inside and out, but the horn is glazed on the outside only.

29. Kingston-type ware: view of drinking horn showing human face (height 104mm).

Lobed cup

(Fig 100, No 388)

Lobed cups which can be identified as Kingston-type ware are uncommon in London. Decorated examples are even more rare. The illustrated fragment of a lobed cup now in the Museum of London reserve collection is unparalleled both in London and Kingston. Only the base of the cup has survived, inside which there is a crudely made model of a horse and rider. The body and head of the legless horse were made in one piece, and were fixed to the base of the vessel, under the belly. The horse's head has stabbed eyes and nostrils, and an incised mouth, ears and mane. The bridle was clumsily formed from separate strips of clay, stabbed at random with a pointed tool. The rider's body was also modelled separately, as were his legs. The head and arms are now missing. There is a handle scar near the base, behind the figure, and both the figure and the inside surfaces of the cup are covered with a thin, clear glaze.

Cup

(Fig 100, No 389)

The one almost complete Kingston-type ware cup known from London was wheelthrown, with two diametrically opposed rod handles. These were attached by the same method used for the handles of certain jug forms. The body was first stabbed from the outside, although the upper join was subsequently smoothed over inside the cup, so hiding the method. The lower end of each handle was pressed against the prepared wall of the cup while the potter pushed his thumb or finger into the stump from inside. The single finger-shaped holes made during this process are still visible. The globular body of the cup is slightly waisted, and has a flaring base, like that of a baluster jug. The base is flat underneath, and there is no obvious knife-trimming. The whole vessel is covered inside and out with a patchy and badly fired glaze, which collected in a pool inside the base, showing that the cup was fired standing upright.

Urinal

(Fig 101, No 390)

Purpose-made ceramic urinals are almost unknown in excavated contexts from London, although they would be difficult to identify from small sherds, and chemical analysis of jugs might well disclose a number devoted to such a usage. However, one almost complete Kingston-type vessel from the Museum of London reserve collection was undoubtedly designed specifically as a urinal. It was thrown as a completely enclosed globular form, rather like a large money-box in shape. A circular hole, 50mm in diameter, was cut off-centre in the top of the dome, and a separately made neck was luted around the opening. A broad bucket handle of strap form was attached across the centre of the dome, to the side of the opening. The ends of the handle were pushed well into the body through slits cut in the walls, and extra clay was wrapped around the join outside. No attempt was made to smooth the inside of the join, or to remove the protruding ends of the handle. The flat base and the lower part of the body were heavily knife-trimmed. Marks on the base show that the vessel was in contact with at least one other pot during firing, and was placed in the kiln in an inverted position. The urinal was green-glazed externally.

Mortar

(Fig 101, No 391)

Only one Kingston-type ware mortar is known from London. It is a large, thick-walled, hemispherical bowl, whose rounded base is now incomplete. The rim is thickened externally and flat-topped. The lower half of the body is glazed outside, and dribbles running towards the rim show that it was fired upside down. The interior has no trace of glaze. Clear wear marks can be seen inside the base, indicating that the vessel was used as a container for pounding or grinding food.

Lids

(Fig 101, Nos 392-93)

Only two Kingston-type ware lids are illustrated here. The more complete example (No 392) is wheelthrown, and shaped like an inverted dish. It is sparingly knife-trimmed above a simple squared rim. A scar on the top shows that some form of knob was originally luted onto the lid. The 'horned' knob is virtually all that has survived of the other lid (No 393). It was secured through a circular hole cut in the top of the lid. It is not known what form of vessel these lids were originally intended to cover, although cooking pots are a likely choice.

Cistern

(Fig 101, No 394)

The bunghole is the only feature that can reliably used to identify this form in sherd material. No complete Kingston-type ware cisterns have yet been found in London. Only the lower part of the body remains of the illustrated example. The sides are straight and the base is flat, with more than one group of three thumb impressions around the circumference. A circular bunghole was cut in the wall of the cistern about 40mm from the base, and a thick disc of clay was luted around the outside of this. The circumference of the disc was then impressed with the thumb and fingers at regular intervals to form an eight-pointed star-shape. No cisterns were identified in the Eden Street kiln waste (Hinton 1980), although a number of sherds were found at the Knapp-Drewett site (McCracken, Nenk and Vince, forthcoming).

Curfew

(Fig 101, No 395)

The illustrated sherd probably comes from a cur-few or fire-cover. The vessel was wheelthrown, with a thick-walled body. The orientation of the throwing-marks suggests a steep-sided dome. A horizontal row of internal finger-impressions gives a minor decorative effect on the outside. The sherd is sooted inside, which supports the suggestion that it came from a vessel used to cover the embers of a fire.

Crucibles

(Fig 101, Nos 396-400)

Kingston-type ware crucibles found in London are all quite small, with thick walls, rounded rims and a slight, pinched pouring lip. They range in shape from a deep, straight-sided form (Nos 396-98), to an open, hemispherical bowl (No 399). All have rounded bases, and one 'bell-shaped' crucible was clearly knife-trimmed (No 400). The latter was the only example with any glaze – a few probably accidental spots. Two of the illustrated crucibles retained deposits of the substance they were used to heat (Nos 397, 400). Fragments of crucibles were found at Eden Street (Hinton 1980, Fig 3, No 25) and Bankside (Dennis and Hinton 1983, Fig 3, No 23).

Storage jar

(Fig 102)

This extremely large vessel from London, here interpreted as a storage jar, is so far without parallel in the Kingston and Bankside waste material, or indeed in any of the Kingston-type ware found in London. The jar is of large rounded form and has two diametrically opposed strap handles. These are broad and thick, and are decorated with two vertical rows of diagonal knife-slashes in a herring-bone pattern. Single wide knife-slashes on either side of the handle/rim and handle/neck joins are probably functional rather than decorative, intended to ensure that the thick clay at these points did not crack during firing. Both handles appear to have been attached by pressing three or four fingers well into the stump from inside the vessel. One of the holes made at the handle/body join was subsequently filled with a large plug of lead. The reason for such an addition is unknown, unless it served as a repair. The other handle was not treated in this way, and there are no traces of lead in any other part of the jar.

The body is decorated with numerous vertical thumbed strips, applied at irregular intervals, and starting at the shoulder. The one surviving base sherd shows that the jar originally had a thick band of thumbed clay, about 20mm deep, added around the circumference. Stab-marks were made with a pointed tool above each thumb-indentation, both inside and outside the base. As with the handle attachments described above, this was probably done to release steam during firing. The vessel has a sparse cover of green glaze outside, and a clear, lead glaze inside.

The storage jar was found at Ludgate Hill, in contexts dated to the late 13th century.

Gaming piece

(Fig 103, No 402)

This piece is unique in Kingston-type ware, and cannot be paralleled in any of the other wares in use in the London area between the 12th and 14th centuries. The stylized figure, probably a knight on horseback, was made in a two-piece mould, and is solid through its central axis. It is decorated in relief, although only the bridle and the horse's mane are easily recognisable. The tail of the horse is broken, and it is not clear how the complete piece would originally have appeared. The whole figure is covered with white slip, under a green glaze. It may have been made simply as a model, a form of toy very popular in the 13th and 14th centuries; alternatively, it may have been part of a chess-set. Pipe-clay toys of the same period were normally quite realistic, whereas chess pieces are known to have become more stylized as the game grew in popularity.

Miscellaneous unidentified vessels

(Fig 103, Nos 403-7)

A number of incomplete vessels of different forms are illustrated because they have been modified in such a way as to make an interpretation of their function difficult. Two rim sherds (Nos 406-407) appear to come from vessels of cooking pot form. However, one (No 407) retains part of the edge of a hole, cut in the body below the rim after throwing; the other (No 406) was cut with a knife or sharp tool in a line that runs almost parallel with the rim. This seems to be the top of a large aperture whose original shape cannot be reconstructed. The lower part of the body and the base of a large, straight-sided, flat-bottomed vessel (No 405) also has part of a small hole drilled or cut cleanly through the wall, about 80mm from the base. The purpose of these holes is unknown.

An unusual, very shallow, flat-bottomed dish-like vessel (No 403) is illustrated in this section because it bears no resemblance to the common Kingston-type form of dish, and because it appears to have been cut down from a taller vessel. The rim is flat and very smooth and was obviously cut to shape. The vessel is unglazed.

The other unusual sherd illustrated (No 404) is the broken leg of a vessel which was probably used for cooking – it shows clear signs of having been heated. It is unglazed, and deeply stabbed at random all round.

Louver

(Fig 104, No 408)

One fragment alone of Kingston-type ware roof furniture has been identified in London, although the precise provenance is unknown. The large sherd comes from the body of a louver or ventilator. The complete form cannot now be reconstructed, but may well have been domed or 'beehive'-shaped, with apertures of various shapes and sizes arranged in a number of tiers. A single circular aperture cut in the body of the louver is flanked by openings which might have been rectangular, or possibly triangular, in shape. Wing-like canopies or 'baffles' were formed from triangular slabs of clay, cut to shape and attached to the sides of the apertures with strips and lumps of clay, both inside and out. There are indications, in the form of straight knife-cuts under the glaze, of a tier of apertures below this, but it is impossible to reconstruct their shape. The body of the louver, into which these apertures were cut, is wheelthrown in the fine Kingston-type clay, and covered outside with a thick, lustrous green glaze, which has seeped through the openings and run down the otherwise unglazed interior. There is no sign of any sooting or blackening of the louver by smoke, although the interior surface is slightly grey in places. This suggests that the structure may have been merely ornamental, or that it was not the principal smoke-extractor for the building to which it belonged.

It is difficult to find parallels for the Kingston-type louver fragment, because so little remains of the original, and because the large apertures are too incomplete for their shape to be reconstructed with any certainty. Triangular, rectangular and circular openings are known in louvers made in London-type ware (Pearce *et al.* 1985, 50-51; Figs 80-83). A large, almost complete, 'beehive-shaped' London-type louver (*ibid.*, Fig 80) may be similar in form to the Kingston-type example. However, most London-type louvers were hand-made rather than wheelthrown, which makes an interesting contrast with the structure under discussion here.

In his classification of medieval roof furniture, Gerald Dunning identified two types of louver (Dunning 1975, 186). The Kingston-type ware louver is most likely to come into Class 1, defined as structures made separately from the roof-ridge, and secured over a hole in the roof in order to extract the smoke, or as decoration.

2. COARSE BORDER WARE

The majority of Coarse Border ware forms found in London are also well-known in London- and Kingston-type wares. However, within the different forms recognised in this book, there appears to be less variety or typological distinction than in the earlier pottery. There was a strong bias towards the production of plain vessels, principally for use in the preparation of food. Cooking pots and jugs are by far the commonest forms in assemblages of Coarse Border ware from the City. Jugs, intended for liquid storage and for serving at table, were functional rather than decorative.

30. Coarse Border ware : baluster jug with stamped decoration (height 245mm).

31. Coarse Border ware : cistern with red-painted decoration (height 285mm).

Since Coarse Border ware vessels are generally thick-walled and robustly made, they often survive in the form of large sherds, and this has made it possible to reconstruct forms with a fair degree of accuracy.

Some Coarse Border ware forms, such as pitchers, are distinctive and easily recognised as different from earlier Surrey whitewares produced at Kingston. However, there are forms, for example, rounded and conical jugs, which bear a close resemblance to Kingston-type ware both in shape and in certain details of construction. These have been classed as Coarse Border ware on the basis of fabric, although the distinction is not always clear. The various forms of Coarse Border ware found in London are described here in terms of shape, details of construction and decoration.

Jugs

Form

Five forms of jug have been identified, and, because there is little variation within each, none has been further subdivided. Some forms, particularly the conical jug, are obviously standardised and uniform in shape and detail. There are too few complete jugs to allow a representative capacity range to be built up for any one form.

1. Baluster

(Figs 30; 105; 106, No 413)

The form is the same as that of the Kingston-type ware cylindrical-necked baluster jug (see p.20; Figs 52-55). The shoulder is often marked by a cordon, and the constricted waist and flared base may be elegantly pronounced (eg Fig 105, No 412). Most baluster jugs in which an adequate proportion of the rim has survived have a pinched and pulled pouring lip. Handles are of strap form, incised and stabbed. Thumbing of the base is common. All the examples illustrated are green-glazed and have applied, anthropomorphic or painted decoration. Undecorated baluster jugs are rare. Apart from cisterns, this is the only form of Coarse Border ware jug to carry body decoration. The capacity of the jug illustrated in Fig 105, No 410, was measured at 1740ml.

2. Barrel-shaped

(Fig 106, Nos 414-15)

The body is ovoid in shape and has either a short, straight-sided neck, or no neck at all. There is typically no pouring lip or spout. Handles are of oval or sub-rectangular section. The form is undecorated, with only a small 'bib' of glaze on the shoulder. It can be compared with the Cheam whiteware barrel-shaped jug (see p.69; Figs 120-21). It is, however, a far less common form in Coarse Border ware. The capacities of the two illustrated jugs are 1900ml and 2000ml respectively.

3. Conical

(Figs 106, No 416; 107-08)

Conical jugs, as their name implies, are straight-sided vessels with no neck or waist, and a base diameter slightly greater than that of the rim. The form has a broad, stabbed and sometimes incised strap or sub-rectangular handle. Bases are generally flat or slightly indented, although a number of vessels have the convex, thumbed base and cordoned body typical of late 14th-century Kingston-type ware conical jugs (Figs 106, No 416; 107, Nos 417-18; see also Fig 65). Jugs with a reasonably complete rim generally have a pinched and pulled pouring lip. Coarse Border ware conical jugs are undecorated and only very sparsely glazed, if at all. It was possible to measure the capacities of only two conical jugs (Fig 108, Nos 421 and 425), which held respectively 1610ml and 1620ml.

4. Rounded

(Fig 109)

The shape is the same as that of the Kingston-type rounded jug, and stylistically close comparisons can be made with the late 14th-century products of the Kingston kilns (see p.28; Figs 74-75). The upper half of the jug, with its long, straight-sided neck and marked shoulder, is similar to baluster forms, so it is possible that the two could be confused in excavated assemblages. The base is flat, or slightly indented. Handles have a strap or sub-rectangular section; all are stabbed, and sometimes incised. Rounded jugs commonly have a pulled and pinched pouring lip. The upper half of the body is covered with a patchy spread or 'bib' of green glaze. This form is otherwise undecorated. The capacities of Nos 428 and 430 were measured at 2700ml and 2360ml respectively.

5. Cistern/large rounded

(Figs 31; 110-112)

Coarse Border ware cisterns are essentially large

rounded jugs with a bunghole positioned approximately one quarter of the height from the base, and at a right angle to the handle. They are thick-walled and heavily built, with a wide strap handle, deeply incised and stabbed in various patterns. The short, straight-sided neck with its thickened rim has no spout or pouring lip. The thumbed base is 'sagging' or convex, and the sides are obviously knife-trimmed. The bunghole was pushed both through a thick disc of clay luted onto the body, and through the wall of the vessel, using a tool of round section, which left a very smooth-sided hole. The circumference of the disc was generally, but not invariably, pinched in at intervals. The thick clay joining the disc to the body might also be incised or stabbed to allow steam to escape in firing (Fig 112, Nos 440-41).

The upper half of the body was glazed in a zone extending approximately from the shoulder to the maximum girth, and commonly including the handle, and may have simple combed decoration. A common feature of Coarse Border ware cisterns is the use of painted red slip as decoration. Not all cisterns were decorated in this way, but the occurrence of red slip on thick-walled sherds from large vessels can almost certainly be taken as a diagnostic feature of the form. Applied, stamped discs of clay are also sometimes found on cistern sherds. Cisterns are one of the commonest Coarse Border ware forms and survive in large quantities from excavations.

Two jugs of large rounded form, but without bungholes, are illustrated here (Fig 110, Nos 432-33). Both are sufficiently complete for it to be certain that they originally had no bunghole. In all other respects they conform to the description of cisterns given above, and sherds from large jugs of this shape could very easily be confused in identification. In the absence of many complete examples, it is impossible to tell how common the form was in London. The capacities of these two large rounded jugs were measured at 6820ml (No 433) and 7420ml (No 432).

6. Biconical

(Fig 113, Nos 459-61)

Biconical jugs are uncommon in Coarse Border ware, but are closely comparable with the Kingston-type ware and Cheam whiteware forms (Figs 82, Nos 182-92; 122, Nos 543-51). The rim is externally thickened, and no examples have any form of pouring lip. The handle is a simple rod, and the base is slightly indented. Patches and spots of green glaze cover the upper half of the body, but the form is otherwise undecorated.

7. Miscellaneous jug forms

Miniature jugs are extremely rare in Coarse Border ware. The one illustrated example (Fig 113, No 464) is in the form of a small baluster jug with anthropomorphic decoration. The rim and face are now missing, and the vessel is green-glazed.

Sherds from a Coarse Border ware puzzle jug are so far unique (Fig 113, No 463). They include part of the rim, at the point where it is joined by the hollow handle, and a single base sherd, which shows that the jug was thin-walled and quite small. The whole vessel was covered with a green glaze.

Rim form

The commonest type of rim on all forms of Coarse Border ware jug is simply thickened externally, and may be either flat-topped (Fig 108, Nos 421-22, 424-25), or slightly bevelled internally (Fig 105, Nos 410, 412). Externally bevelled rims (Fig 107, No 417) are less common. The thickened clay at the top of the jug was finished to give a variety of external profiles to most forms, ranging from rounded (Fig 109, No 426), to squared (Fig 108, No 421) or triangular (Fig 106, No 413). Particularly deep rims may also have a central groove, made while the jug was still on the wheel (Fig 106, No 415). A large number of conical jugs have a flat-topped rim which is bent out at a right-angle, giving a distinctly L-shaped profile (Fig 108, Nos 421, 423-24). The rim may also be slightly thickened internally (Fig 108, No 423), but not to the extent of forming a 'hammer-head' rim. There is far less typological distinction in Coarse Border ware rim forms than in London- or Kingston-type wares, and because of this it is often difficult to assign small, isolated rim sherds to any particular form of jug. The rims of baluster and rounded jugs, for example, could easily be confused. However, the very short neck, if any, of the barrel-shaped jug, the wide diameter and thickness of cistern rims, and the neckless profile and L-shaped rim of the conical jug are all aids to identification.

No Coarse Border ware jugs identified in London have any form of spout made separately and added to the rim. Barrel-shaped, biconical and large rounded jugs and cisterns were all made without a pouring lip. Cisterns, of course, did not need one, since their contents were drawn off through the bunghole. However, baluster, conical and rounded jugs commonly, but not invariably, have a pinched and pulled pouring lip, made in the same way as on Kingston-type ware jugs (see p.30). In some baluster jugs the depth of the lip extends almost the entire length of the neck, a form which is also found on Kingston-type ware (see p.30; Fig 105, No 410). At the rim, clear thumb and finger-prints can often be seen on either side of the lip. In the case of baluster jugs, the decorative scheme of the body may also extend to the lip. This is most clearly shown by the anthropomorphic jugs whose makers obviously took advantage of the deep lip, and made a feature of it by turning it into a vehicle for applied decoration in the form of a human face (Fig 106, No 413).

Handle form

Strap handles are the commonest type on almost all forms of Coarse Border ware jug. Particularly broad and heavy strap handles were made for cisterns and large rounded jugs (Figs 110-11), and all examples have pronounced grooves running down the upper surface, made as the potter smoothed his fingers along the length of the handle. Barrel-shaped jugs invariably have handles of sub-rectangular or oval section (Fig 106, Nos 414-15), although this type of handle was also applied to a number of conical and rounded jugs (Figs 108, Nos 423-24; 109, No 430). Rod handles are limited to biconical jugs (Fig 113, No 461).

Most Coarse Border ware handles were stabbed with a sharp knife or pointed tool. This can give a certain decorative effect, especially when it was carried out with care to make one or more neat lines running the length of the handle (Figs 105, No 409; 107, No 417). However, the main reason for stabbing handles was undoubtedly to ensure the successful firing of the complete jug by allowing steam to escape from its thickest parts. Some handles are very deeply stabbed, so that in places the point of the tool came through the other side (Fig 106, No 413). The handles of baluster and large rounded jugs and cisterns are often incised as well, either in a single, central, vertical line with stab-marks on each side (Figs 105, No 409; 110, Nos 432, 434), or in two or three lines with stabbing in between (Figs 111, No 435; 112, No 437). A line of deep stab-marks across, or even all round, the upper handle join was necessary at the point where extra clay was used to make the

attachment of the handle more secure, and which was therefore thicker than any other part of the jug (eg Figs 105, No 409; 107, No 417). The bottom of the handle was also sometimes stabbed around the join (Figs 112, No 444; 113, No 450). On many jugs, however, the procedure of stabbing the handle was obviously carried out hurriedly and with little care. Jug handles carrying other forms of decoration are extremely rare – the cistern handle illustrated in Fig 112, No 442 is a notable example. A broad, thick strap was pinched at regular intervals down each side of the upper, concave surface, and a single thumbed strip of clay was applied down the centre. A pointed tool was used to stab evenly-spaced holes in two rows, one each side of the central strip, and across the top of the handle. Another handle whose decoration is so far unparalleled is unfortunately incomplete (Fig 113, No 449). The remaining portion, which comes from the area near the join with the rim and neck, has four ring-and-dot stamps, rather than stab-marks. However, it is impossible to reconstruct the original arrangement or number of stamps on the complete handle.

The methods by which jug handles were attached differ in certain respects from those used by the Kingston- and London-type ware potters (see Pearce 1984). As with these other wares, the means of attachment varies according to the shape and size both of the vessel and the handle, and can be seen more clearly from the lower join simply because the potters did not find it necessary to hide a join which could not be seen by the user. The upper join, inside the neck of the jug, was always covered by clay smoothed into the walls and disguising the method used to secure it. However, a number of excavated sherds have been broken in such a way as to show that the end of the handle was pushed through the wall of the jug, and was then worked back into the neck. Pads or strips of clay were wrapped around the join outside and smoothed into the walls, often rather carelessly, so that their edges can clearly be seen (Fig 109, No 428).

Various different methods were used to attach the lower end of the handle to the body. In the case of barrel-shaped and rounded jugs, most conical jugs and some baluster jugs, the end of the handle was simply luted onto the outside of the jug. It was often made more secure by pressing the thumb or finger into the soft clay, leaving a single clear print at the base of the handle (Figs 107, No 419; 109, No 426). The marks left by the potter's fingers as he smoothed the clay of the handle into the body are clearly visible. Cracks often appeared around the join during firing, but were obviously not considered to have weakened the handle, or to have made the pot unsaleable. In the jug illustrated in Fig 109, No 427, the lower end of the handle has completely come away from the body, leaving a clean, circular scar. Luting causes no disruption of the walls of the jug and often the only indication of a join inside is a slight depression made by the potter's fingers as he supported the body while pressing the end of the handle onto the outside. Luted handles are extremely rare in London- and Kingston-type wares and in Mill Green ware, in all of which the wall of the jug was broken in some way, either to insert the handle through a hole cut in the body, or to push the wall into the end of the handle (Pearce 1984). The latter method was used by the Coarse Border ware potters on their larger vessels, in particular for large rounded jugs and cisterns, as well as some conical and most baluster jugs. The size of these jugs and their handles made it necessary to have a more sturdy join than on smaller jugs. Baluster and conical jugs may have a single finger-hole pushed into the end of the handle from inside the vessel, but large rounded jugs and cisterns required an even more secure join, and three or four fingers were pushed right through the body, well into the handle. This had the advantage not only of strengthening the join, but also of reducing the thickness of the clay and so improving the chances of a successful firing.

Base form

Thumbed bases are found on some baluster and conical jugs and on large rounded jugs and cisterns. When applied to a flat base, the act of thumbing tended to produce a very slight recess by drawing the clay of the base-angle out and down, a little below the level of the rest of the base (Fig 105, Nos 409-10, 412). The effect is less noticeable when the base profile is convex, as, for example, in the large rounded jugs and cisterns (Figs 110-11). The commonest pattern of thumbing is in a continuous line of closely spaced, separate impressions, although a few conical jugs have three or four groups of two to three impressions at intervals around the base (Fig 107, Nos 417-18).

Flat or slightly indented bases are common on conical and rounded jugs (Figs 108, Nos 421-23;

109, Nos 427-28), and on barrel-shaped jugs (Fig 106, Nos 414-15). A concave profile may have been produced by wiping the base with the palm of the hand after the pot had been removed from the wheel, or it may have resulted from the use of a trimming tool. In such cases the soft clay of the base-angle was pushed up at various points around the circumference and was not subsequently trimmed away.

Evidence for knife-trimming to any marked degree is seldom obvious on Coarse Border ware jugs, although marks resulting from wiping and smoothing the clay are often apparent underneath the base. However, baluster jugs, by the nature of their shape, required knife-trimming of the lower part of the body to accentuate the waist. Examples showing both vertical knife-trimming (Fig 105, Nos 409, 411) and trimming in horizontal arcs (Fig 105, Nos 410, 412) are illustrated. Jugs with 'sagging' bases, ie certain conical and rounded forms and large rounded jugs and cisterns, are also knife-trimmed, sometimes heavily, and this emphasises the shape of the base profile.

Decoration

Combed and incised horizontal bands are the simplest form of decoration on Coarse Border ware jugs of all forms. Their use is, however, limited mostly to the application of a single incised line around the neck, made while the jug was turned on the wheel. Large rounded jugs and cisterns often have one or more lines and bands of combing (eg Figs 110, No 433; 111, No 435). Conical jugs, however, are generally completely undecorated. The jug illustrated in Fig 106, No 416 is an exception. The upper half of the vessel is now missing, but from the lower handle join down to the zone of knife-trimming the body was combed while on the wheel in a broad, continuous band.

Painted decoration is limited almost entirely in Coarse Border ware to cisterns. It takes the form of groups of more or less vertical lines of red slip painted with a thick brush around the shoulder, under the glaze. The number of lines or strokes in each group varies from two to four, and their arrangement may be orderly (Figs 31; 110, No 434), or rather more casual (Fig 111, No 436). The strokes generally meet at the top and splay

32. Right: *Coarse Border ware: details of various stamps from miscellaneous jugs.*

32a

32b

32c

32d

32e

32f

out in an inverted 'V' or arrow formation. One unusual example of a baluster jug with this form of decoration is illustrated in Fig 105, No 409; the brush strokes are arranged in groups of three, producing an arrow-head.

Applied polychrome decoration is not common. The only reasonably complete Coarse Border ware forms on which this type of decoration is found are baluster jugs. The decorative scheme of the one illustrated jug (Figs 30; 105, No 410) is very simple. Three vertical strips of thick, 'buttery', red slip were applied at even intervals around the body. They were then pinched and thumbed, leaving clear nail marks on either side. Between these, three vertical rows of three thick discs of 'buttery' red slip stamped with a grid-pattern were luted onto the neck and body. The whole jug was then covered with a green glaze. Smears of red, the result of careless handling, were left around the lower half of the jug. A few of the discs have subsequently come away from the body, leaving uneven, unglazed circular scars.

Although known only from sherds, clay discs stamped with a grid pattern were also used on cisterns (Figs 32c-f; 113, Nos 452-54), in addition to painted or applied red or white slip strips and lines. Two other patterns of stamp, both similar in design, have been found in London. The sherds illustrated probably come from jugs rather than cisterns (Fig 113, Nos 455-57). Both are applied to circular discs of fine white clay. The one stamp takes the form of an equal-armed cross with small, raised pellets in each quarter. Exactly the same stamp was used on two different jugs, one in the reserve collection of the Museum of London (Figs 32a; 113, No 456), and the other in the British Museum (No 455). In both cases, the discs were applied over areas of painted red slip, defined by raised strips of plain or thumbed clay. The other design of stamp consists of two intersecting equal-armed crosses, with eight pellets, one between each cross-arm (No 457).

Anthropomorphic decoration is almost entirely limited to baluster jugs. The green-glazed jug illustrated in Fig 106, No 413 is the only example from London which is sufficiently complete for the overall scheme of decoration to be reconstructed. The deep pinched and pulled pouring lip was crudely made and the human facial features were built around it. The jutting chin, the beak-like nose, and the ears were all made separately and smoothed into the clay of the jug body. The chin was incised with four vertical lines to represent

a beard, and the mouth indicated by a deeply incised horizontal line. The eyes were impressed with a blunt, round-ended tool. Vertical applied strips, nicked at regular intervals with the thumb- or finger-nail and pinched in between the nicks, were used to represent arms. These extend from just below the rim, down either side of the face, to the maximum girth where they curve round and turn slightly upwards to end in hands which clasp a large, applied, annular brooch. The hands were formed as part of the brooch – the ends of the arms were simply laid over the brooch at the wrist, and were then incised to represent fingers. The ring and separately applied pin of the brooch were made from broad strips of fine clay, decorated with closely spaced, circular, finger-tip impressions. Nail-marks can be seen in some of the impressions. Two more vertical, nicked strips were applied, one on each side of the jug, between the arms and the handle, but are otherwise unrelated to the human representation. Elements of this scheme of decoration are found in the other two baluster jugs illustrated here (Fig 105, Nos 411-12), although No 412 has no brooch. The arms were each made from two strips of clay, joined at the elbow. The hands are represented by incised fingers, and are simply clasped together at the shoulder of the jug. The design of No 411 is more stylised, so it is not clear exactly what the potter intended to depict. The arms are vertical, thumbed, applied strips, bent at the elbows, but do not end in clearly defined hands as in the other examples. An arrangement of incised lines may represent either a hand or the cuff of a garment. Four plain circles of applied clay grouped between the arms may represent parts of a brooch or details of dress.

Only one Coarse Border ware miniature jug with anthropomorphic decoration has been found in London (Fig 113, No 464). Strips of clay were applied to the body to indicate arms, bent up at the elbow. Large hands rest on the shoulder of the pot, but are not clasped. Both arms and the belly of the jug between them are covered, in no particular pattern, with closely-spaced ring-and-dot stamps. The jug is green-glazed. The scarcity of surviving Coarse Border ware miniature anthropomorphic jugs contrasts with Mill Green ware (Pearce *et al.* 1982, Fig 9) and Kingston-type ware (Figs 84; 85, Nos 221-25), in both of which the type is well represented in the museum collections studied.

33. Coarse Border ware : details of anthropomorphic decoration from lobed cups.

Cooking vessels

A variety of vessels for use in cooking were made in Coarse Border ware, and during the late 14th and 15th centuries the industry was the main supplier of London's needs in this respect. Cooking pots form by far the largest proportion of all cooking vessels from excavations in London. Other forms supplied to the capital include cauldrons, frying pans and large bowls. Less common are pipkins, dripping dishes and small dishes (see Appendix 6 for the relative frequency of forms from large excavated ceramic assemblages). Since Coarse Border ware cooking vessels tend to be thick-walled and more substantial than, for example, Kingston-type ware and Cheam whiteware, they often survive in the form of large sherds which can generally be identified with a reasonable degree of confidence.

1. Cooking pots

(Figs 114-15; 116, No 479)

Three main types of cooking pot were made in Coarse Border ware. The commonest (Type 1 – Fig 114, Nos 465-68) can be closely compared both in shape and size with Kingston-type ware cooking pots (Fig 94, Nos 296-97). It has a globular body, constricted at the shoulder, and a short, straight-sided, flared neck. Rims are simply bevelled internally (Nos 466, 468), or, more commonly, externally thickened and flat-topped or bevelled (Nos 465, 467). In some cases, a slight internal thickening may give a hammer-head effect (No 467). All Type 1 cooking pots have a convex base profile, heavily knife-trimmed, both underneath and around the lower part of the body, in series of overlapping, horizontal strokes. Trimming, to reduce the thickness of the clay, was carried out when the pot was in a leather-hard state, as shown by the holes and drag-marks in the clay, where large inclusions were pulled along by the trimming-tool. Inside the base, a thin cover of green glaze sealed the surface of the pot, and the few spots that occur elsewhere on the body are likely to be accidental. The majority of cooking pots are poorly finished, and careless trimming, warped bases and rims, dents from handling and kiln scars are common (eg No 468). The running of glaze shows that cooking pots were generally fired in an inverted position. Pots of this type are typically heavily sooted and blackened over the lower part of the body and base, and often right up to the rim.

The second main type of Coarse Border ware cooking pot (Type 2) is the same shape as Type 1, although it is often much larger (Figs 115, Nos 476-78; 116, No 479). It differs in having an internal lid-seating or bifid rim, and no neck. The top of the rim may be rounded or thickened externally. The base, as with Type 1, is convex and knife-trimmed, and is glazed internally. There may also be a band of glaze outside, around the upper part of the body from the rim to the shoulder. Spots, splashes and dribbles show that most vessels were stacked in an inverted position in the kiln. Sooting and blackening are again common. A further difference between Type 2 and Type 1 cooking pots is in the provision of one or more handles (Figs 115, No 478; 116, No 479). However, it is impossible to tell how common this was in the absence of more complete examples. Certainly, not all Type 2 cooking pots have handles. In one of the illustrated examples (No 478), and in other sherds (not illustrated), the handle is a broad incised and stabbed strap, attached directly below the rim. The form and treatment of the handle closely resemble those of cisterns (Fig 113, Nos 446-47), and fragments from excavations could easily be wrongly attributed. The handle of No 479 has broken away completely from the shoulder, leaving a clean scar. A hole, stabbed through the body from the outside is clearly visible. This shows that the end of the handle was originally pushed through to form a 'plug' or dowel. The outside surface, around the hole, was also roughened with criss-cross marks from a knife-blade. This method of attaching handles was commonly used for jugs (see p.32). A row of tiny holes across the top of the handle was made after it had been attached.

The third type of cooking pot (Type 3) may have been used either for cooking or for dry storage (Figs 114, Nos 469-74; 115, No 475). Some examples are blackened, others are not (eg Nos 470, 475). Type 3 cooking pots are generally much larger than either of the types described above, and some would have had a considerable storage capacity. They may also be very tall, their height up to twice the maximum girth. In other respects they are similar to Type 1 cooking pots, with a short neck and an externally thickened, flat-topped rim which may also be slightly thickened internally. The base is convex and heavily knife-trimmed and wiped by hand. Glaze was commonly used to cover the inside of the base. Running of glaze again suggests firing upside down (Fig 115, No 475). A number of large Type

3 cooking pots/storage jars have vertical applied strips at intervals around the upper half of the body (Figs 114, Nos 469, 473; 115, No 475). The strips are plain or thumbed, and may be partly decorative and partly a help in handling such a large pot.

2. Pipkins

(Fig 116, Nos 480-82)

Pipkins are not a common Coarse Border ware form in London (see Appendix 6), and no complete examples have been found to date. Sherds show that they took the form of a small cooking pot, with a slightly constricted shoulder and straight-sided or flared neck. Rims can also be compared with cooking pots, and have an externally thickened, flat-topped or bevelled profile. However, pipkins are distinguished from cooking pots by having a short strap handle which springs from the shoulder at an angle of approximately 45° to the level of the rim. Two methods of attaching handles are known: the commoner was to push the end of the handle through a hole in the body of the pipkin and to smooth the 'plug' into the walls inside, adding extra pieces of clay if necessary, both inside and out. One to three clear thumb- or finger-impressions were made underneath the handle where it was attached to the body to make a more secure join. The thickest part of the handle, near the body, was sometimes deeply stabbed (No 481) to prevent damage in firing. Alternatively, the handle was simply luted onto the pipkin leaving only a slight dent inside at the point of attachment, but not otherwise disturbing the throwing marks. Pipkins are unglazed except for a thin spread inside the base. Blackening of the exterior is common.

3. Cauldrons

(Figs 116, Nos 483-89; 117, Nos 490-91)

Coarse Border ware cauldrons are commoner in excavated assemblages than their Kingston-type ware counterparts, although they share the same main characteristics and shape. In form, cauldrons are simply cooking pots adapted for a particular use by the addition of two diametrically opposed vertical loop or angular handles, and three long legs. Handles are of sub-rectangular, square, strap or oval section, and are generally slightly concave on the outer surface. Stabbing is not common, probably because cauldron handles tend not to be thick or heavy. They were generally luted onto the body at the rim and shoulder, although there are a few examples of handles 'plugged' or pushed through the neck inside. As with luted jug handles (eg Fig 106, Nos 414-15), a single thumb impression at its lower end, where it was smoothed into the body, made for a better join, although poorly bonded handles are quite common (Nos 484, 487). Angular handles, with a 90° bend at the mid-point (Nos 483, 488) appear to have been made from two lengths of clay, joined together. Rims are thickened externally with a flat or rounded top (Nos 487, 489), or are simply everted or rounded (Nos 484, 488). The neck flares from a constriction at the shoulder. Examples in which a large proportion of the rim has survived show that pinched and pulled pouring lips were commonly made at the mid-point of the circumference between the two handles (No 489). The base, as with cooking pots, is convex in profile and knife-trimmed. The legs are thick and heavy. Although few complete examples have survived, they tend to be shorter than London-type ware cauldron legs (Nos 490, 491; see also Pearce *et al.* 1985, Fig 69, Nos 368-70). They were luted onto the bottom of the cauldron at the base-angle, and slight depressions inside at the point of contact show that the potter supported the walls behind the legs as he secured them. A few particularly heavy legs were more firmly attached: the end was pushed through a hole cut in the body, and the excess clay smoothed into the walls inside (No 491). Cauldron legs are invariably either stabbed or deeply incised. Two or more vertical lines were cut into the outer, and sometimes the inner surface of the leg, and can be as much as $\frac{3}{4}$ of the thickness in depth (Nos 487, 490). Alternatively, a pointed tool was used to stab holes behind the leg and around the point of attachment (No 491). Spreads of green glaze were applied inside the base and often inside the rim and neck; running shows that most cauldrons were stacked upside down in the kiln. The pattern of surface blackening from use in cooking is interesting. Heavy encrustations of soot are common, particularly around the lower half of the body. However, the base is generally much blacker than the ends of the legs, and in many instances one half of the vessel, from base to rim, is blacker than the other.

4. Frying pans

(Fig 117, Nos 492-97)

The form described here as a 'frying pan' is the same in Coarse Border ware as in Kingston-type ware (see p.47; Figs 96, Nos 331-33; 97, No 334) ie an open, shallow, wheelthrown vessel with a handle, used for heating food. Frying pans closely resemble bowls in shape (Fig 118, Nos 500-505) and may be difficult to identify from sherds in the absence of handles. Consequently, analysis of excavated assemblages may not accurately reflect the relative proportions of the two forms. Rims are externally thickened and flat-topped or bevelled, often to the extent of producing a broad flange. The hollow tubular handle was generally hand-made from a slab of rolled clay. Wheelthrown, tubular handles are rare – the one illustrated example has very clear throwing marks inside (No 495). The end of the tube was attached over the rim of the bowl and smoothed into the body inside so that the handle stood at an angle of approximately 45° to the level of the rim. Additional small pieces of clay were built up around the join, often with little care, leaving the edges still visible. A single deep thumb- or finger-impression was made just below the rim, under the end of the handle, to make the attachment more secure, and sometimes broke right through the wall (No 494). The hollow handle was probably intended to act as a socket for a wooden handle, which would have been necessary to hold the frying pan when hot. Very few complete frying pans survive, so it is impossible to tell whether the form typically had a pouring lip. Only one example is illustrated here (No 493), but, since the handle is missing, its position in relation to the lip cannot be determined. Most vessels are poorly finished, with the flat base and lower half of the body heavily knife-trimmed. Frying pans are glazed inside the base, with patches, spots and runs of glaze outside. Heavy burning and sooting of the base and walls are common.

5. Dripping dishes

(Figs 117, No 498; 118, No 499)

Coarse Border ware dripping dishes are shallow, open, handmade vessels with handles, but differ from frying pans both in plan and construction. The form is uncommon, and is generally represented in excavated assemblages by small sherds only. Reconstruction is generally impossible, and the variety of shapes and details of construction, such as number and type of handles cannot be determined. Only one dripping dish which is anywhere near complete is known from London (No 498). It is semi-circular in plan with the

diameter a straight side, and was slab-built from rolled out clay. The flat base was bent up to form the sides, which were folded round each other at the ends of the straight side. Marks left by the potter's fingers as he formed the vessel and smoothed the base in line with the diameter can still be seen inside. The base and sides were knife-trimmed outside to reduce the thickness of the clay. The rim is simply flat-topped on the straight side, and slightly bevelled externally around the rest of the vessel. The tubular handmade handle is attached over the rim at an angle, by the same method used for the frying pan handles described above, with a deep finger impression inside, just below the rim. Inside, the dripping dish is well covered with a thick green glaze. Parts of the straight side, but not the base, are blackened externally, showing that it was this side which was exposed to heat. This is consistent with the suggested function as a dripping dish, which would have been pushed into the embers beneath a roasting joint to catch the juices, and would therefore be unevenly blackened.

Bowls and dishes

Bowls

(Fig 118, Nos 500-509)

As with Kingston-type ware (see p.47), any distinction between bowls and dishes is made largely on the basis of relative dimensions. Complete profiles are extremely rare in excavated material from London, and only two, unusual, forms are illustrated here (Nos 508-9). Consequently, classification of sherds as 'bowl' or 'dish' becomes meaningless, and the term 'bowl' alone is again used to describe open forms larger than 'saucers'.

Coarse Border ware bowls were made in a number of different shapes ranging from wide-rimmed, shallow vessels (Nos 501, 505) to deep, straight-sided types (No 506). Rims are thickened externally with a broad, flat or bevelled top. Many rims are also slightly thickened internally. The rim of No 509 is unusual in having a wide flange with an external, vertical bevel. Although very few complete profiles can be reconstructed, bases are usually convex in profile, and some 'sag' to a pronounced degree. The convexity was produced both by pressure from the inside, as shown by finger-prints and other marks, and by knife-

trimming outside. Heavy knife-trimming of the lower part of the body might also alter what was originally a straight-sided profile. The process was generally carried out with little care so that some vessels are over-thin in places, with gouge-marks where the trimming-tool cut into the clay (No 509).

A number of bowls have pinched and pulled pouring lips (Nos 506-7), although their frequency cannot be determined in the absence of complete examples. The majority of bowls have a covering of green glaze inside the base, with dribbles and spots both inside and out. Running of glaze shows that they were stacked upside down in the kiln. Unglazed examples (No 509) are rare. Blackening and sooting of the exterior surface, sometimes as far as the rim, shows that many were used for cooking. Unblackened bowls were probably used in food preparation and serving (eg No 505).

Only one bowl with any form of decoration is illustrated (No 502). This takes the form of a simple roller-stamped design running around the top of the rim. Another unusual bowl, in the collection of the Bank of England, is completely hemispherical in shape with only a slight constriction just below the simple, everted rim to break the even rounded profile (No 508). The lower part of the body and rounded base are heavily knife-trimmed, and the vessel is unglazed. It is uncertain exactly how it would have been used — whether it was suspended above a fire for cooking, or whether it was rested in the embers to keep it upright, or even if it was used for cooking at all.

Small dishes or 'saucers'

(Fig 118, Nos 510-13)

Coarse Border ware small dishes or 'saucers' closely resemble the form common in Kingston-type ware (see p.47; Fig 98, Nos 349-366) and also made in Cheam whiteware (Fig 125, Nos 579-82). Bases are generally flat, and rims are simply rounded. Pouring lips are uncommon — No 513 is the only example from recent excavations — although this may be no more than an accident of survival. Knife-trimming of the base and sides is unusual and many dishes appear to have been smoothed across the base. This had the effect of smudging the clay at the base angle onto the sides in places. This was not trimmed or tidied. As with Kingston-type ware, liquid glaze was poured into the dish, swilled around the base and then poured out over the rim. Accidental spots

34. Left: *Coarse Border ware: lobed cup with polychrome glazing and internal zoomorphic decoration (height 92mm).*

and splashes of glaze inevitably occur over the rest of the body.

Other forms

A number of Coarse Border ware forms which do not fit into any of the categories outlined above have been found in London. From their limited occurrence in excavated material, none constituted an important element in the pottery supplied to the capital by the Surrey coarseware industries, whose main emphasis lay on cooking and storage vessels. Most of the forms described here were either supplied principally by other contemporaneous potteries, or were more commonly made in other materials.

Lobed cups

(Figs 33-34; 119, Nos 514-19)

Undecorated lobed cups are a common element in assemblages of late Surrey finewares or 'Tudor Green' from London (Fig 127). They are not common in Coarse Border ware (see Appendix 6), although a number of fragments from large, decorated cups, and one very impressive complete cup have been found. These Coarse Border ware lobed cups differ from the 'Tudor Green' cups both in scale and in the presence of decorative features, which suggest that they may have been intended to be used as communal drinking vessels at important functions or feasts. The smaller, plain 'Tudor Green' cups are more likely to have held individual servings. There are very few undecorated Coarse Border ware lobed cups, and only one fragmentary example is illustrated (No 519).

The one complete Coarse Border ware lobed cup (Figs 34; 119, No 514) is essentially a bowl with a pedestal foot. Above a carination at the mid-point of the body, the walls were pinched together, from inside, at regular intervals, forming a series of seven lobes. Seven strap handles were attached, one at each of these points, separating the lobes. They were luted onto the body at the carination, and folded over the rim. The rim is rounded and not thickened, and the base is flat, with no sign of knife-trimming. The cup is covered with a thick green glaze outside, and a clear, lead glaze inside, appearing yellow.

A finely modelled figure of a stag at bay sits inside the 'well' formed by the interior of the base. The legs and head were made from separate pieces of clay and added to the body, all in the same clay as was used for the body of the cup. The antlers were also made separately, but from red-firing clay. The hooves, mouth and nostrils are all incised, and the body and tail are also decorated with a pattern of incised lines. The eyes are stabbed with a pointed tool. Around the stag, three stylised trees, made from red clay, presumably represent a forest. The clay at the base of each tree is smoothed into the white body of the cup. Three incised lines, containing two rows of stab-marks, radiate from the base of each trunk. The tops of the trees are lobed around a central pinnacle of clay.

The other decorated lobed cups illustrated are probably similar in size to No 514, and appear to follow the same pattern in having modelled figures both in the centre of the cup, and around the inside walls. It is impossible to tell from the surviving fragments how many lobes each cup originally had, or how the complete decorative layout appeared. A second figure of a stag (No 517) may well have formed part of a scheme similar to No 514. It is very crudely made, with no legs, and its body and head formed from a single lump of clay. The antlers, now missing, were made from red-firing clay. The eyes and nostrils were stabbed and the mouth incised. The body is otherwise undecorated. The figure was fixed to the base of the cup with a large lump of clay, into which its belly was pressed. The clay was then clumsily smeared up the sides of the stag and pinched together over the chest and wrapped behind the neck. The stag, and probably the interior of the cup, were covered with a green glaze which had bubbled badly in firing.

Two illustrated lobed cup sherds are decorated with human figures (Nos 515-16). Both are placed inside the body of the cup, facing the centre, in the position occupied by the trees of No 514. It is impossible to tell how many such figures each cup would have had, or what kind of centrepiece, if any, they surrounded. The complete profile of No 515 remains (see also Fig 33b), although the diameter of the cup cannot be accurately measured. A strap handle was attached in the same way as those of No 514, with a small finger-tip impression at the lower end. A lightly incised cross marks the top of the handle at the point where it was wrapped over the pinched rim, between the lobes. The outside of the cup was green-glazed, and the inside, including the figure, was covered with a clear glaze. The cup was poorly finished – numerous small lumps of clay stuck to the surface under the glaze were not removed before firing. The figure was crudely made, and has no features to distinguish its sex. The head and body were made from a single lump of clay, and the arms, now broken, were added separately. The body was fixed to the cup with a large piece of clay wrapped over the waist and smoothed down into the walls. This was stabbed with the point of a knife, and the edges on each side were defined by an incised line. The nose and chin were pinched out of the clay of the face, the eyes were stabbed, and a row of incised lines suggests hair.

The other figure (Figs 33a; 119, No 516) is shown by details of dress to be that of a woman. Nothing of the cup remains except for a small part of the body behind the figure, which is green-glazed. The body, head and arms were all made from separate pieces of clay. The headdress was made from two strips of clay fixed, one over the other, around the face, which is deeply set within it. The eyes are stabbed, and the mouth, hair, fingers and headdress are incised. One arm is broken, and the other is bent round so that the hand rests on the waist.

One lobed cup sherd with zoomorphic decoration is illustrated (No 518). A small modelled bird is attached to the inside, and the remains of the lower end of a handle can be seen outside. Both surfaces, and the bird, are covered with a thick green glaze. The bird was fixed to the wall of the cup by a separate lump of clay, which was stabbed with a knife-point. The bird's legs and claws were incised in the cup beneath the body. The wings are neatly folded and stand out in slight relief, and the body and tail are incised. The head is missing.

Lids

(Fig 119, Nos 520-22)

Coarse Border ware lids were made in the shape of a small dish, inverted in use. Although complete examples are rare, most lids appear to have been thrown with a foot which served as a knop for lifting them from the vessel they were intended to cover. The knop, or base of the lid as thrown, tends to be flat and slightly indented, and was probably wiped or smoothed by hand after removal from the wheel. Knife-trimming was seldom carried out, and excess clay around the knop and on the body was generally left untouched. All surviving lids are unglazed, except for accidental spots from other vessels in the same firing. Rims are simply rounded, and correspond closely in diameter with the rims of cooking pots.

Since lid-seated cooking pots were made in Coarse Border ware (Figs 115, Nos 476-78; 116, No 479), it is a reasonable assumption that these were the vessels which the lids were principally made to cover. None, however, have been found archaeologically in definite association.

Money-box

(Fig 119, No 523)

One almost complete Coarse Border ware money-box is illustrated here. The form is better known in Kingston-type ware (Fig 99, Nos 373-83), and the same method of construction was used (see p.48). In shape, the money-box resembles a small, slightly squashed, enclosed cone. The apex is now missing, but was probably simply pointed, and the coin-slit was cut vertically just below this. The base is slightly convex in profile, but there are no obvious signs of knife-trimming. The upper half of the body was green-glazed, with spots and patches around the base. As with most medieval money-boxes, it was broken around the coin-slit at some time to remove the coins.

Condiment

(Fig 119, No 524)

Condiments are difficult to recognise from sherds which otherwise resemble parts of a small dish. The one Coarse Border ware sherd from London excavations which can be positively identified has part of a basket handle attached over the rim. Little else remains of the original form, although it is clear that the strap handle had a single central incised line, each side of which diagonal stab-marks were made with the point of a knife. Too little of the rim survives for the diameter to be reconstructed, but the dish was clearly small and shallow, comparing closely with the Kingston-type ware condiment illustrated in Fig 99, No 372.

Chafing dish

(Fig 119, No 525)

Part of what was probably a pedestal base has been identified as coming from a chafing dish by the presence of sooting and blackening inside the vessel. Nothing remains of the bowl which would have been set on this pedestal. The base is slightly indented and was knife-trimmed or smoothed underneath. A thin spread of pale green to clear glaze covers the outside walls.

Curfew

(Fig 119, No 526)

A single sherd from a Coarse Border ware curfew comes from a vessel which was originally domed or bowl-like in shape, intended to be inverted in use to cover the embers of a fire (cf the Kingston-type ware curfew, Fig 101, No 395). The vessel was thick-walled with a patchy, thin glaze externally. The rim is flat-topped, trimmed to this shape with a knife or similar tool. Rows of small holes were made with the point of a knife around the body of the curfew, and closed up noticeably on the outside during firing. The inside walls are burnt in patches.

Louver

(Fig 119, No 527)

One Coarse Border ware sherd from London has been identified as part of a louver, and probably came from a baffle or hood built around an aperture or vent in the body of the structure. It is impossible to form any idea as to the shape of the complete piece, or to reconstruct the shape of the aperture, although this was clearly rounded in part. The baffle was formed by hand from a thick slab of clay, fixed around the aperture with additional lumps of clay in the same way as the baffles on the Kingston-type ware louver illustrated in Fig 104. Diagonal lines were incised in the upper, or outer, surface under a green glaze which ran through the aperture onto the interior walls of the louver. The internal surface is red-brown in colour, but shows no sign of blackening caused by smoke-laden air rising through the roof-hole which the louver, if not decorative, would be intended to cover.

Roof furniture made in Surrey whiteware is extremely rare in London. There would probably have been little demand for it, since local potteries could more easily and conveniently supply the market (see Pearce *et al*. 1985, Figs 78-83).

Crucibles

(Fig 119, No 528)

Two small dishes almost identical in shape and size were found in a single context at Trig Lane (only one, therefore, is illustrated). They are interpreted as crucibles since they had both clearly been placed in a strong heat which resulted in heavy burning and blackening, and produced a thick, red encrustation around the base and outside walls of one of them. The vessels have a smoothly rounded base, and rounded rim, and were probably handmade, then finished on a turntable. The base and sides are smoothed and trimmed to the desired shape. Both crucibles had a pinched and pulled pouring lip, although very little of these now remains. A few spots of glaze externally are likely to have been accidental.

Urinal

(Fig 119, No 529)

The upper part of a Coarse Border ware urinal, now in the British Museum reserve collection, comes from a bottle-shaped vessel, different from the Kingston-type ware urinal illustrated in Fig 101, No 390. The wheelthrown body is globular in shape with a narrow neck, closed at the top. A large circular hole was cut in the wall of the vessel just below the neck, which suggests that it was made to be used as a urinal. The lower part of the body is now missing.

3. CHEAM WHITEWARE

All the major whiteware forms made at the published Cheam kilns are found in London in similar relative proportions, both from recent excavations and from the museum reserve collections. The material from Parkside (Marshall 1924) and from 15-23 High Street (Orton 1982b) is closely comparable in fabric, form and methods of construction with pottery identified as Cheam whiteware from the City. The pottery found at the kiln sites was discarded as waste and was therefore largely fragmentary – few complete profiles could be reconstructed from the High Street site. Consequently, the large number of complete, or nearly complete, Cheam pots in the Museum of London reserve collection (63 different vessels) form a particularly useful complement to the kiln material.

In the late 14th and 15th centuries, Cheam provided London principally with fine, undecorated, white-bodied vessels for storing, serving and drinking liquids, for use both in the kitchen and at the table. It was never as important a source of cooking vessels as the coarse whiteware industries of the Surrey–Hampshire borders, which provided the bulk of the capital's everyday kitchen pottery.

Jugs

As at the kiln sites, the commonest Cheam whiteware jugs found in London are barrel-shaped, biconical and rounded (see Appendix 6; Orton 1982b, table 3). The other forms of jug described here are of minor importance in excavated assemblages. The form found at Parkside and referred to by Orton as a 'bunghole pitcher' (*ibid.*, 81; Marshall 1924, 90, 93) has not been recognised in any significant quantity in London. This may, however, be the result of difficulties in distinguishing the form from the larger jug types when represented by body sherds alone. There are no Cheam whiteware 'bunghole pitchers' or cisterns in the Museum of London reserve collection.

1. Barrel-shaped

(Figs 120-21)

The form is the same as that of the Cheam High Street barrel-shaped jugs (Orton 1982b, Figs 16; 17, Nos 20-23; see also Marshall 1924, Fig 11). It can also be compared with the Coarse Border ware jugs already described in this book (see p.55; Fig 106, Nos 414-15). The body has a rounded profile, which, as at Cheam, may be smoothly convex (Fig 121, No 535) or more biconical in appearance (Fig 121, No 539). Each type may, or may not, have a short, straight-sided neck (Fig 121, Nos 539-40 and 536-37 respectively). None of the London finds has a pouring lip. Handles have an oval or rod section, and bases are invariably flat and slightly indented. Glaze is limited to the upper half of the body, generally in a small 'bib' on the shoulder. No other form of decoration is known.

Fourteen more or less complete barrel-shaped jugs in the Museum of London reserve collection were examined. Analysis of their capacity and height suggests that they fall into three different ranges of size: a) 400-580ml/125-145mm; b) 930-1200ml/165-190mm; c) 1550-2020ml/195-280mm. Of those jugs illustrated, Figs 120, Nos 530-32 and 121 No 535 are in category c); Fig 121, Nos 536-39 are in category b); and Fig 121, Nos 540-42 are in category a). Rim diameters range from 40-100mm, although the majority of rims are 50-60mm across.

2. Biconical

(Figs 35; 122, Nos 543-51)

The form of the biconical jug has already been described in the section on Kingston-type ware (see p.28; Figs 82, Nos 182-92; 83, Nos 193-97). It is also well represented at the Cheam kiln sites (Orton 1982b, Fig 17, Nos 24-30; Marshall 1924, Fig 6). The Cheam vessels from London show little variation in shape, and most have a markedly biconical body, more noticeably so than the Kingston-type ware forms. The central carination may be marked by a slight bulging of the walls, or ridge, although a few jugs have a rather more rounded profile (Nos 543, 546). The neck is straight-sided, or very slightly flared towards the rim. All vessels have a rod handle, and a flat, indented base. They are glazed on the upper half of the body, either in a small 'bib' or all round the shoulder. The only form of decoration used consists of incised horizontal lines around the carination or shoulder.

There are twenty-five complete or almost complete biconical jugs in the Museum of London reserve collection. The capacities of thirteen were measured, and when analysed in relation to height, appear to fall into two groups: a) 740-930ml/230-245mm (Nos 543-46); b) 280-490ml/160-190mm (Nos 547-51). Rim diameters range from 50-60mm.

3. Rounded

(Figs 36; 122, Nos 552-54; 123, Nos 555-56)

This is the same form as Orton's 'standard' jug (Orton 1982b, Figs 17, Nos 31-5; 18, Nos 36-42) and as Marshall's 'pitchers' and 'ewers' (Marshall 1924, Fig 7). Since comparable Cheam whiteware jugs found in London conform closely in shape, if not in constructional detail, to Kingston-type ware and Coarse Border ware jugs classified in this book as 'rounded', the same term is here preferred to cover all Surrey whiteware jugs of this form.

The body has a smoothly rounded profile from shoulder to base, with a straight-sided, or slightly inverted neck. Rounded jugs may, or may not, have a pinched and pulled pouring lip (eg Fig 122, Nos 552-54 fall into the latter category, and Fig 123 No 556 into the former). Presence, or not, of a pouring lip was the criterion used by Marshall to classify his rounded jugs as either pitchers (no lip), or ewers (with lip; Marshall 1924, 86). This seems a tenuous classification, given that the jugs have the same form, and that fragmentary material from excavations could well be impossible to identify as one or the other.

Handles are generally of oval to sub-

35. Cheam whiteware : biconical jug with green glaze (height 235mm).

36. Cheam whiteware : rounded jug with red slip decoration and clear glaze (height 240mm).

rectangular, or rod section, and bases are flat and slightly indented. The body is very smooth, both inside and out, and throwing marks are not obvious. The upper half of the body is glazed, either in a 'bib' or all round, with a pale to dark green, patchy glaze. Decoration is limited to the use of incised horizontal grooves. Only one complete red-painted rounded jug is known from London (Fig 123, No 556). Rim diameters range from 80-110mm, and the height from 200-250mm. Measured capacities vary widely, ranging from 1180-3050ml.

4. Conical

(Fig 123, No 557)

One complete conical jug in the Museum of London reserve collection is the only example of this form in Cheam whiteware to have been found in London. None have been recorded in excavated assemblages. The shape of the vessel compares closely with the almost complete conical jug from Cheam High Street (Orton 1982b, Fig 18, No 54) and with late Kingston-type ware and Coarse Border ware forms (Figs 65; 107-08). The sides are almost straight and the rim diameter is only slightly smaller than that of the base. The body is very smooth outside, with no evidence of the throwing marks which are clearly visible inside. The jug has a pinched and pulled pouring lip, and a handle of sub-rectangular section. Five shallow, horizontal grooves run around the body at widely-spaced intervals, giving a stepped profile. The base is indented. The vessel is unglazed and has a capacity of 1750ml.

5. Baluster

(Fig 123, No 558)

The waisted lower half of the body and base of a baluster jug are the only evidence for this form in Cheam whiteware from London. The outer surfaces are smooth, but inside the base throwing marks and twisted stretch-marks can be seen. The base is almost flat underneath and slightly indented in places. Spots and patches of glaze show that the jug was probably originally glazed over a large proportion of the body. A red-painted baluster jug was found at Cheam Parkside (Marshall 1924, Fig 13), and the London example may also have been decorated in this fashion. No baluster jugs were recorded at Cheam High Street.

6. Small rounded drinking jug

(Fig 123, No 559)

This jug, in the Museum of London reserve collection, is without parallel at any of the Cheam kiln sites, or in excavated pottery from London. In shape, it resembles the Kingston-type small rounded form (Figs 79-81), but differs from it in detail. It appears to have been made as a copy of 14th-century German stoneware drinking jugs (for parallels, see Beckmann 1974, Fig 14). The neck has a cordon below the rim and closely-spaced, shallow, horizontal grooving from rim to shoulder. There is no lip. Pronounced throwing marks can be seen around the body, and the base is thumbed in a manner that recalls the suggested German prototypes. There are a few spots of pale green glaze on the body, probably accidental.

Rim form

The rims of Cheam whiteware jugs are all relatively simple in shape and show little variation between the major forms. However, vessels can often be identified from rim sherds alone by the presence, or not, and type of neck in relation to the rim diameter. For example, biconical jugs have a fairly narrow rim diameter and a long, straight-sided neck. Barrel-shaped jugs, on the other hand, have a very short neck, if they have one at all, and may be wider-mouthed.

Biconical jugs typically have an externally thickened rim, flat-topped or slightly bevelled internally (Fig 122, Nos 543-51). The bevel effect is probably produced, as suggested by Orton, by 'turning' (Orton 1982b). Exceptions are very few (eg Fig 122, No 550). Barrel-shaped jugs (Figs 120-21) also have externally thickened rims, but often to a more pronounced degree, producing what Orton called a 'flange'. The rim may be squared or more or less triangular in section, and may, in addition, show signs of having been turned (Fig 121, No 542). The same types of rims are associated with rounded jugs (Figs 122, Nos 552-54; 123, Nos 555-56). The conical jug (Fig 123, No 557) also has the typical externally thickened, squared rim. By comparison with these jug forms, the small rounded drinking jug (Fig 123, No 559) is unusual in having a simple, rounded, unthickened rim, comparable with German stoneware forms.

Rounded jugs may, or may not, have a pinched and pulled pouring lip, as does the conical jug. However, none of the barrel-shaped or biconical jugs examined show any sign of a lip or spout. This agrees with Orton's findings in the Cheam High Street material.

Handle form

All the handle forms used by the Cheam whiteware potters can be found in the other medieval pottery industries of the London area. Cheam jug handles were simply plain and functional, and display little variety in shape. The methods used to attach them to the body of the jug also compare closely with the techniques of contemporary and earlier potteries, with one very distinctive exception, the occurrence of which on a whiteware jug gives a good clue as to its origin (see below).

As with other Surrey whitewares, the upper handle join with the rim or neck of the jug was invariably covered with clay, so that it is difficult to see exactly how it was secured. However, close visual examination and the evidence of a number of conveniently broken sherds suggest that the majority of Cheam jug handles were either pushed through the jug neck from outside, or were simply luted onto a prepared surface. If the first method was used, the end of the handle was smoothed back into the neck inside the jug, or extra lumps of clay were pressed over the join. Pieces of clay were also wrapped around the join on the outside, and smoothed well into the neck. These did not always bond properly and subsequently cracked or even broke partly away during firing. However, although it can be difficult to see how the upper end of a handle was attached, the lower joins were not hidden, sometimes because this was impossible, and generally because it was unnecessary.

Strap handles are uncommon in Cheam whiteware forms from London and are found only on larger jugs. The two illustrated examples belong to a large barrel-shaped jug (Fig 120, No 532) and a rounded jug (Fig 123, No 555). They are not typical of either form. In most medieval potteries of the London area, strap handles were attached in a manner particularly suited to their width (see Pearce 1984, 20-1). The potter pushed two or three fingers from inside the jug into the end of the handle as it was pressed onto the body, so breaking through the wall. Extra pieces of clay were then added around the join outside the jug.

Barrel-shaped and rounded jugs generally have a handle of oval or sub-rectangular section, which

may also have a shallow groove running down the outer surface (Fig 121, Nos 537, 539). The smaller barrel-shaped jugs tend to have rod or squared handles (Fig 121, Nos 540-42). The method of attaching the handle to the jug varied with the size. Handles of jugs in the smallest capacity range were generally luted onto the body, causing only a slight bulge to appear inside the vessel, but not breaking through the walls. A very acute angle resulted between the inner surface of the handle and the body of the jug, and this was left untouched. The ends of the handle were pinched across onto the body on each side. Although now missing, the handle of the small rounded drinking jug was also attached in this way (Fig 123, No 559). Larger barrel-shaped jugs (Figs 120; 121, Nos 535-37) seldom have luted handles – because of their size, a more secure means of attachment was required. The potter either stabbed the body to prepare it (this method, which was also used on the one Cheam conical jug, is described in detail below), or pushed his finger into the end of the handle through the wall of the jug from inside the vessel. Extra lumps of clay were also smoothed around the outside of the join to fill in cracks and make it stronger. All but two of the fourteen complete barrel-shaped jugs recorded have a single, long, vertical impression at the base of the handle, where it joins the body. This was made as the potter drew his thumb or finger though the clay from base to rim. An accident which took place during this procedure is illustrated by Fig 120, No 534 – the potter's hand slipped and his finger went deep into the side of the handle, causing the body of the jug to bulge inside.

Biconical jugs typically have a rod handle, although a few are slightly squashed and oval in shape. They appear invariably to have been attached by the method, mentioned above, which was described by Marshall as 'skewered' (Marshall 1924, 88). The technique is particularly suitable for small and/or narrow-mouthed, long-necked jugs into which the potter could not easily insert his hand or fingers. It is also a method which is unsuitable for broad or heavy strap handles. It involved preparing the body of the jug at the point where the lower end of the handle was to be attached by stabbing it right through the wall with a pointed tool, from three to six times, in an inverted V-formation. In one vessel examined the tip of a knife was used, leaving wider gashes, rather than circular holes. The end of the handle was then pressed onto the body over the holes so that the soft clay squeezed through them. This was left completely untouched inside. Small pieces of clay were smoothed around the join outside, and, as with barrel-shaped and rounded forms, the handle was finished with a long, vertical thumb- or finger-impression across the join (only three out of twenty-five complete biconical jugs in the Museum of London reserve collection were not finished in this way).

The majority of Cheam whiteware jug handles are completely plain, carrying no form of decoration. A few handles of larger forms were stabbed, which this was probably a practical rather than a decorative measure. Strap handles appear always to have been stabbed (Figs 120, No 532; 123, No 555). A pointed tool was used rather clumsily in both illustrated examples, and not in any particular pattern. The handle of the rounded jug (No 555) was both stabbed and lightly incised with two narrow, vertical lines. Other handle forms were also occasionally stabbed (Figs 120, No 533; 122, No 552). Of all the smaller barrel-shaped and biconical jugs examined, only one (Fig 121, No 540) had any form of handle-stabbing – a cluster of four, uneven holes across the top of the handle/rim join.

Base form

All Cheam whiteware jugs have a flat and indented base. The degree of indentation may be only slight (Fig 122, Nos 547-49), or quite pronounced (Fig 121, Nos 535, 538, 542). No entirely flat bases are known, and no 'sagging' or convex bases. With one exception, Fig 123, No 559, no bases are thumbed. Jug forms can be identified from base sherds by the diameter and base angle – biconical jugs are generally easy to recognise, although rounded and barrel-shaped jugs are difficult, if not impossible to distinguish.

Where it is still possible to see, jugs of all forms appear to have been removed from the wheelhead by bringing a length of wire or gut under the base and looping it round in an arc to free the pot. This left a characteristic fan-shaped impression in the clay which was generally obscured afterwards, either partially or completely, by smoothing. The only exception was the a conical jug (Fig 123, No 557) which has parallel drag-marks in the clay under the base, produced by pulling a taut length of wire straight across the bottom of the jug.

The majority of jugs, particularly the smaller barrel-shaped and biconical forms, were probably wiped underneath the base after they had been removed from the wheel, perhaps with the palm of the hand, or even just with the thumb. This left smooth, but unevenly distributed depressions in the base, and caused the clay around the circumference to spread up the sides in places. Some jugs show signs of having been slightly flattened around the edges from being stood to dry. Plant impressions, principally grass or straw, and small lumps of clay picked up from the workshop bench or floor, are still visible in a number of cases.

None of the Cheam whiteware jugs from London show any sign of the heavy knife-trimming common to earlier medieval jugs, for example, London-type ware (Pearce *et al.* 1985, 26). However, many jugs have a few shallow, uneven grooves running around the sides just above the base-angle, and may well have been 'shaved' after throwing, while being 'turned'. This could have been carried out at the same time as the turning of the rim suggested above.

Decoration

Cheam whiteware jugs from London are essentially plain and functional vessels. Glaze was used sparingly on all forms, and the conical jug is completely unglazed. The glaze colour can vary from pale yellow with green mottling to a deep, lustrous green obtained by the addition of copper to the lead glaze. Jugs may have only a small 'bib' on the shoulder opposite the handle, or they may have a larger glazed area around the upper half of the body.

None of the barrel-shaped jugs found in London have any form of body decoration. Biconical and rounded jugs (Figs 122; 123, No 555) commonly carry a very basic form of decoration, which can be paralleled at Cheam High Street (Orton 1982b, Fig 17). This consists of from one to three shallow, incised, horizontal grooves running around the maximum girth. There may also be a single groove around the neck. These grooves were made with a pointed tool or comb while the jug was being turned. A variation on this can be seen on the conical jug (Fig 123, No 557) which has a series of five shallow, horizontal grooves, wider than those described above, running around the body from the upper handle join to just above the base. A trimming-tool was held at a slight angle against the body of the jug as it was turned, leaving a narrow ledge and shaving away the clay above it. This gave the finished jug the appearance of having several tiers. Another variation on this form of decoration is seen on the small rounded drinking jug (Fig 123, No 559) whose neck carries a series of closely-spaced horizontal grooves running from rim to shoulder.

Red-painted decoration, as found at Parkside (Marshall 1924, 89-92; Figs 12-14), but not at Cheam High Street, is not common in London – one complete rounded jug and a few sherds are known. The rounded jug (Figs 36; 123, No 556) was decorated using a wide brush – marks from the bristles can still be seen – to apply a thin red slip, which was, nevertheless, not so thin as to run. A broad horizontal band was painted around the angle of the neck and shoulder, and a second band just below the maximum girth. In each case, more than one brush-stroke was needed to make the lines. Within them, a simple, curvilinear design was repeated three times around the body, again using several short brush-strokes rather than single, long strokes. A very thin, patchy, clear to pale green glaze was applied in a 'bib' over this design. The pattern can be paralleled at Parkside (Marshall 1924, Fig 14).

No other form of decoration was used by the Cheam potters who supplied London. Applied plastic decoration, anthropomorphic and zoomorphic decoration, roller-stamps and stamped bosses were not in their repertoire.

Measures

(Fig 123, Nos 560-63)

The term 'measure' was coined by Marshall, and is retained here – the possible function of the form is discussed below (Marshall 1924, 86). Measures are small, hollow vessels whose form is 'very comfortable for holding in the hand' (ibid., 86). They resemble an elongated baluster jug in shape, their height at least three times the diameter of the rim, and have a short, slightly flared neck. The rim is rounded or triangular in shape, but not thickened. The base is not flared to the same extent as that of a baluster jug, and the form has no pouring lip or handle. The lower third of the body and the base are thick-walled in comparison with the rest of the vessel, and show stretch-marks inside, resulting from the twisting of the clay during throwing. The base is indented in the same way as jug bases, and the fan-shaped impression made when the measure was removed from the wheel may still be visible underneath. Measures

do not appear to have been knife-trimmed, and tend to be poorly finished, with kiln scars, handling marks and wipe-marks in all directions still visible. A clear or pale green glaze was applied inside, with spots and patches outside, and sometimes a band of glaze around the neck. None has any form of decoration. The internal glazing suggests that they were used to store liquids, which would otherwise permeate the fabric. Moreover, their shape and size are not ideally suited for use as drinking vessels, especially since purpose-made drinking jugs formed an important part of the Cheam whiteware industry. Therefore, Marshall's term 'measure' may well be a reasonable indication of the intended usage of these vessels. However, there are as yet too few complete examples whose capacities can be measured for any sort of gradation in size to be recognised. The capacities of only two complete measures (Nos 560, 563) were recorded as 150ml and 220ml respectively.

Measures were found at the Parkside kiln site, but not at Cheam High Street. The vessels described as 'bottles' in the High Street interim report (Orton 1979, 303), and compared with Marshall's measures, were reclassified in the subsequent report as barrel-shaped jugs (Orton 1982b).

Cooking vessels

The only Cheam whiteware cooking vessels represented in significant quantities in London excavations are cooking pots and pipkins. This makes an interesting contrast with Kingston-type ware and Coarse Border ware, in both of which a greater variety of forms for use in the kitchen were made (see Appendix 6).

1. Cooking pots

(Fig 124, Nos 564-70)

Two types of Cheam whiteware cooking pot are known from London – those with lid-seating (Nos 569-70) and those without (Nos 564-68). The latter are commoner in excavated assemblages, and are represented by four complete examples in the Museum of London reserve collection. They are jar-shaped in form and have a more angular profile than other Surrey whiteware cooking pots, with a high shoulder, and either a short, straight-sided neck (Nos 564, 566, 567), or no neck at all (No 565). The angle between the rim and the shoulder may be emphasised by an incised line. Rims are thickened externally, and are either bevelled internally (Nos 564-67), or almost flat-topped (No 568). Some cooking pots may also have been turned – for example No 566, which has an incised groove running unevenly around the top of the rim. Bases are flat and slightly indented – *the* Cheam whiteware base form for all vessel types (cf jugs, Figs 120-23). They appear generally to have been wiped or smoothed underneath, and were lightly knife-trimmed in a narrow band around the lower part of the body, just above the base-angle – No 567 still has a rather jagged groove cut into the body by the blade of the trimming-tool about 10mm from the base. All cooking pots of this type have a spread of pale to dark green glaze inside the base, and spots on the body. Running of glaze shows that they were fired upside down. None are decorated or well-finished, and palm-prints, finger-marks, dents, lumps of extraneous clay and kiln scars all indicate something of a rapid 'production-line'.

Orton commented on the flat base as being an unusual form for medieval cooking pots, and suggested that the vessels from Cheam High Street were instead jars used for dry storage, rather than for cooking (Orton 1982b, Fig 18, Nos 47-9). However, all the illustrated London vessels and most excavated cooking pots are burnt and sooted, some quite heavily, even as far as the rim. This seems to justify the use of the term 'cooking pot' which Orton applied to the same form in his interim paper on the High Street site (Orton 1979, 303; Fig 3, Nos 21-3).

The other type of cooking pot made in Cheam whiteware has a bifid rim or internal lid-seating (Nos 569-70). No complete examples have been found in London, but the evidence of sherds from excavations suggests that they may have been larger and less angular in profile, more like Coarse Border ware forms (Fig 115, No 477). Rims have a hooked internal ledge and rounded top, not thickened externally. In addition to the use of glaze inside the base, bifid cooking pots have a band of glaze around the top part of the body outside, from the rim to the shoulder.

2. Pipkins

(Fig 124, Nos 571-73)

Cheam whiteware pipkins are similar in form, and presumably in function, to Kingston-type ware and Coarse Border ware vessels of the same name (Figs 95, Nos 311-17; 116, Nos 480-81 respectively). Their shape mirrors that of the cooking pot, but they are smaller and more squat – the maximum girth is up to twice the height. The majority are so similar to each other in shape and detail that they were probably made in the same workshop over a relatively short period of time. Rims are thickened externally, with a flat top and slight internal thickening. Vessels with a reasonably complete rim are rare, and most pipkins are represented only by their handle and the corresponding profile. Consequently, very few pouring lips survive. However, on the basis of other Surrey whitewares (see p.46), it seems that a lip was a necessary part of this particular form. Part of a pinched and pulled lip can be seen on No 571, situated on the rim at approximately 90° from the handle. The pipkin illustrated in Fig 124, No 573, although it shares the same basic characteristics of the type described above, may come from a different workshop. It is taller in relation to the maximum girth than the common Cheam form, and has an internally bevelled rim. The handle is missing.

Pipkin bases are indented in the same way as other Cheam forms, and may be smoothed underneath. However, No 573 was left untouched after throwing, showing very clearly how the vessel was removed from the wheel. A length of wire was drawn under the base, then looped around to cut the pipkin from the wheel-head, leaving the tell-tale fan-shaped mark (cf jug bases, p.74). Pipkins have a short, stubby strap handle luted onto the body at an angle of about 45° to the rim. The upper surface is concave, as a result of smoothing with the fingers during manufacture. A single thumb- or finger-impression was made below the handle outside the vessel, at the point where it joins the body. The end of the handle was cut, or 'nipped' off with the fingers from a longer strap, and 'tipped' over as it was pushed flat with the thumb. This tended to give the handle a slightly hooked shape. As with cooking pots, pipkins have a spread of green glaze inside the base. The majority of vessels found had obviously been used for heating food. This may be shown simply by a slight sooting around the circumference of the base, or by a more general blackening – No 573 is very heavily burnt both inside and out.

Pipkins of the same form as the London examples were found at Cheam Parkside (Marshall 1924, 85; Fig 5), but not in the High Street excavations.

3. Lids

(Fig 125, Nos 574-77)

Cheam whiteware lids are simply small dishes made to be inverted in use, probably over some form of cooking vessel, such as lid-seated cooking pots (Fig 124, Nos 569-70). Small sherds from either lids or dishes could easily be confused, particularly rim sherds, The only difference is the presence, or not, of glaze – dishes are generally glazed inside, and lids are completely unglazed.

Lids are wheelthrown, with an indented 'base', which acts as the knop or handle by which they were lifted. Many have twisting marks around the base/knop, resulting from the stretching of the clay during throwing. Rims are rounded and not thickened so that they could fit easily into the lid-seating of the vessel they were made to cover. Most lids are very poorly finished. For example, No 576 has a knop whose edges were roughly, and presumably accidentally, folded downwards to meet the body around half the circumference. Small lumps and particles of clay are scattered all over the surface, and the top of the knop looks as if it was stood in grass or straw while still soft.

One unusual form is illustrated (No 577), and has been classified as a lid, although with no great certainty. It is unglazed, and has a rounded rim, with a flat 'base' or top, slightly indented. There is no knop or handle. It is much shallower and smaller than the forms described above, and the sides are slightly convex in profile. The rim appears to have been in contact with another vessel in the kiln, leaving a number of broken surfaces.

Lids were found at Cheam High Street, although the only knop from this site was both narrower and taller than the London examples (Orton 1982b, Fig 18, No 46R). Lids were also found at Parkside (Marshall 1924, probably Fig 12), although Marshall did not recognise the form as described here.

4. Frying pan

(Fig 125, No 578)

A very shallow, wheelthrown dish, whose rim diameter is about eight times the height, was probably used for cooking, as shown by heavy sooting outside. It has, therefore, been classified as a frying pan, on the basis of parallels with other Surrey whitewares (Figs 96, Nos 332-33; 117, Nos 492-97). The rim is thickened externally and squared. The base is flat and was knife-trimmed, both inside and out, to reduce the thickness of the clay. The vessel is green-glazed inside and over the top of the rim. Although a complete profile has been reconstructed, far too little of the vessel has survived for it to be possible to tell whether it had a handle, as would be expected if its interpretation as a frying pan is correct.

Other forms

Small dishes

(Fig 125, Nos 579-82)

Cheam whiteware small dishes are similar in form to those made in Kingston-type ware (Fig 98, Nos 349-66) and Coarse Border ware (Fig 118, Nos 510-13). They have a rounded rim, which is sometimes slightly thickened or bevelled, giving a flanged appearance (No 580). The base, as usual with Cheam whitewares, is flat and indented, rather unevenly, as if it had been wiped with the palm of the hand. There is no sign of knife-trimming. In most cases, the clay around the circumference of the base was smeared up the sides of the dish in several places. Dishes are glazed inside, and are uniformly poorly finished. Quality was obviously not a prerequisite of production. An interesting usage is suggested by No 580, which is sooted inside and around the upper half of the body outside, although not under the base. This pattern of blackening may have resulted from the dish having been used as a lamp.

Small dishes were found at Cheam Parkside, although they were not clearly differentiated from lids (Marshall 1924, Fig 8). None were found at the High Street site.

Money-box

(Fig 125, No 583)

Only one reasonably complete Cheam money-box is known from London. It can be closely paralleled by the Kingston-type ware money-box illustrated in Fig 99, No 373. Its enclosed form resembles a bishop's mitre in shape, with a vertical coin-slit. It is wheelthrown, and has an indented base. There is a spread of green glaze on the outside. The vessel was broken around the coin-slit to extract the coins.

37. '*Tudor Green*' *ware : anthropomorphic baluster jug with green glaze (height 285mm).*

4. 'TUDOR GREEN' WARE

There is very little pottery from recent London excavations that can be classified with any certainty as 'Tudor Green' ware, as defined earlier in this book, ie finewares made in the later, 15th-century phases of the Surrey whiteware industries. This very fine, thin-walled pottery tends to break into very small sherds which can easily be confused with the later 16th- and 17th-century products of the Surrey-Hampshire borders ('Border ware'). However, on the basis of material from dated, excavated contexts, a type-series has been constructed for London 'Tudor Green' by cross-reference to complete, or nearly complete, vessels in the reserve collections of the Museum of London and British Museum. Very few forms, principally tablewares, are represented.

Jugs

(Figs 37; 126, Nos 584-86)

There is one complete 'Tudor Green' anthropomorphic baluster jug in the Museum of London reserve collection (Figs 37; 126, No 584). The shape compares closely with late Kingston-type ware and Coarse Border ware baluster jugs (Figs 54-59; 105; 106, No 413), although the fabric is extremely fine and the walls thin. The throwing-marks are light and close together, and the clay has twisted and stretched around the constricted 'waist'. The base is indented and was lightly knife-trimmed underneath. However, the sides of the jug were left untouched by trimming or smoothing. The strap handle was luted onto the body at the lower end, although it might have been pushed through the wall of the jug at the neck – subsequent covering of the join has obscured the method of attachment at this point. A thumb- or finger-impression was made over the lower join outside, and the handle was stabbed across the upper join and in a single line down the centre. Two incised, horizontal lines run around the shoulder. The rim is externally thickened, with a flat top and slight internal thickening, and has a single cordon, forming a collar. This distinguishes it from the Kingston-type and Coarse Border ware parallels noted above. Highly stylised human facial features were added to the pinched and pulled pouring lip. The nose and

38. 'Tudor Green' ware: lobed cup with green glaze (height 65mm).

chin were made from separate pieces of clay, and the chin has a row of deeply incised vertical lines to represent a beard. The eyes are simply slits made with the tip of a knife. There are no nostrils or mouth. Applied strips of clay were made into arms which extend down the body either side of the face, from just below the rim cordon. The strips are bent up at the maximum girth, each forming an 'elbow', so that the hands almost meet on the belly of the jug. The fingers are incised lines, four on one hand and five on the other. The jug has an even, apple-green glaze with dark speckles over the upper half of the body, and a thick pool of glaze has collected under the base. Particularly good parallels for the decoration are provided by the Coarse Border ware anthropomorphic jugs illustrated in Fig 105, Nos 411-12 and Fig 106, No 413.

The rim and neck sherd illustrated in Fig 126, No 585, may have come from a baluster or rounded jug. The rim is similar to that of No 584, and is externally thickened, with a flat top. The handle, which is incomplete, has a sub-triangular section with a flat outer surface. There is a single row of stab-marks made with a pointed tool across the top of the rim/handle join, and another line of stab-marks down the centre of the handle. The only other illustrated sherd which may have come from a jug (No 586) has an applied disc of clay stamped with a grid pattern which recalls Coarse Border ware jug decoration (Figs 105, No 410; 113, Nos 452-54).

Costrels

(Fig 126, Nos 587-88)

Two 'Tudor Green' costrels or portable flasks are illustrated. Both are in the Museum of London reserve collection – one is complete, the other less so. They are 'mammiform' in shape, a type which is also known from sherds excavated in London and can be paralleled at Farnborough Hill (Holling 1977, Fig 1, No 15). They were wheelthrown as enclosed vessels with a flat 'base', knife-trimmed after removal from the wheel. In the case of No 587, the surface opposite the flat base, ie the top of the vessel as thrown, was also flattened, but had a smaller diameter, defined by a single incised line, enclosing a central, incised spiral. A band of three incised lines runs around the carination at the mid-point of the body. This part of the other costrel (No 588) is now missing. The costrels were made to be used in the same way as a modern water canteen, and so a tubular neck

was formed over a hole made in the side of the vessel, which became the top when in use. In both cases, the neck was luted onto the costrel around the hole and secured with extra pieces of clay smoothed well into the body. The hole was not made in either vessel by cutting and removing a disc of clay, but was simply pushed through the wall, and the clay either folded back around its circumference into the vessel (No 588), or smoothed up inside the neck (No 587). The top of the neck was cut straight across, leaving it flat and smooth. Lugs were provided to enable the user to suspend the costrel from a thong of leather or other suitable material. These were made from flat, 'ear-shaped' pieces of clay, luted onto the neck and body along the circumference of the vessel. However, No 587 is unusual in having three rather than just two lugs – two were positioned as normal, and the third was placed between them at right angles to each. A circular hole was pushed through the centre of each lug, although neither costrel shows any sign of wear at these points. A very practical feature of No 588 is the slight flattening of the body diametrically opposite the neck, forming a sort of base when in use to enable the pot to be stood upright. Both costrels are green-glazed over most of the body. The capacity of the complete costrel (No 587) was measured at 1700ml.

Lobed cups

(Figs 38; 127)

There are a number of complete, or nearly complete, lobed cups in the reserve collections of the Museum of London and the British Museum (six are illustrated here). Those which can be classed as 'Tudor Green' by comparison with sherds from dated, excavated contexts, are generally undecorated and made for individual rather than communal use, contrasting with the large, decorated lobed cups made in Coarse Border ware (Fig 119, Nos 514-18). They can be compared with the Farnborough Hill forms (Holling 1977, Fig 1, Nos 8a, 8b), and were wheelthrown as wide-mouthed, thin-walled cups with a flared rim and waisted, flat or slightly indented base. They were not generally knife-trimmed. There is a carination more or less at the mid-point of the body, above which the walls were pinched in up to the rim from inside the cup, at regular intervals around its circumference. This produced the characteristic lobed effect – six lobes seems to be an average number. Rims are rounded and unthickened, as appropriate for a drinking vessel. A short handle of strap, sub-rectangular, squared or oval section was attached either in the middle of a lobe, or between two lobes. The top end was wrapped over the rim and smoothed down inside the cup, and the lower end was luted onto the body, marked by a single finger- or thumb-impression outside. The size of the handles makes them rather difficult to hold, and they are better suited for hanging the cups from hooks on a dresser. Body decoration is uncommon – the only illustrated example is No 593, which has three deeply incised, horizontal lines running around the upper half of the body, above the carination. In all cases, the entire inside surface is green-glazed; outside, the body may be glazed from the rim to the base, or only as far as the carination.

Applied internal decoration is uncommon in 'Tudor Green' lobed cups. A stylised, crudely-made 'tree' luted onto the inside wall of one cup (No 597) was probably one of a number, perhaps three or four, surrounding a centrepiece (cf the Coarse Border ware stag cup, Fig 119, No 514). It was made from several separate, rolled pieces of clay, stuck as branches onto a central trunk, the base of which was smoothed into the body of the cup and stabbed with the tip of a knife. A similar decorative idea is represented by No 596, although the added figure, possibly another tree, has broken away, and so cannot be reconstructed. This cup is also interesting in that the base is blackened around the edges, presumably as a result of being heated.

III ORIGINS AND AFFINITIES OF THE SURREY WHITEWARES

The white-firing clays used in the Surrey whiteware industries were known to medieval potters in the 11th century (see p.13). However, there was a period of about a century, from *c.*1150 to just before *c.*1250, during which no contemporaneous Surrey whitewares were used in London. This period corresponds to the *floruit* of the London-type ware industry, and it may well be that there was no real market for Surrey pottery at this time. Early Surrey coarsewares, which had been used in London from the mid-11th to mid-12th century, were continuously produced in Surrey for local use during this period.

The Kingston-type ware industry appears not to have started until the first half of the 13th century. Its pottery is not found in London in contexts dated earlier than the middle of the century, and there is a little evidence from sites in Kingston upon Thames for a phase during which London-type ware Rouen style jugs and other non-local glazed red earthenwares, but no whitewares, were used in the town (unpublished material in Kingston upon Thames Heritage Unit and Art Gallery). Since Rouen style jugs came into use at the very end of the 12th century (Pearce *et al.* 1985, 132), this phase in Kingston must date to the early 13th century, forming a *terminus post quem* for the Kingston whiteware industry.

The London sequence shows that a wide variety of jug forms were made in the early Kingston-type ware industry (see Figs 41-42 for a diagrammatic summary of the life-span of the main Kingston-type ware vessel forms). However, there is insufficient evidence to show that they were all being produced during the initial, mid-13th-century, phase. Those which were definitely made at this time, that is baluster, conical, pear-shaped and rounded jugs, with applied and stamped decoration and sometimes polychrome glaze (Fig 39), are closely paralleled, both in form and decoration, in the contemporaneous London-

type ware industry (for example see Pearce *et al.* 1985, Figs 41-4; 52; 55). There is little doubt that the potters who founded the Kingston-type industry came from London. The reasons why they should have moved away from London are less clear. London was always the main market for Kingston-type ware, so that the Kingston potteries can hardly be seen as a daughter industry set up on the edge of the London-type ware market area to supply the local region. It is more likely that the desire to make pots in a white-firing clay was an important deciding factor, even though Kingston upon Thames is not situated on a bed of white-firing clay.

By the late 13th century, the Kingston-type ware potters were making vessel forms and using decorative techniques which were not found in the London-type ware industry. These include the elegant baluster jugs made in imitation of

39. Kingston-type ware: mid-13th-century assemblage. Left, highly decorated pear-shaped jug (height 312mm); right, highly decorated cylindrical-necked baluster jug (height 324mm).

metal forms, and the use of stamped bosses. The metal copy baluster jug is not found in other industries in the London area, nor has it been recognised by the authors further afield, and must be considered a local invention. The shape of the body, with its narrow waist, straight neck and decorated handle all show clear affinities with contemporary metal jugs as illustrated in late 13th- and 14th-century illuminated manuscripts (Randall 1966, Pl LVII, No 276; Pl LXXXVIII, No 423; Pl XCV, No 459). Stamped bosses, however, are a form of decoration which was used extensively in southern and eastern England – for example, at Rye in Sussex (Barton 1979, 201-5, 242). 'Aardenberg ware' from the Low Countries provides a particularly close parallel for this type of decoration (Dunning 1976, Figs 1, Nos 1-2; 3), but there is no evidence for the use of the same dies at more than one centre. Although the dating evidence is uncertain, it seems likely that the Low Countries vessels are earlier than their English counterparts, and that knowledge of this technique could have been brought from the continent by the Kingston-type potters. Independent invention is unlikely with such a complicated technique, although it is possible that similar moulds were used for confectionery

40. Kingston-type ware: late 13th- to 14th-century assemblage. From left to right, back row: small rounded anthropomorphic jug (height 180mm); metal copy baluster jug (height 336mm); conical jug with stamped boss decoration; large storage jar. Front row: tripod pipkin; pipkin (height 96mm).

and butter, and that potters in different areas independently hit on the idea of adapting them to decorate pottery.

The early 14th-century Ludgate Hill assemblage is similar in composition to groups of late 13th-century date from Swan Lane and Trig Lane, showing that, over quite a long period, little major change took place in the forms or methods of decoration used in the Kingston-type industry (Fig 40 illustrates an assemblage of late 13th- to early 14th-century Kingston-type ware vessels). At some time in the middle of the 14th century, however, the Kingston-type ware assemblages from London change in character. Metal copy baluster jugs are no longer found, and are replaced by plain jugs copying the London-type ware tulip-necked baluster form (Pearce *et al.* 1985, Fig 37). Large rounded jugs, as found at the Knapp-Drewett site, are the main type of jug at this period. This type of jug was also an important product of the Coarse Border ware industry, and

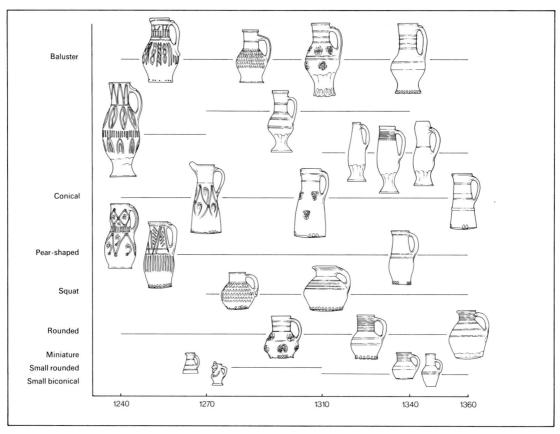

Baluster

Conical

Pear-shaped

Squat

Rounded

Miniature
Small rounded
Small biconical

1240   1270   1310   1340   1360

41. Diagram to show the time-span of the main Kingston-type ware jug forms as dated by large pottery assemblages from London excavations.

the Kingston-type potters were probably copying them. Applied decoration and polychrome glaze were no longer used. These changes suggest that a less varied and plainer range of pots was being made, but that most of the forms and decorative techniques in use at this time were already known, either within the industry, or locally. These mid-14th-century types continued in production until the end of the century, when the industry came to an end. A comparison of the forms, rim types and decoration found at the Knapp-Drewett kiln in Kingston (McCracken, Nenk and Vince forthcoming) with late 14th-century Kingston-type wares from London reveals certain differences, which suggests that only a small proportion of the London material came from the Knapp-Drewett kiln. Even at the end of the industry's life, when Kingston-type ware formed only a fraction of the pottery used in London, there were still a number of workshops in operation, each employing its own, slightly different, techniques.

Sherds of Coarse Border ware are occasionally found in the London sequence as early as the mid-13th century, when Kingston-type ware came

into use in the capital. The forms represented at this period are cooking pots with everted, infolded rims, and green-glazed large rounded jugs with decorated strap handles and combed decoration. Both these forms are common in earlier industries in southern England. The rounded jugs, for example, are similar in size and shape to 12th- and early 13th-century London-type ware early rounded jugs and tripod pitchers (Pearce *et al.* 1985, Figs 10-23). Even in the late 14th and 15th centuries, when Coarse Border ware was the commonest type of pottery used in London, the range of forms and decorative techniques employed was remarkably small and appears to have been developed mainly from the earlier products of the kilns (see Figs 43-44). The only new ideas in the industry at this time were the use of decorative strips of red clay, and the introduction of the cistern. It is not difficult to see where both innovations might have originated.

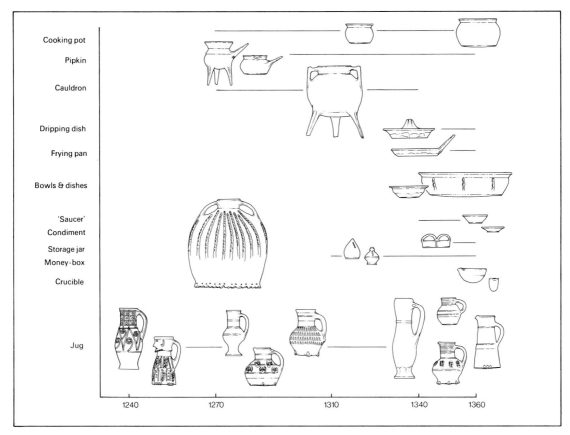

Cooking pot					
Pipkin					
Cauldron					
Dripping dish					
Frying pan					
Bowls & dishes					
'Saucer'					
Condiment					
Storage jar					
Money-box					
Crucible					
Jug					
	1240	1270	1310	1340	1360

42. Diagram to show the time-span of the main forms of Kingston-type ware as dated by large pottery assemblages from London excavations.

The use of applied red strips would be a natural development in any workshop where more than one colour clay was available, and the form of the cistern, with its characteristic bunghole, could well be a translation into clay of a form common in leather and wood.

The only other obvious changes in typology recognised in the Coarse Border ware found in the London sequence concern cooking pot and bowl rims. By the mid-14th century, flat-topped rims were being made on these forms alongside, or instead of, the everted rims of the 13th and early 14th centuries. However, the major change took place at the end of the 14th century, with the introduction of lid-seating. 'Bifid' rims seem to have become the standard form very quickly, and predominate in early 15th-century groups. Ceramic lids are also present in these groups, and there is little doubt that the two features are connected. In south-east England, the introduction of the 'bifid' rim can be seen in other industries, such as Late London Slipped ware (Vince 1985, Fig 31 No 3), together with the increased use of lids in Cheam whiteware. Although these are functional changes, there was

also a stylistic preference, in that when lid-seating was adopted by, for example, the Malvern Chase potters in the 16th century, the form of rim they chose was quite different from that prevalent in the south-east (Vince 1977, 268, Fig 3).

The origins and affinities of the Cheam whiteware industry have already been discussed elsewhere (Orton 1982b, 79-82). Orton sees the industry as coming into existence as a response to an increasing demand for small jugs, to be used for drinking rather than for pouring. This demand, he argues, was the result of the adoption of a continental fashion, although there is only the barest similarity between the actual form of the Cheam whiteware biconical jugs and their proposed Siegburg stoneware counterparts. Alternatively, it is possible that the Cheam vessels had metal prototypes, as suggested by their sharp, angular profiles. There are also no local parallels for the use of a neat arrangement of stab-holes to

key the body surface for the attachment of the handle.

In the early 15th century the Cheam potters began making barrel-shaped jugs in preference to the biconical forms prevalent in the late 14th century (see Figs 45-46 for late 14th- and early 15th-century assemblages of Cheam whiteware from London; see also Fig 47). The new form is simple in shape, but does not appear to have been widely used in other industries, except where it might have been copied from the Cheam products, for example in Late London-type ware (Pearce *et al.* 1984, Fig 59, Nos 241-2).

The Cheam whiteware industry was almost certainly larger in scale than a single potter working at any one time during its life. At least three workshops are known in the village of Cheam (for a list of sites, see Orton 1982b, 78). At least one of these, the 1969 High Street site, was used repeatedly over a long period of time, from the late 14th to the late 15th centuries. Although there is some evidence that certain features of Cheam whiteware were copied in Kingston-type ware (ie the form of the biconical jug), there is little to suggest that Kingston

43. Coarse Border ware : assemblage of miscellaneous forms. From left to right, back row : conical jug (height 285mm) ; rounded jug (height 215mm) ; cistern (height 285mm). Front : cooking pot (height 120mm).

products influenced the Cheam potters. After the Kingston-type ware industry had come to an end, in the 15th century, the only whitewares being made in Surrey were Cheam whiteware and Coarse Border ware. Both produced a similar range of forms. However, the Cheam potters concentrated on the production of smaller vessels, principally for use at the table, and the Coarse Border ware industry, as represented in London, was based on the production of large forms for cooking and storage. The two industries may have started in direct competition, but appear to have settled into a state of equilibrium in which their wares were complementary in serving the needs of the London market (see Appendix 6 for a statistical analysis of the London material). Similarities in forms and methods of decoration suggest mutual copying. For example, red slip 'painting' on the bodies of large rounded jugs and cisterns and other forms, is found in both

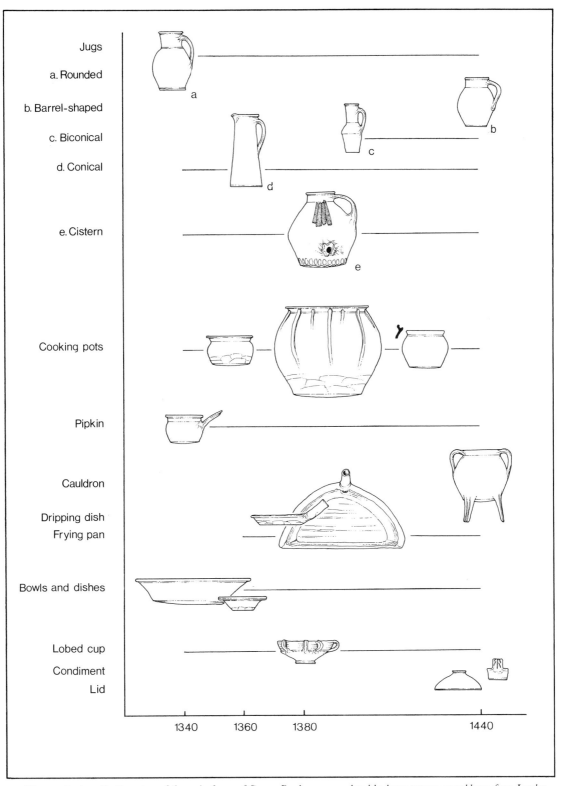

Jugs
a. Rounded
b. Barrel-shaped
c. Biconical
d. Conical
e. Cistern

Cooking pots

Pipkin

Cauldron

Dripping dish
Frying pan

Bowls and dishes

Lobed cup
Condiment
Lid

1340   1360   1380   1440

44. *Diagram to show the time-span of the main forms of Coarse Border ware as dated by large pottery assemblages from London excavations.*

industries, although the decorative schemes favoured differ.

Untempered, thin-walled cups were made in all three main Surrey whiteware industries. Although they may have been produced as early as the late 13th to early 14th century, they became more common in the late 14th century, and it is to this period that evidence for their production at Kingston and Cheam belongs. Most are represented by body-sherds, and too few complete profiles can be assigned to a particular source for any similarities or differences to be noticeable. However, the few profiles from the Knapp-Drewett kiln in Kingston differ from the standard 15th-century type both in profile, and in the use of incised decoration, applied on the wheel.

THE END OF THE MEDIEVAL SURREY WHITEWARE INDUSTRIES

The Kingston-type whiteware industry had definitely stopped sending pottery to London by the early 15th century, and production had most probably ceased, although the kilns were still in existence towards the end of the 14th century.

45. Cheam whiteware: late 14th-century assemblage. Left, cooking pot with flat-topped rim (height 170mm); right, biconical jug (height 195mm).

Since it may have included workshops in Southwark as well as in Kingston, the demise of the industry was probably not due to purely local circumstances. The source of the white clay was obviously the same as, or similar to, that used by the Cheam potters, as demonstrated by Neutron Activation Anaylsis (see Appendix 4), so that there can be no question of the raw clay supply having been exhausted. It seems more likely that the end of the industry was part of a long process whereby potting was driven away from London, perhaps by market forces, even though the early 15th century actually saw the re-establishment of pottery production in the London area.

The Cheam and Coarse Border ware industries were thriving in the early 15th century. However, after this time the London sequence becomes very unclear, since the rate of waterfront reclamation in the City was decreasing as stone revetments were introduced. The fate of these industries cannot yet be established archaeologically in London. Even so, the Cheam kilns may still have

been in production in the early 16th century, to judge by a few vessels from groups of this date from London. Although the Coarse Border ware industry had probably declined before then, the production of 'Tudor Green' was at its peak.

CONCLUSION

The Surrey whiteware industries began in the mid-13th century, although white clay, which was probably obtained from the Reading Beds in Surrey, was known to potters by the late 11th century.

Three main industries can be distinguished.

46. Cheam whiteware: 15th-century assemblage. From left to right, back row: rounded jug (height 250mm); barrel-shaped jug (height 275mm). Front row: small barrel-shaped jug (height 130mm); measure (height 150mm).

The Kingston-type industry consisted of workshops along the south bank of the Thames, from Kingston to Southwark. In the late 13th century potters at Kingston were supplying the royal palace at Westminster, although the only archaeological evidence from either Kingston or Southwark dates to the late 14th century. This industry ceased production at the end of the 14th century, although redwares were being made in

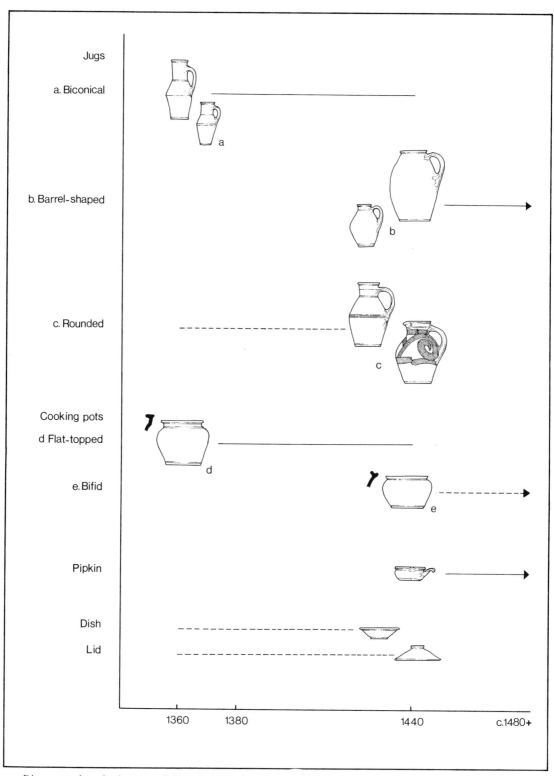

47. *Diagram to show the time-span of the main forms of Cheam whiteware as dated by large pottery assemblages from London excavations.*

Kingston in the late 15th or early 16th centuries.

The Cheam whiteware industry began in the mid-14th century and grew in the early 15th century. Its fortunes in the late 15th century are at present unknown, although it may still have been operating in the early 16th century. The Coarse Border ware industry covered a wide area of north-east Hampshire and west Surrey, and was already in existence by the mid-13th century. It was not until the mid-14th century that its products started to appear in London in large quantities. At that time the industry grew to become the largest pottery source in south-east England. Coarseware production had probably ceased by the early 16th century, although finewares, which had been produced in all three industries during the late 14th century, continued to be made. In the 16th century, this led to the emergence of an industry which supplied much of England with thin-walled green-glazed cups and jugs.

Kingston-type ware was the first pottery in England known to have relied on imported clay. It came into existence as a response to the demand for fine whiteware vessels, stimulated perhaps by French imports. By the time of its demise in the late 14th century, there were two other whiteware pottery centres, at Cheam and the Surrey/Hampshire border. Both these centres were situated near potential sources of white clay.

The study of stratified assemblages from London has enabled the relative fortunes of these industries to be established, and has shown that for decades, if not longer, the products of each industry were standardised and stable, but that at certain times – namely c.1350 and c.1400 – there were typological changes which affected both the range and relative frequency of vessel types. Why the medieval pottery industry should have behaved in this way is at present unknown.

Acknowledgements

The preparation of this book would not have been possible without free access to the reserve collection of the Museum of London. We are indebted to Brian Spencer, John Clark, Peter Stott and Rosemary Weinstein for making this available to us and for all their advice and help during work on the project. We are also extremely grateful to John Cherry who allowed us to study the pottery in the Department of Medieval and Later Antiquities of the British Museum.

Invaluable help and advice were given by those directly involved with the various kiln sites which produced Surrey whitewares. We would especially like to thank Clive Orton for information on Cheam whiteware; Marion Shipley of Kingston upon Thames Heritage Office; Stephen Nelson and Andrew Penrose of Kingston upon Thames Archaeological Society; and Beverley Nenk and Scott McCracken for access in advance of publication to the Knapp-Drewett material.

We would also like to thank the following for their help in showing us pottery from museums and excavated sites in London and the Home Counties: R. J. C. Hildyard of the Victoria and Albert Museum; G. J. Dawson of the Cuming Museum; J. Arthur of Castle Arch Museum, Guildford; D. B. Kelly of Maidstone Museum and Art Gallery; C. Breen of Dartford Archaeological Society; C. Baker of Dartford Museum; C. Saunders and A. Havercroft of the Verulamium Museum, St. Albans; P. M. Wilkinson of the Passmore Edwards Museum; D. W. Phillipson and M. D. Cra'ster of the University Museum of Archaeology and Anthropology, Cambridge; and J. E. Poole of the Fitzwilliam Museum, Cambridge.

A number of individuals associated with the DUA in various capacities over the past few years have been involved in different aspects of research and preparation ranging from quantification to typing. Their help is gratefully acknowledged. We would particularly like to mention T. W. M. Anderson, J. Barker, J. Edwards, M. Elliott, J. Hetherington and B. Nenk. E. M. Pratt drew the pot illustrated in Fig 111, No 436. Tony Dyson and Clive Orton read through the completed draft and offered much helpful advice. We are also very grateful to Suzanne Lang, a practising potter, for technical information and experimental work on decoration.

We are grateful to the following museums for permission to publish illustrations of pottery in their collections: the British Museum for Fig 59, No 45; Fig 60, No 54; Fig 61, No 55; Fig 66, No 80; Fig 70, No 103; Fig 71, Nos 110, 111; Fig 73, Nos 117, 122; Fig 74, No 126; Fig 75, No 132; Fig 79, Nos 149, 158; Fig 80, Nos 166, 170; Fig 81, No 174; Fig 82, Nos 186, 187, 191; Fig 83, Nos 193, 203; Fig 84, Nos 215, 216; Fig 85, No 229; Fig 86, No 230; Fig 90, Nos 263, 267; Fig 91, Nos 274, 275; Fig 93, Nos 291, 292; Fig 98, Nos 349, 364; Fig 99, Nos 369, 371, 376, 380, 383; Fig 100, No 386; Fig 101, Nos 394, 399; Fig 107, No 420; Fig 108, Nos 422, 424; Fig 113, No 455; Fig 114, No 467; Fig 119, Nos 519, 529; Fig 127, Nos 590, 595; the Victoria and Albert Museum for Fig 50, No 4; Fig 63, No 68; Fig 74, No 128; Fig 75, No 137; Fig 86, No 233; Fig 108, No 423; the Cuming Museum for Fig 92, Nos 279, 284; Fig 98, No 344; Castle Arch Museum, Guildford for Fig 58, No 39; Fig 106, No 416; Fig 111, No 435; Stevenage Museum for Fig 84, No 214; Maidstone Museum and Art Gallery for Fig 69, Nos 97, 99; the University Museum of Archaeology and Anthropology, Cambridge for Fig 101, No 400; the Fitzwilliam Museum, Cambridge for Fig 61, No 59; Fig 62, No 63; Fig 85, No 228; Fig 105, No 411. Fig 63, No 66; Fig 75, No 135 and Fig 118, No 508 are reproduced by permission of the Governor and Company of the Bank of England.

The photographs reproduced in Figs 10-13; Figs 15-16; Fig 26a-c; Fig 27 and Fig 29 are by John Edwards of the Museum of London. Figs 30-38; Fig 43; Figs 45-46 and the cover transparency were taken by Louise Woodman of English Heritage. All other photographs are by Jon Bailey until recently of the Department of Urban Archaeology.

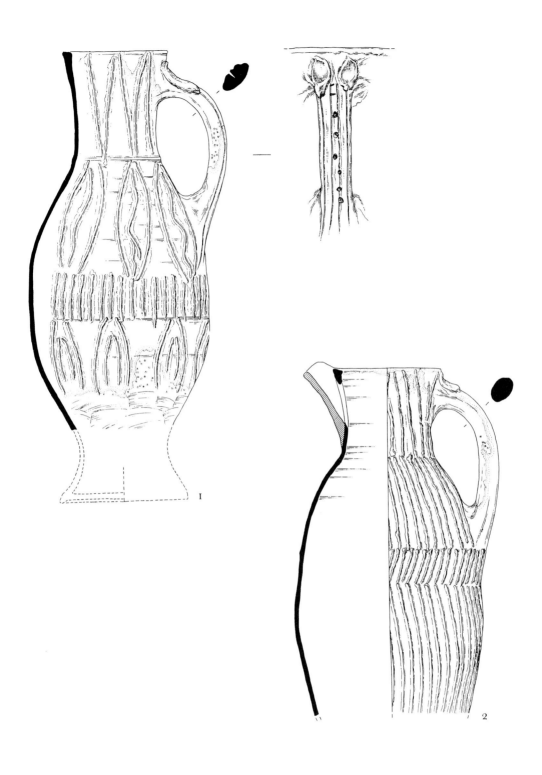

48. Kingston-type ware: large baluster jugs in the highly decorated style. (Scale 1/4)

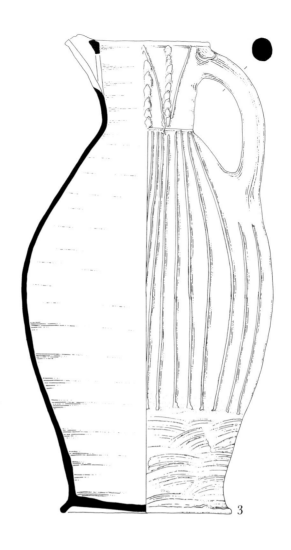

49. Kingston-type ware : large baluster jug in the highly decorated style. (Scale 1/4)

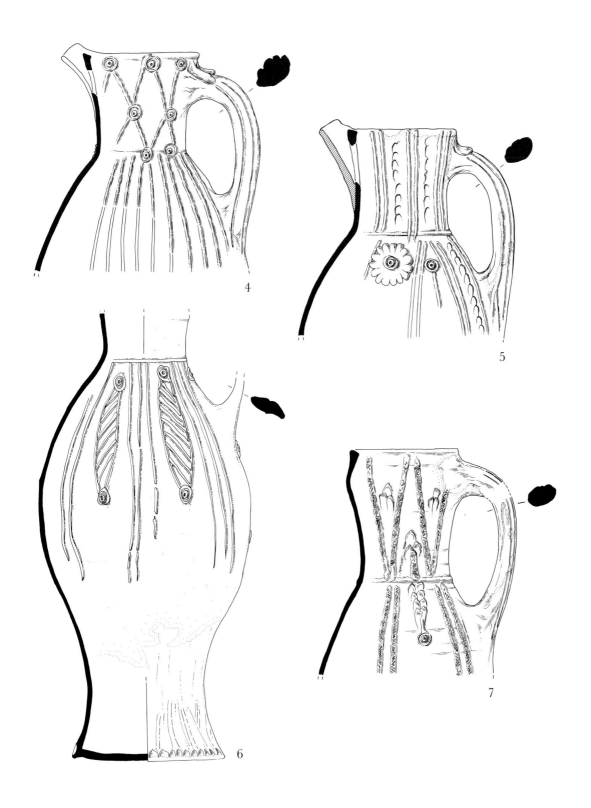

50. *Kingston-type ware: large baluster jugs in the highly decorated style. (Scale 1/4)*

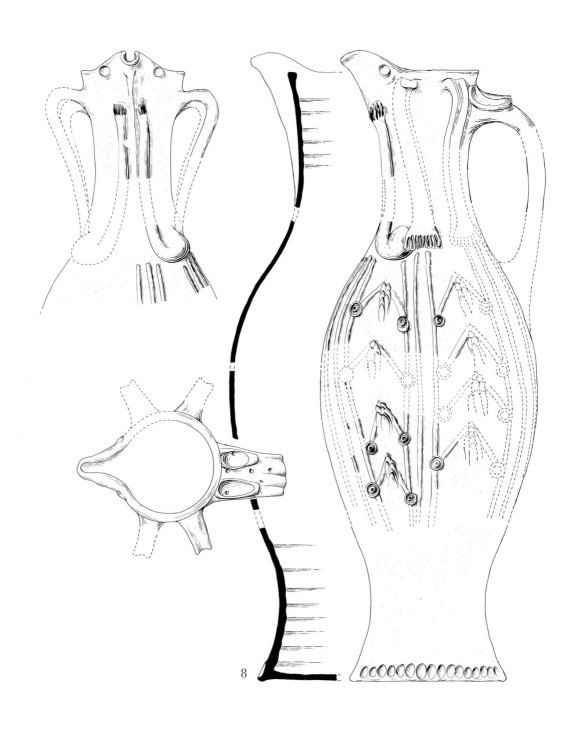

51. Kingston-type ware: large anthropomorphic baluster jug in the highly decorated style. (Scale 1/4)

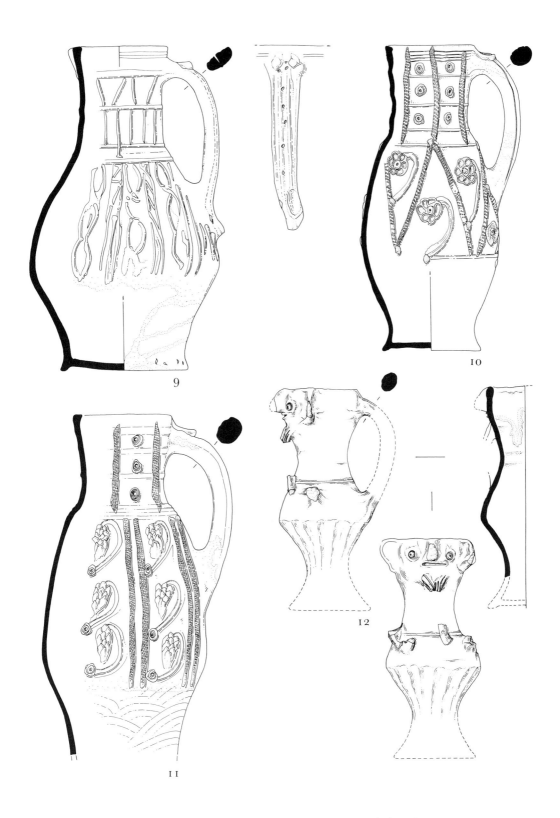

52. Kingston-type ware : cylindrical-necked baluster jugs in the highly decorated style. (Scale 1/4)

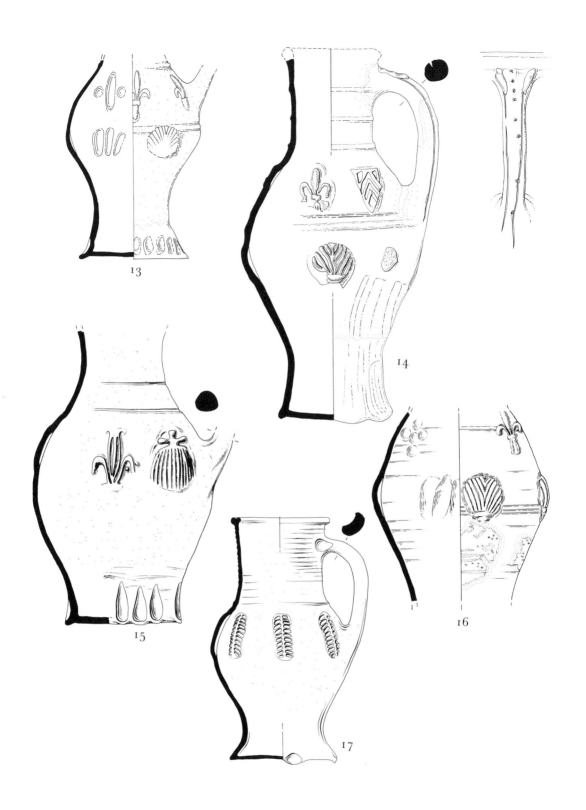

53. Kingston-type ware: cylindrical-necked baluster jugs with stamped boss decoration. (Scale 1/4)

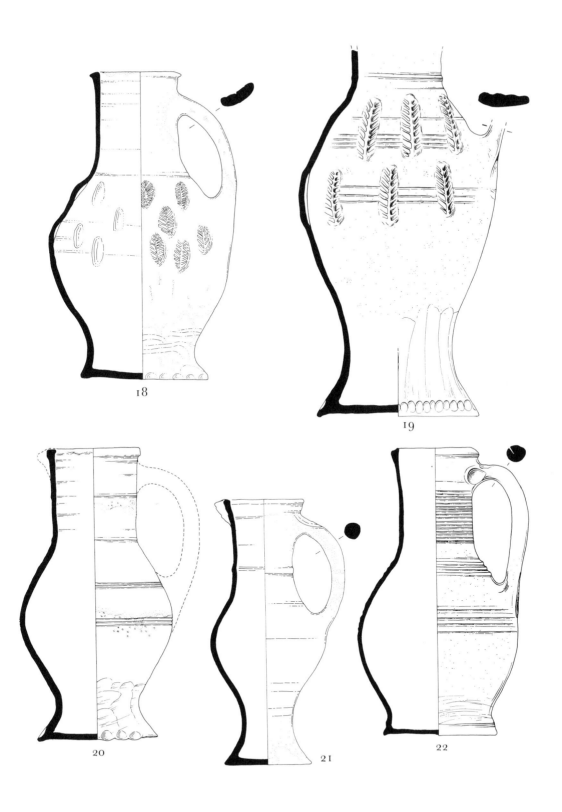

54. *Kingston-type ware: cylindrical-necked baluster jugs, Nos 18-19 with stamped boss decoration. (Scale 1/4)*

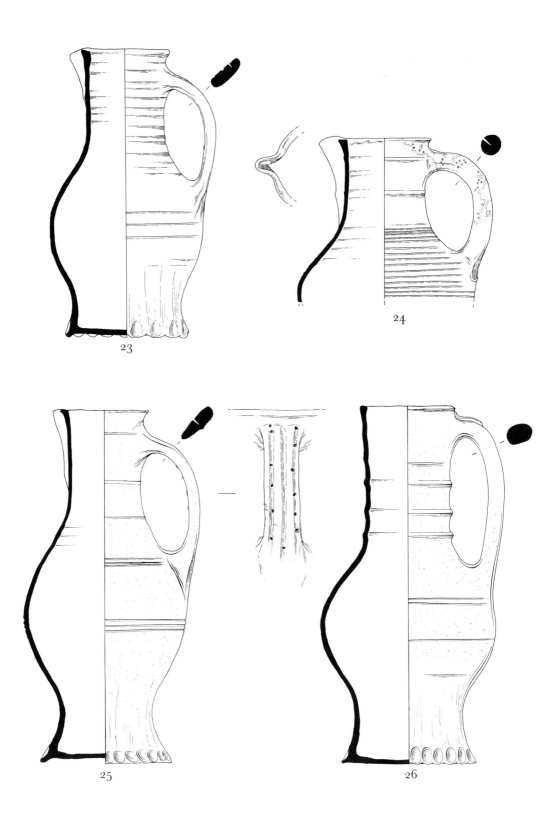

55. Kingston-type ware: cylindrical-necked baluster jugs. (Scale 1/4)

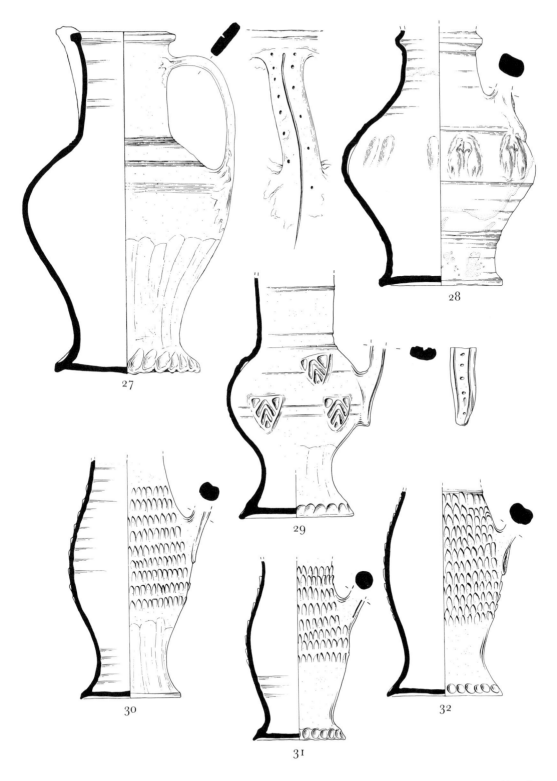

56. *Kingston-type ware : cylindrical-necked baluster jug (No 27) ; metal copy baluster jugs, Nos 28-29 with stamped boss decoration and Nos 30-32 with pellet decoration. (Scale 1/4)*

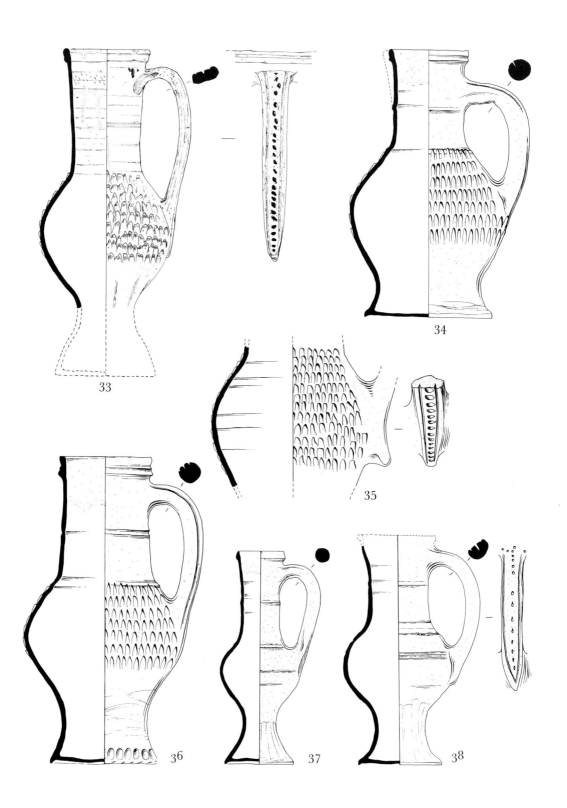

57. Kingston-type ware: metal copy baluster jugs, Nos 33-36 with pellet decoration. (Scale 1/4)

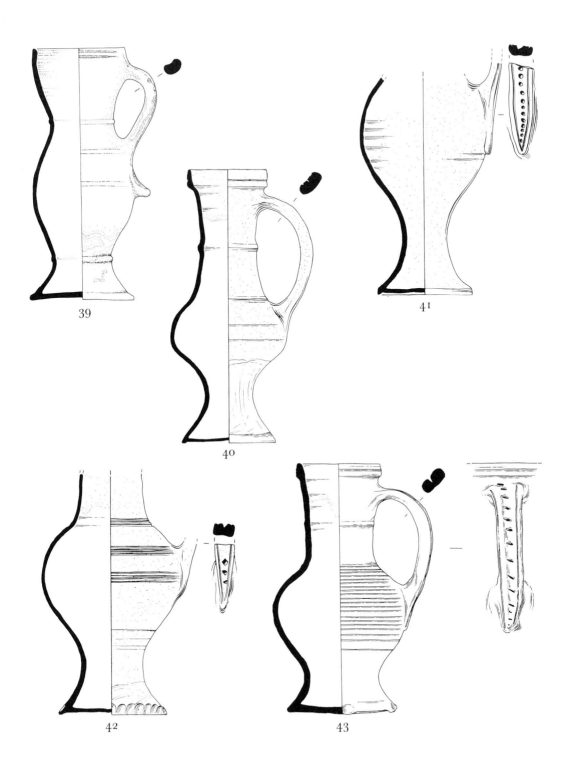

39

40

41

42

43

58. Kingston-type ware : metal copy baluster jugs. (Scale 1/4)

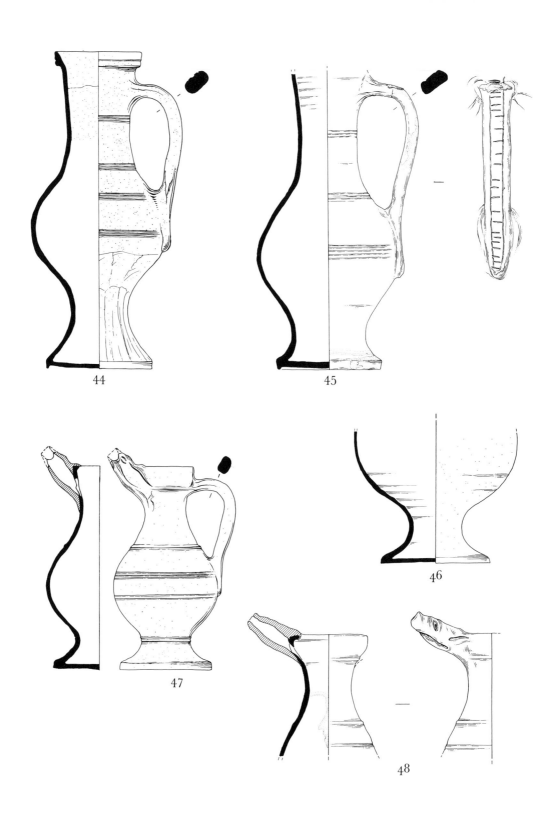

59. Kingston-type ware: metal copy baluster jugs (Nos 44-46); ewers (Nos 47-48). (Scale 1/4)

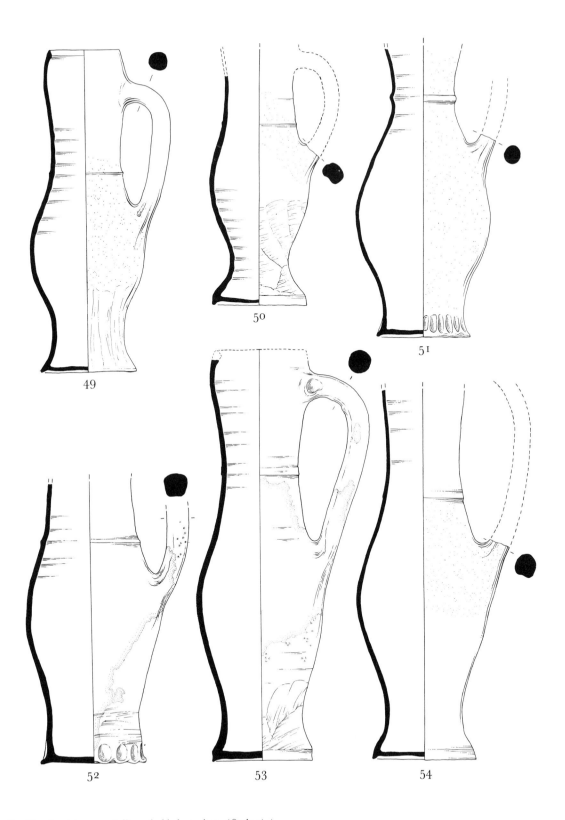

60. Kingston-type ware: tulip-necked baluster jugs. (Scale 1/4)

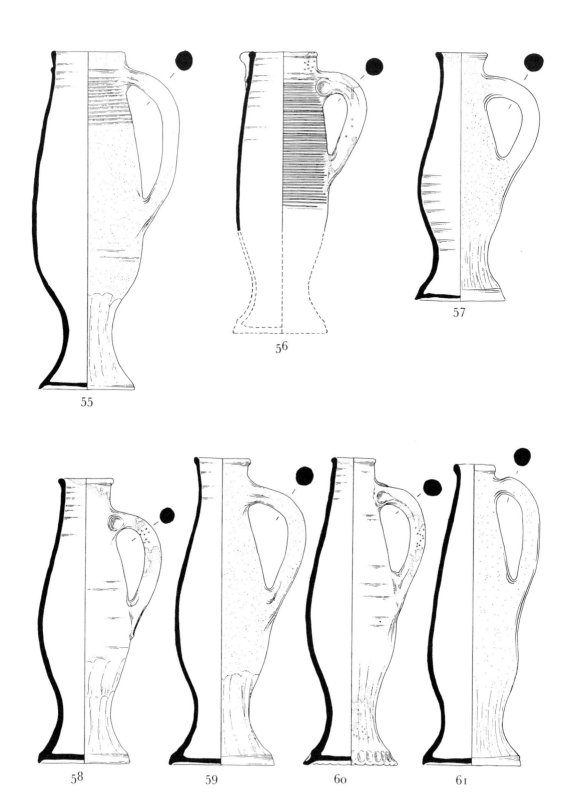

61. Kingston-type ware: rilled baluster jugs (Nos 55-56); narrow-necked baluster jugs (Nos 57-61). (Scale 1/4)

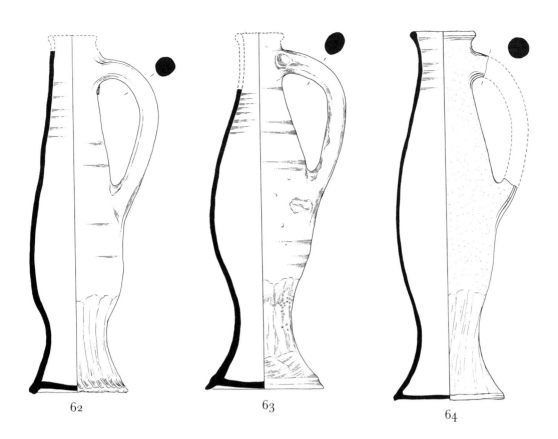

62. *Kingston-type ware : narrow-necked baluster jugs. (Scale 1/4)*

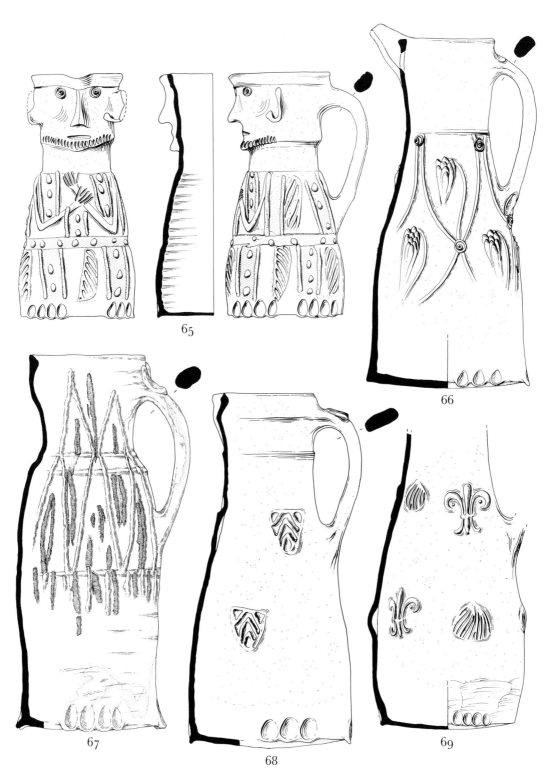

63. *Kingston-type ware: conical jugs in the highly decorated style (Nos 65-67); and with stamped boss decoration (Nos 68-69). (Scale 1/4)*

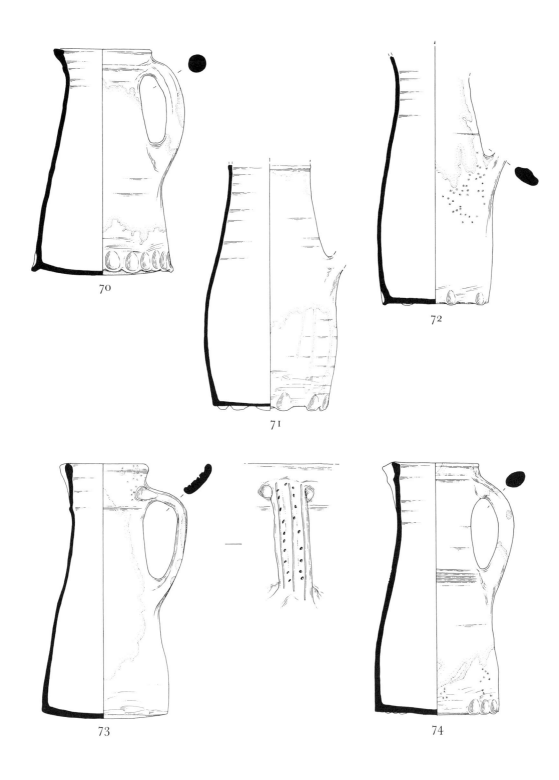

64. *Kingston-type ware : conical jugs. (Scale 1/4)*

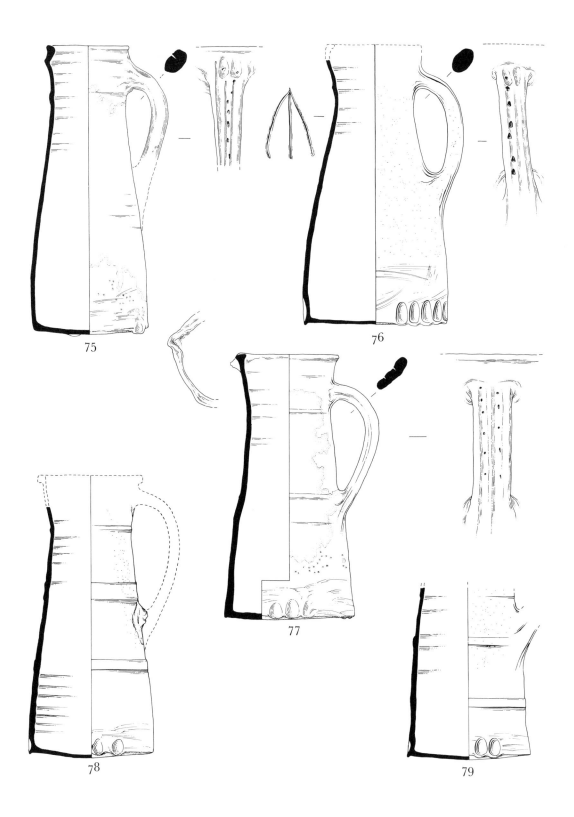

65. *Kingston-type ware : conical jugs. (Scale 1/4)*

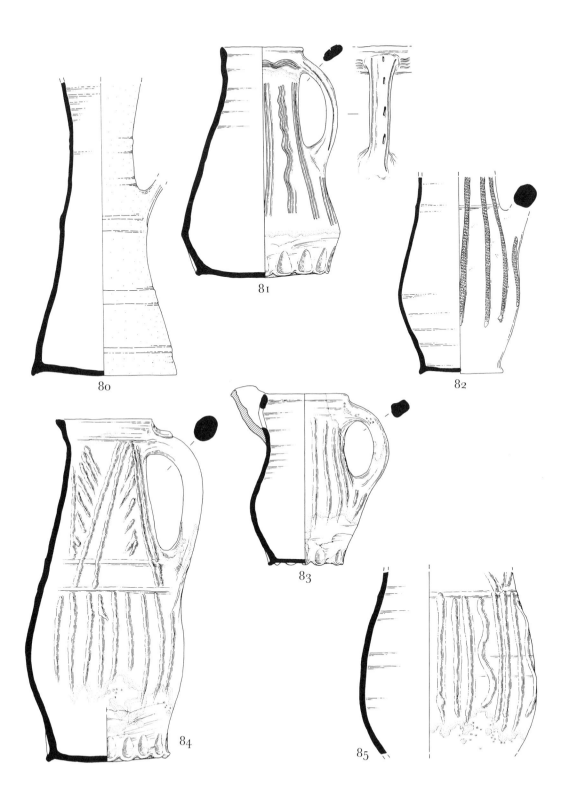

66. *Kingston-type ware: conical jug (No 80); pear-shaped jugs, with combed decoration (No 81); and in the highly decorated style (Nos 82-85). (Scale 1/4)*

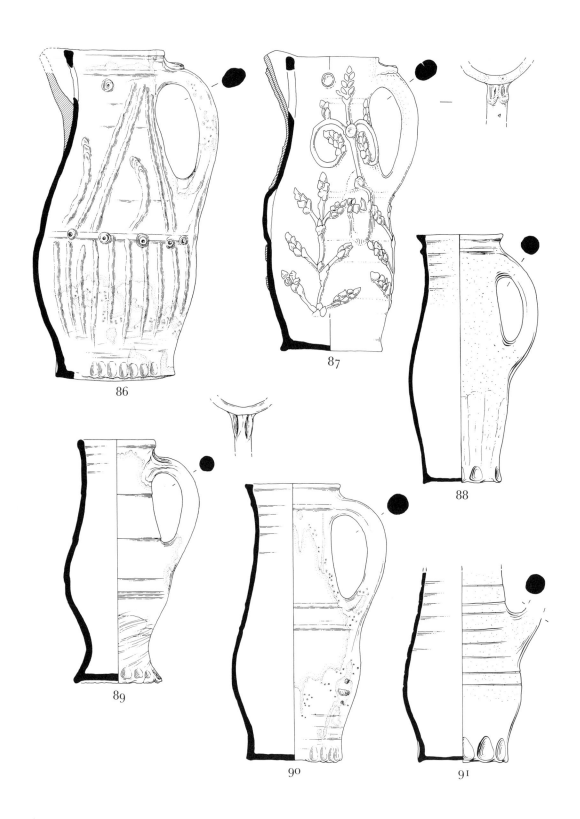

67. *Kingston-type ware: pear-shaped jugs, Nos 86-67 in the highly decorated style. (Scale 1/4)*

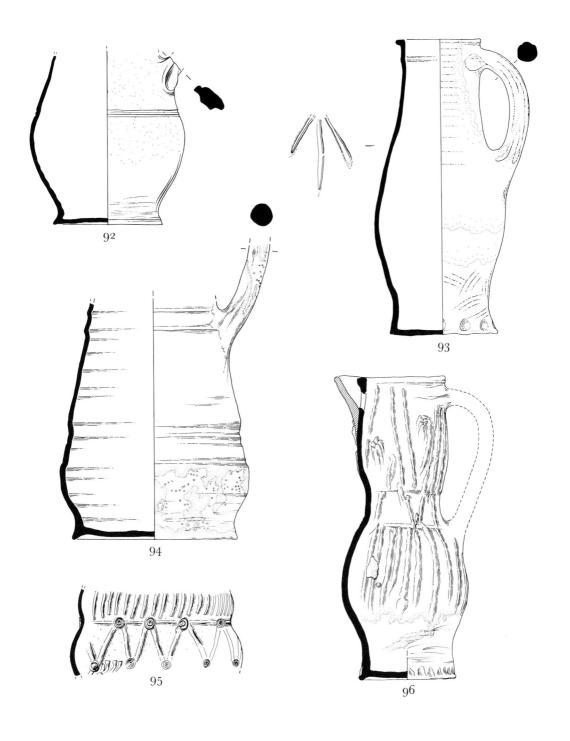

68. Kingston-type ware: pear-shaped jugs (Nos 92-94); waisted pear-shaped jugs in the highly decorated style (Nos 95-96). (Scale 1/4)

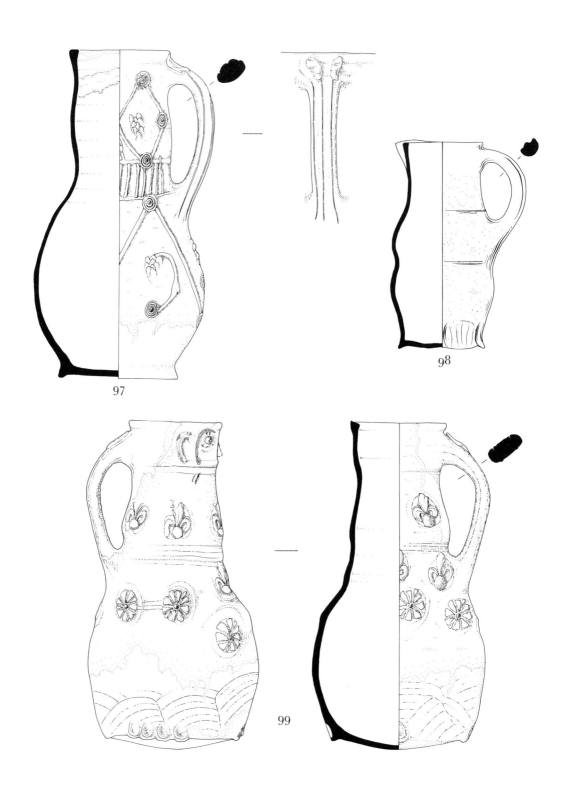

69. Kingston-type ware: waisted pear-shaped jugs with no decoration (No 98); in the highly decorated style (Nos 97); and with stamped boss and anthropomorphic decoration (No 99). (1/4)

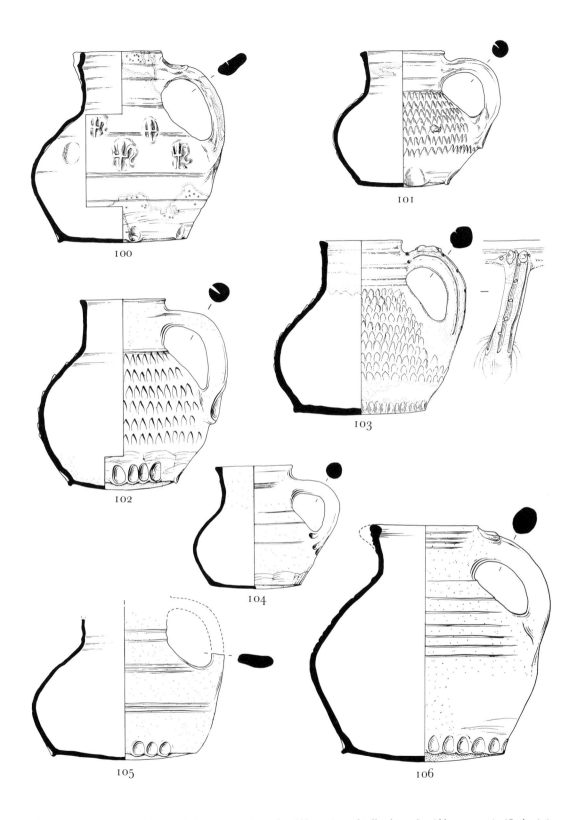

100

101

102

103

104

105

106

70. Kingston-type ware : squat jugs with stamped boss decoration (No 100) ; and pellet decoration (Nos 101-103). (Scale 1/4)

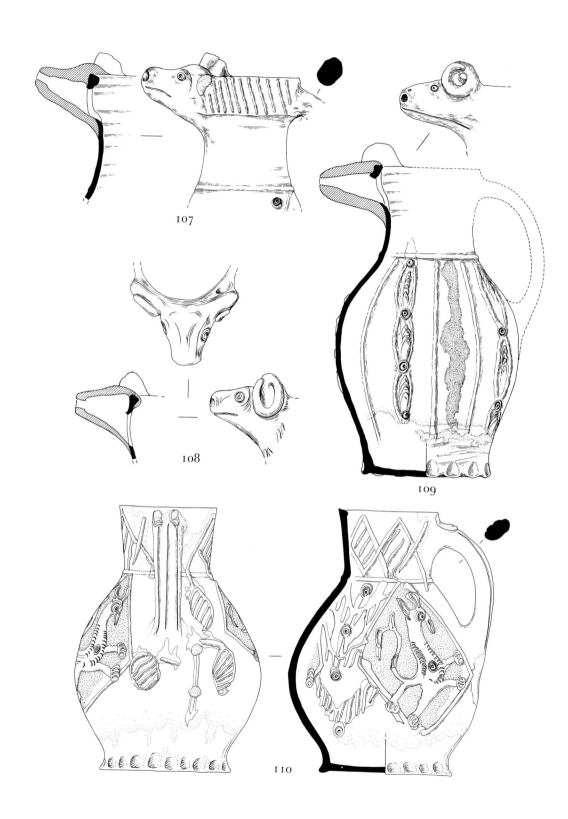

71. *Kingston-type ware: rounded zoomorphic jugs in the highly decorated style. (Scale 1/4)*

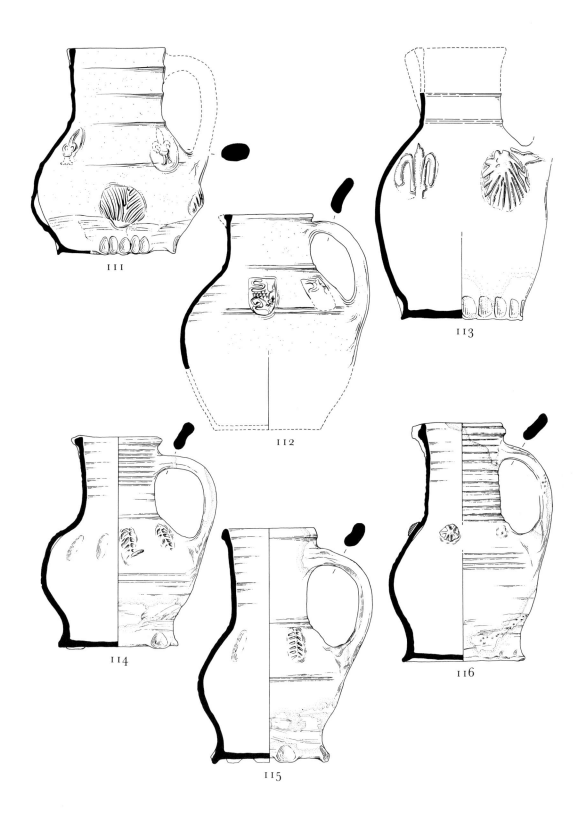

111

112

113

114

115

116

72. *Kingston-type ware : rounded jugs with stamped boss decoration. (Scale 1/4)*

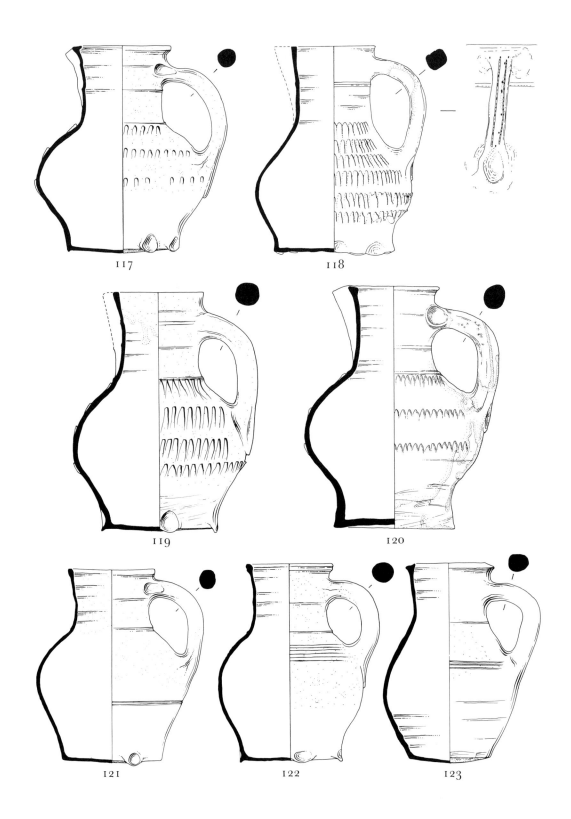

73. *Kingston-type ware: rounded jugs, Nos 117-120 with pellet decoration. (Scale 1/4)*

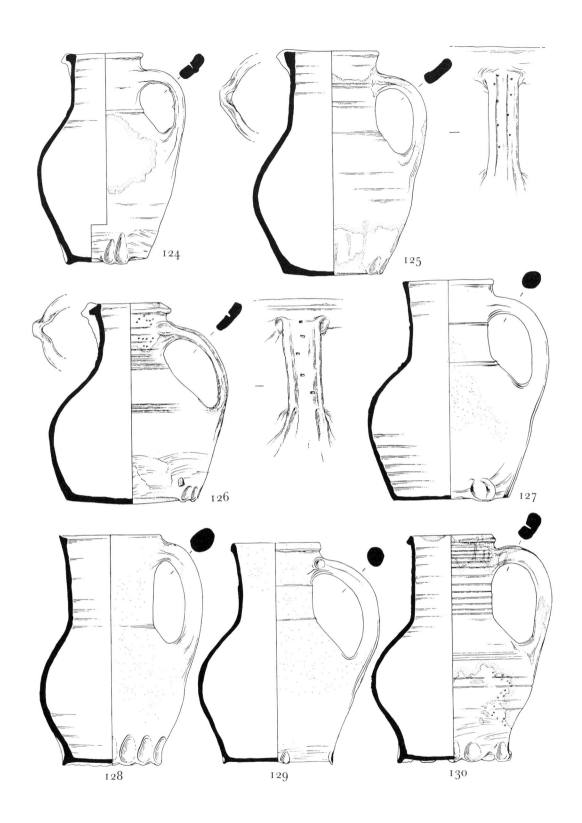

74. *Kingston-type ware: rounded jugs. (Scale 1/4)*

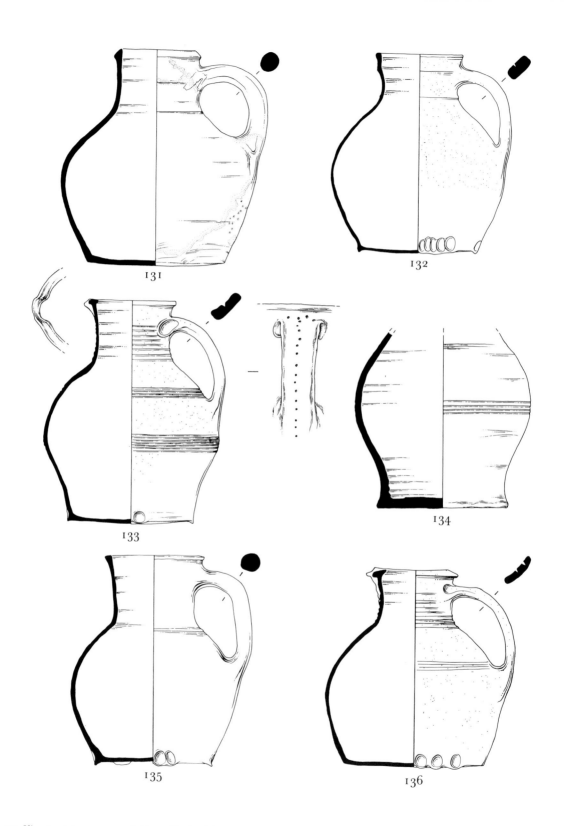

131

132

133

134

135

136

75. Kingston-type ware : rounded jugs. (Scale 1/4)

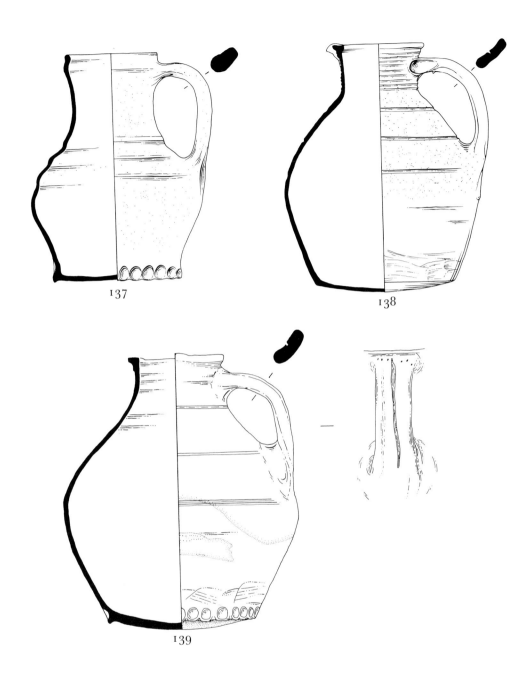

137

138

139

76. Kingston-type ware : rounded jugs. (Scale 1/4)

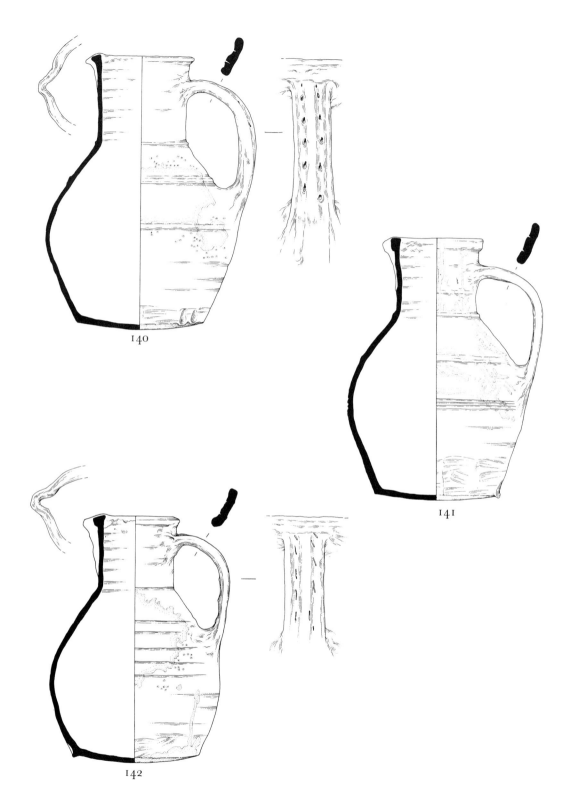

140

141

142

77. Kingston-type ware : rounded jugs. (Scale 1/4)

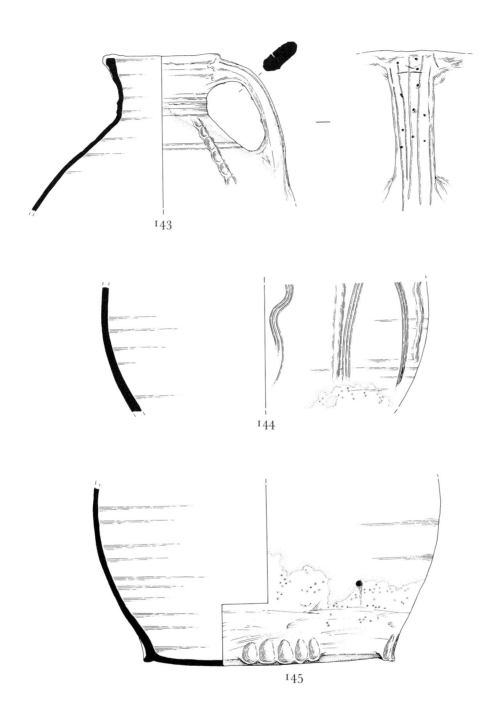

143

144

145

78. Kingston-type ware: large rounded/squat jugs, Nos 143-144 with applied and incised decoration. (Scale 1/4)

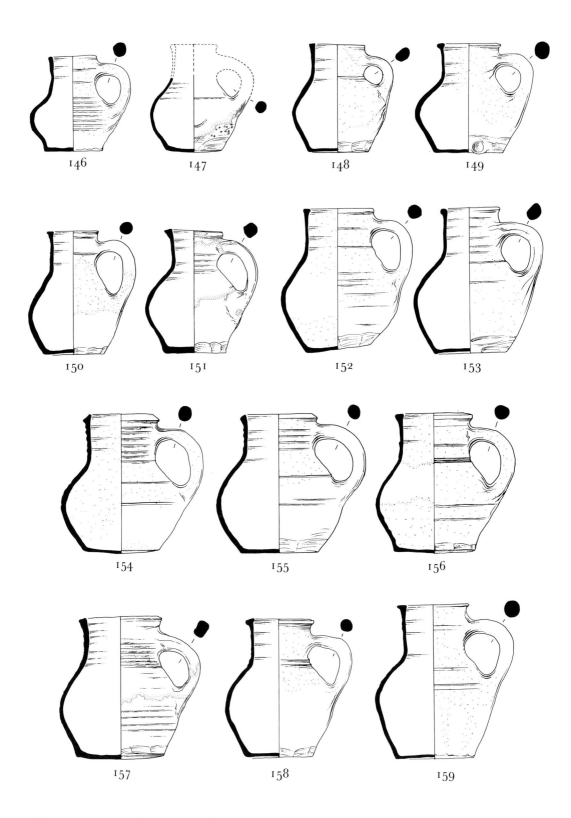

146 147 148 149

150 151 152 153

154 155 156

157 158 159

79. Kingston-type ware: small rounded jugs. (Scale 1/4)

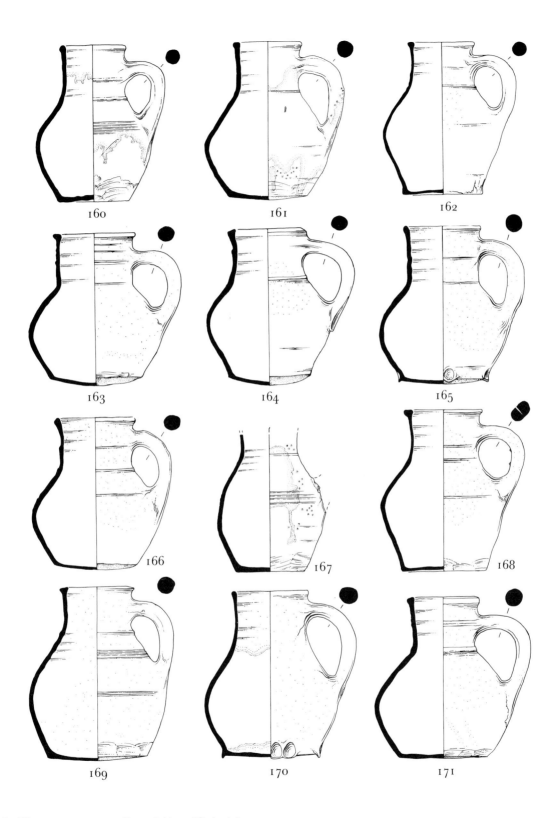

80. Kingston-type ware : small rounded jugs. (Scale 1/4)

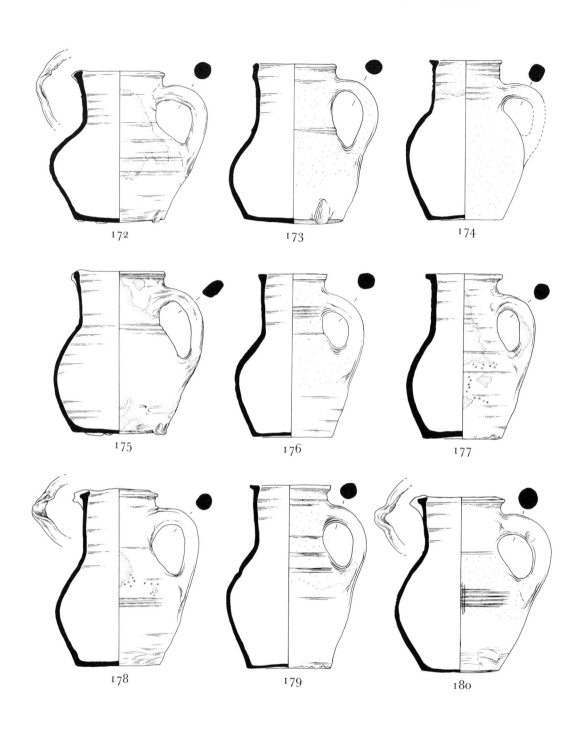

81. Kingston-type ware: small rounded jugs. (Scale 1/4)

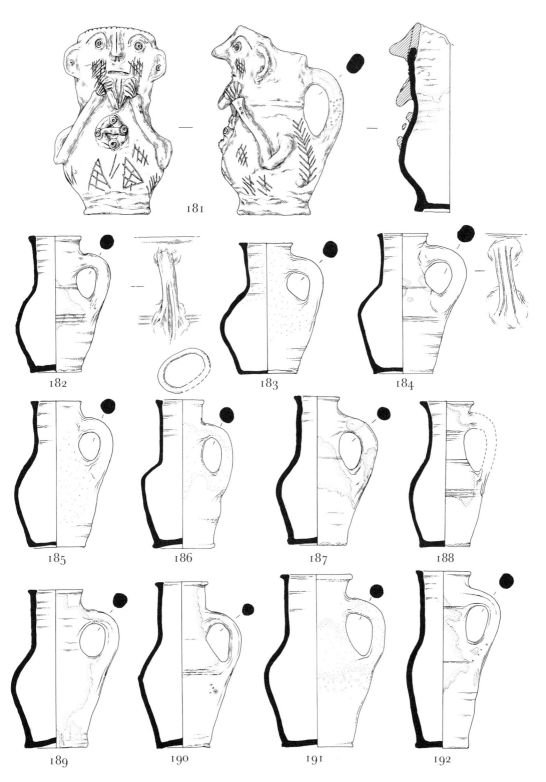

82. Kingston-type ware : small rounded jug with anthropomorphic decoration (No 181) ; biconical jugs (Nos 182-192).
(Scale 1/4)

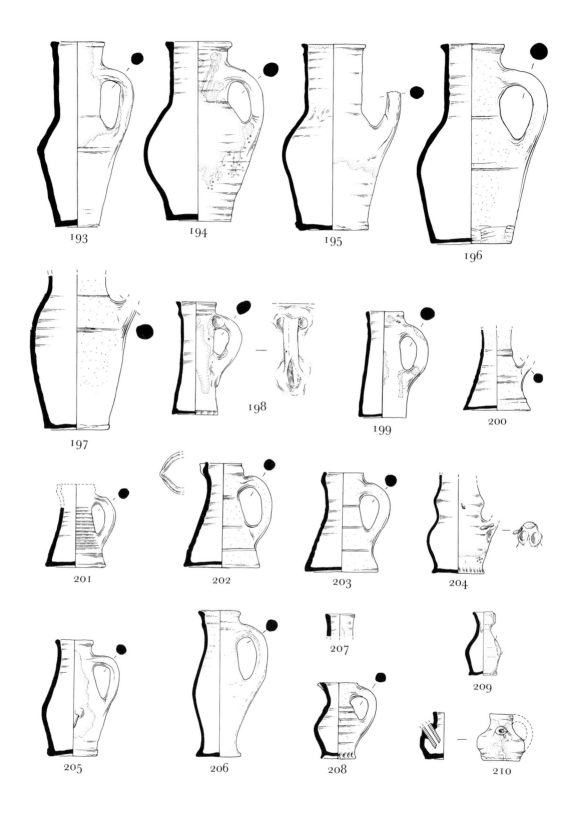

83. Kingston-type ware : biconical jugs (Nos 193-197) ; miniature jugs (Nos 198-210). (Scale 1/4)

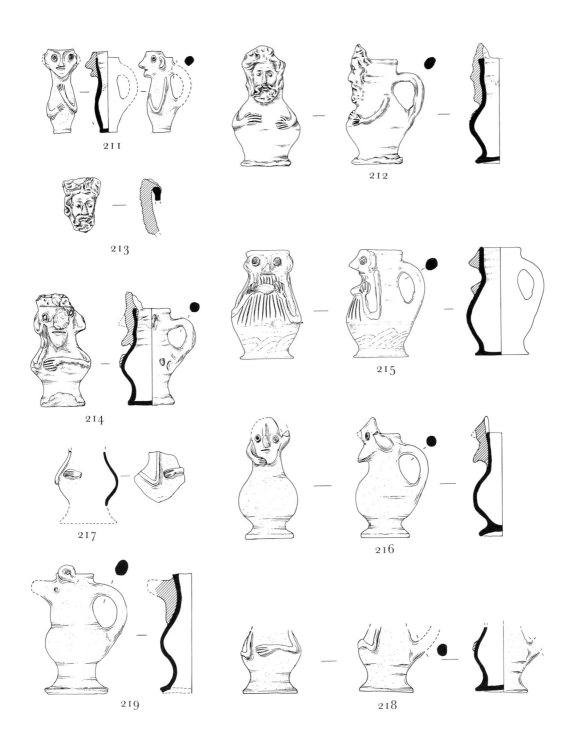

84. Kingston-type ware : miniature anthropomorphic jugs (Nos 211-218) ; zoomorphic jug (No 219). (Scale 1/4)

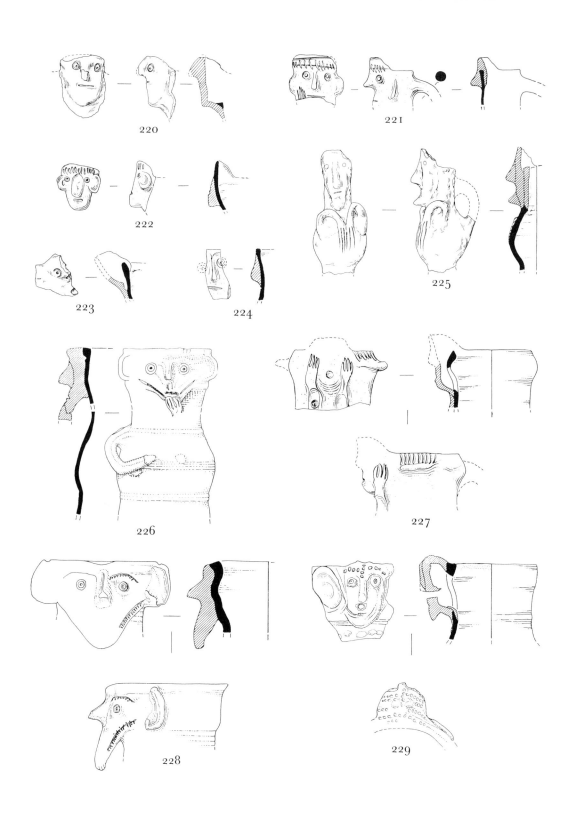

85. Kingston-type ware: miscellaneous anthropomorphic jugs. (Scale 1/4)

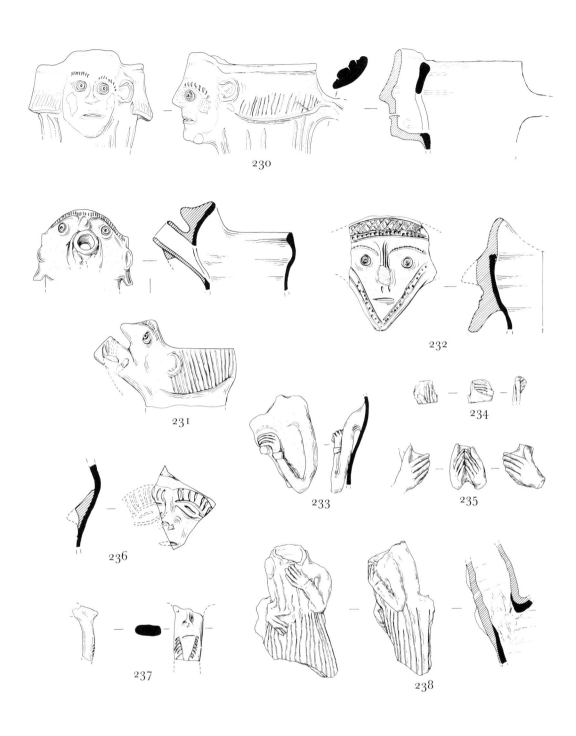

86. Kingston-type ware : miscellaneous anthropomorphic jugs. (Scale 1/4)

230

231

232

233

234

235

236

237

238

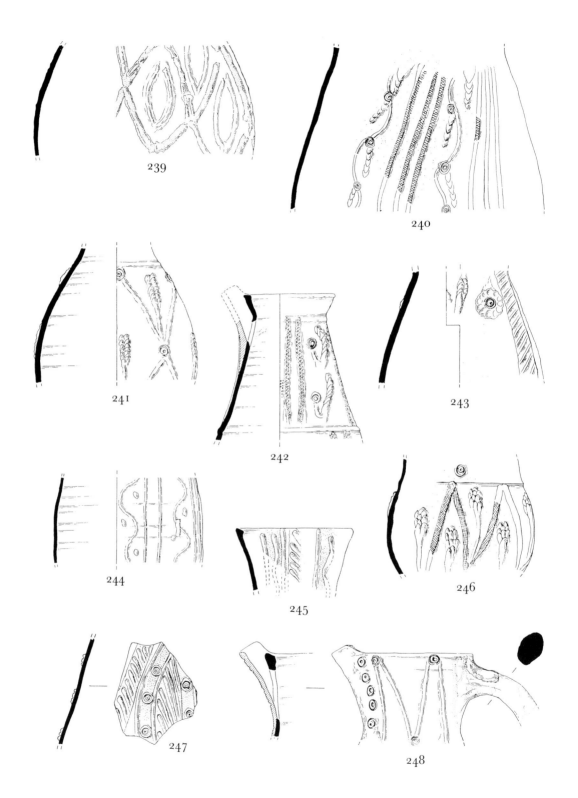

87. Kingston-type ware : miscellaneous jug fragments in the highly decorated style. (Scale 1/4)

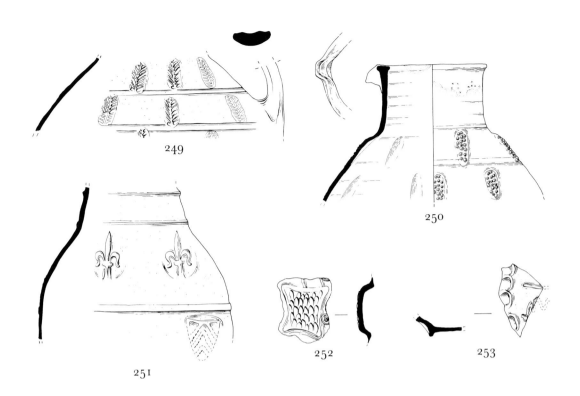

249

250

251

252

253

88. *Kingston-type ware: miscellaneous jug fragments with stamped boss decoration (Nos 249-251); square boss with pellet decoration (No 252); base fragment with incised marks (No 253). (Scale 1/4)*

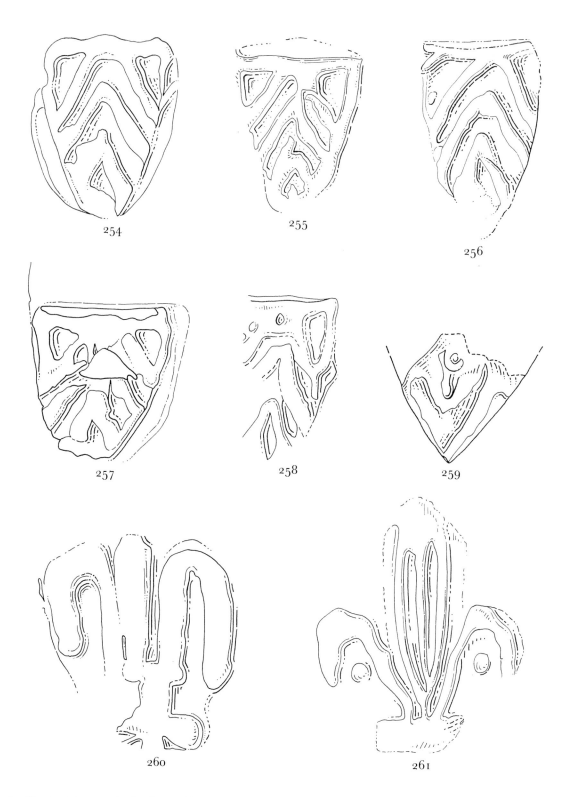

89. *Kingston-type ware: details of stamped bosses, with shield device (Nos 254-259); and* fleur-de-lys *pattern (Nos 260-261).* (*Scale 1/1*)

262

263

264

265

266

267

268

269

90. Kingston-type ware: details of stamped bosses of fleur-de-lys *pattern. (Scale 1/1)*

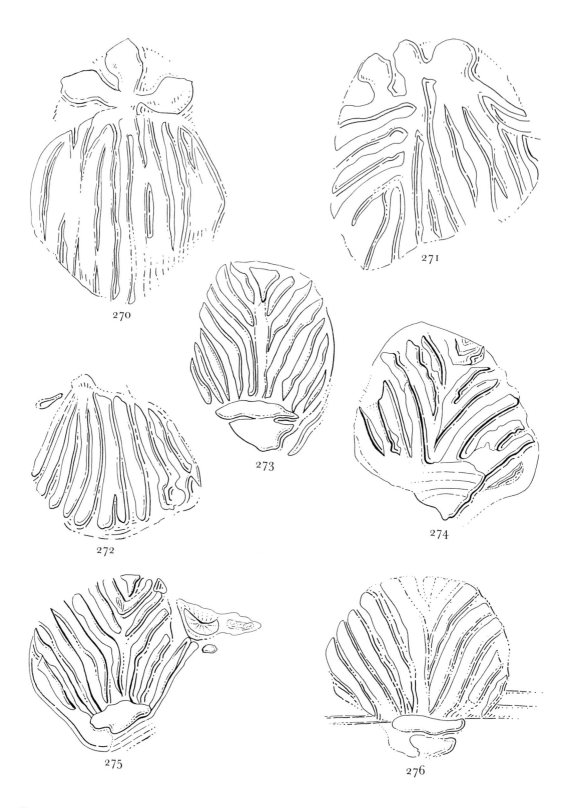

270

271

272

273

274

275

276

91. Kingston-type ware: details of stamped bosses of shell pattern. (Scale 1/1)

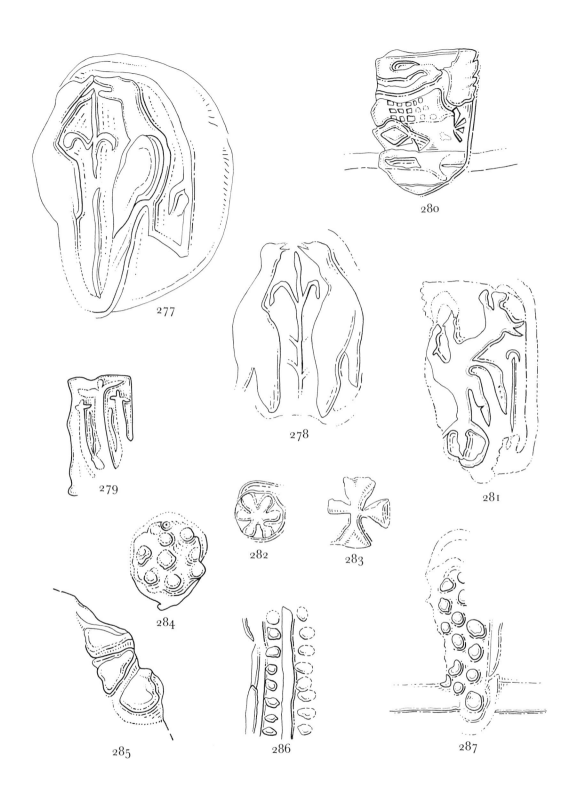

92. *Kingston-type ware: details of miscellaneous stamped bosses. (Scale 1/1)*

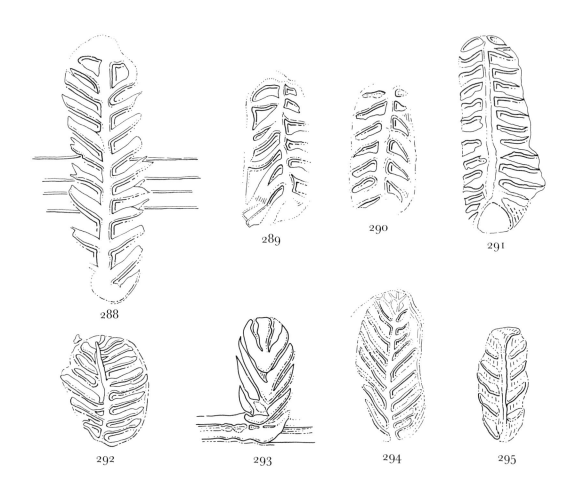

288 289 290 291 292 293 294 295

93. Kingston-type ware: details of stamped bosses of 'wheatear' pattern. (Scale 1/1)

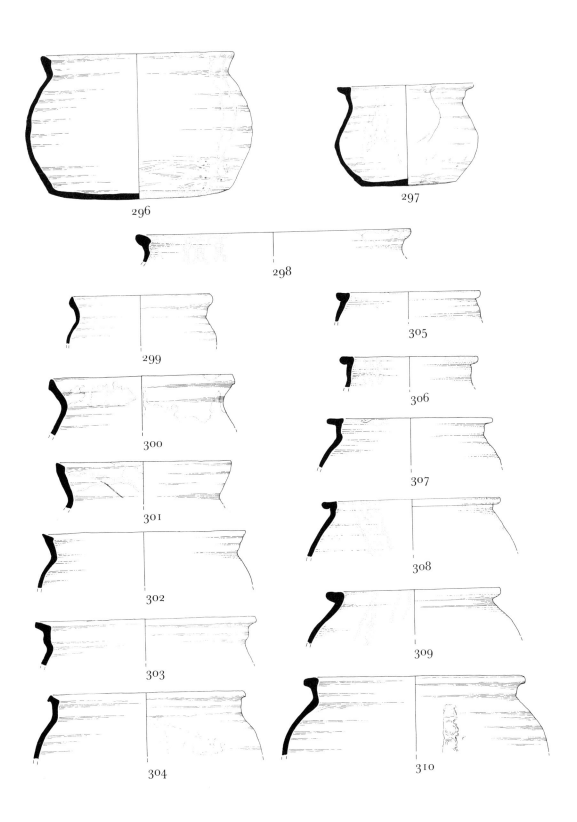

296

297

298

299

305

300

306

301

307

302

308

303

309

304

310

94. Kingston-type ware: cooking pots. (Scale 1/4)

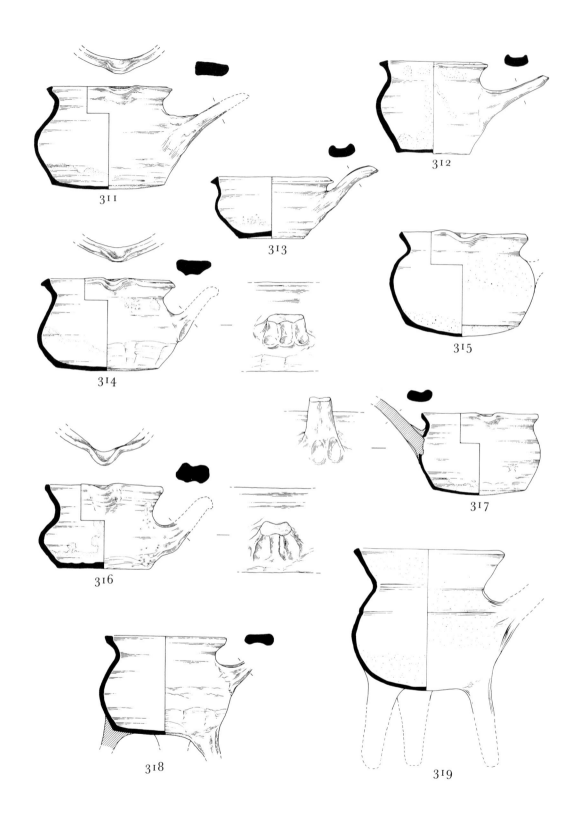

95. Kingston-type ware: pipkins (Nos 311-317); tripod pipkins (Nos 318-319). (Scale 1/4)

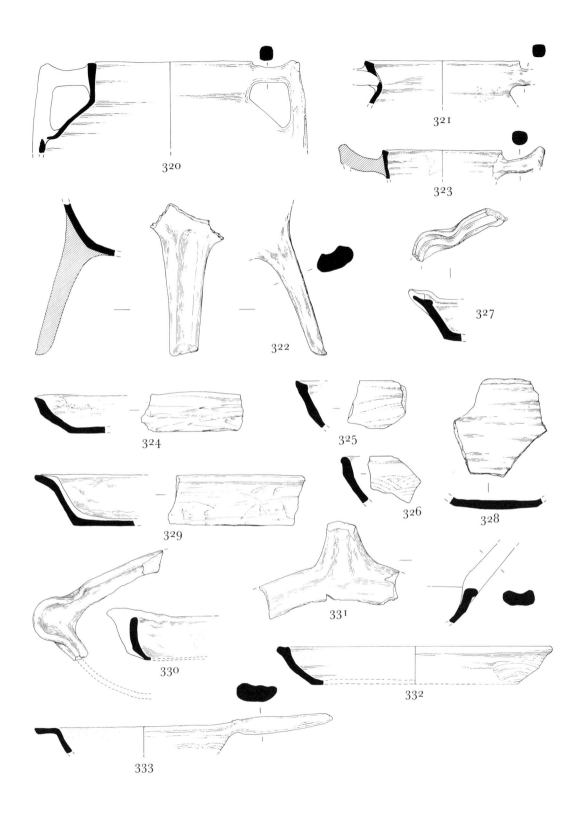

96. *Kingston-type ware : cauldrons (Nos 320-323) ; dripping dishes (Nos 324-330) ; frying pans (Nos 331-333). (Scale 1/4)*

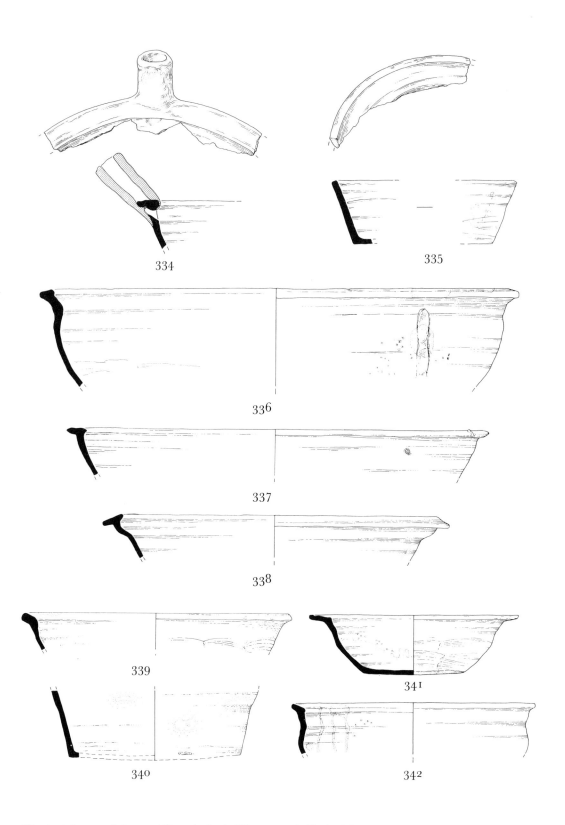

334

335

336

337

338

339

340

341

342

97. *Kingston-type ware: frying pan (No 334); bowls (Nos 335-342). (Scale 1/4)*

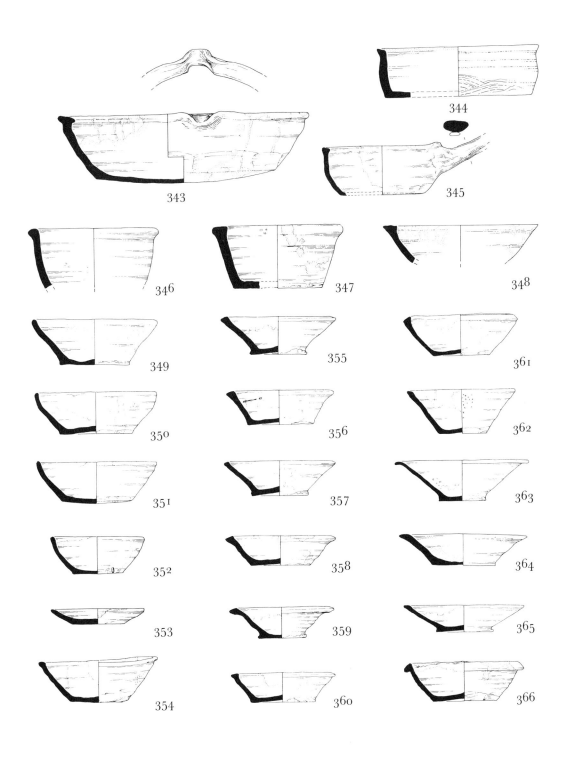

98. *Kingston-type ware: bowls (Nos 343-347); small dishes or 'saucers' (Nos 348-366). (Scale 1/4)*

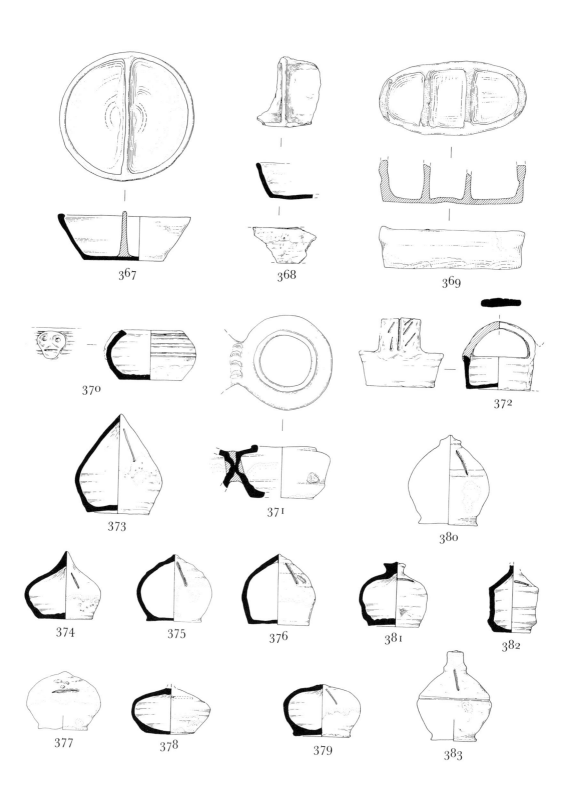

99. Kingston-type ware: condiments (Nos 367–372); money-boxes (Nos 373–383). (Scale 1/4)

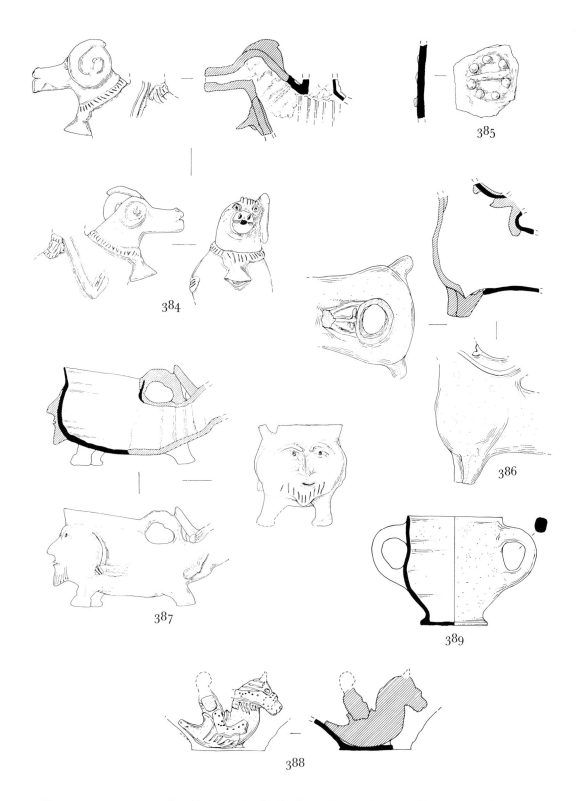

100. *Kingston-type ware: aquamaniles (Nos 384-386); drinking horn (No 387); lobed cup (No 388); cup (No 389).*
(Scale 1/4)

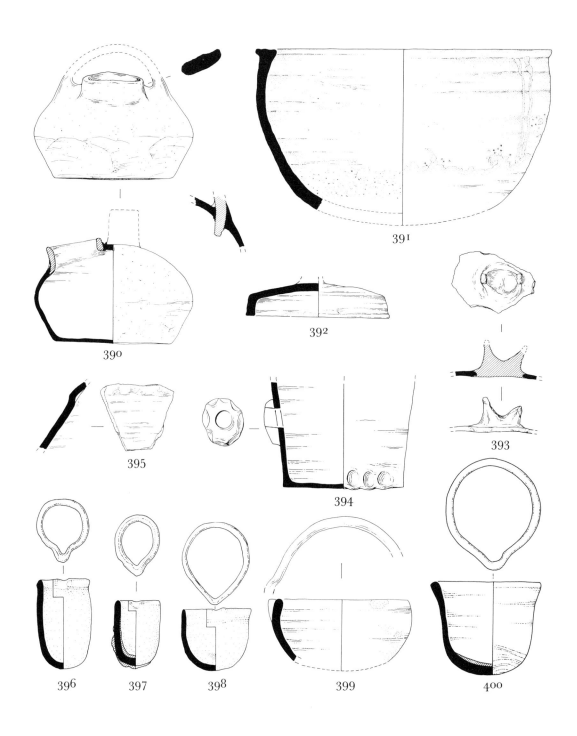

101. Kingston-type ware: urinal (No 390); mortar (No 391); lids (Nos 392-393); cistern (No 394); curfew (No 395); crucibles (Nos 396-400). (Scale 1/4)

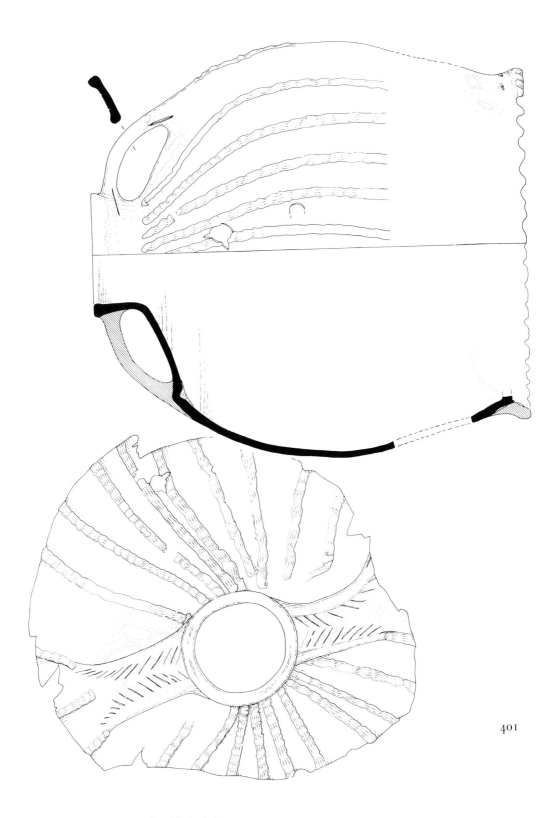

401

102. Kingston-type ware : storage jar. (Scale 1/4)

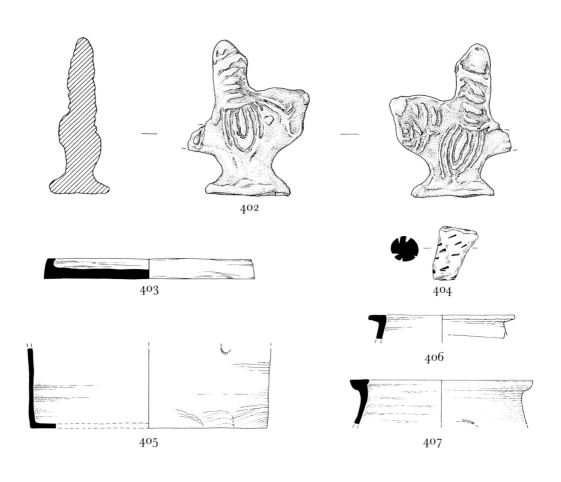

103. Kingston-type ware: gaming piece (No 402); miscellaneous unidentified fragments (Nos 403-407). (Scale 1/4; No 402 1/2)

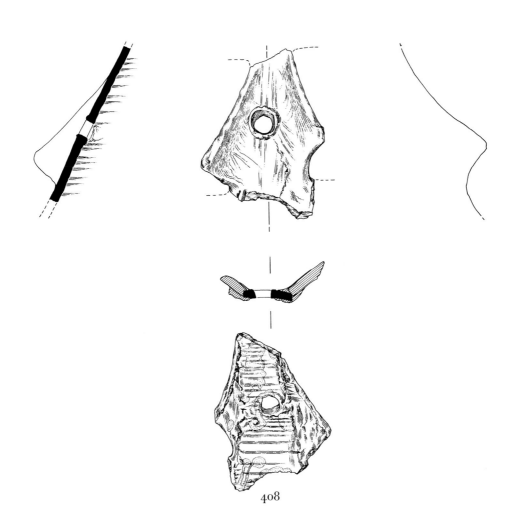

408

104. Kingston-type ware : louver. (Scale 1/4)

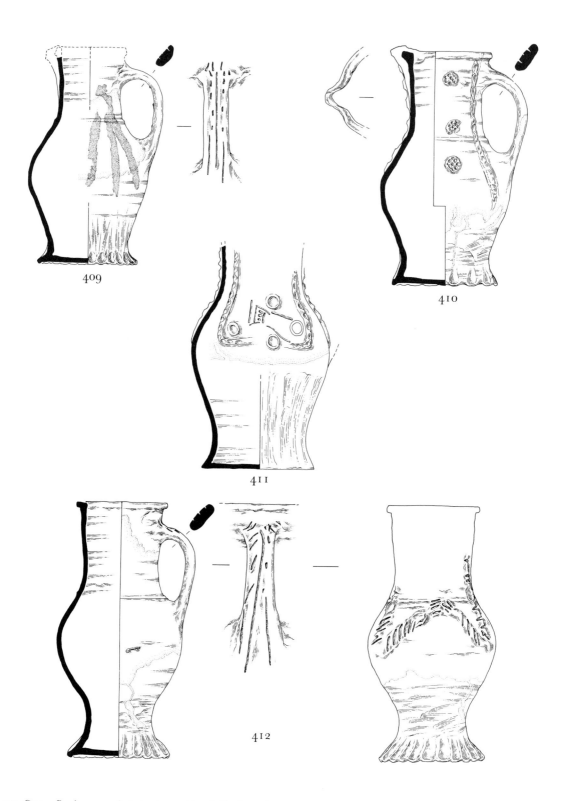

105. Coarse Border ware: baluster jugs, with red slip decoration (No 409); stamped decoration (No 410); anthropomorphic decoration (Nos 411-412). (Scale 1/4)

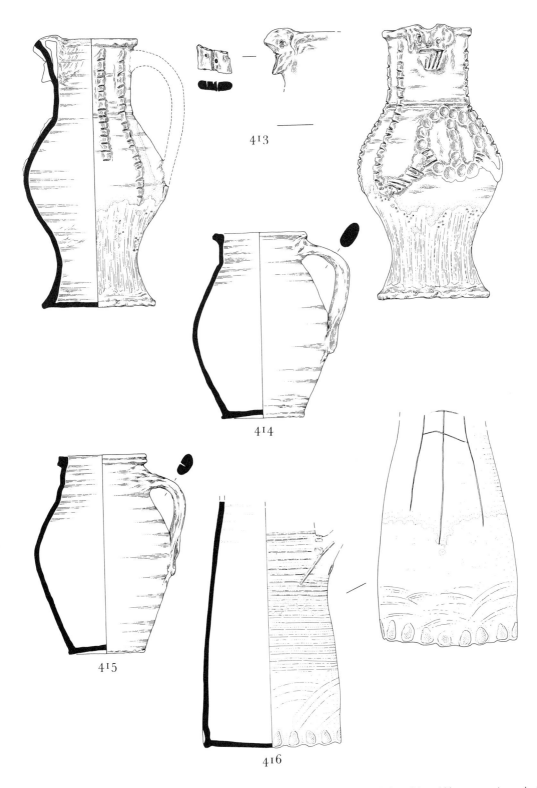

413

414

415

416

106. Coarse Border ware: baluster jug with anthropomorphic decoration (No 413); barrel shaped jugs (Nos 414-415); conical jug with 'maker's mark'? (No 416). (Scale 1/4)

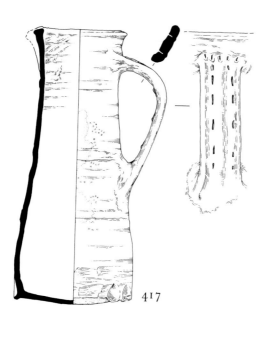
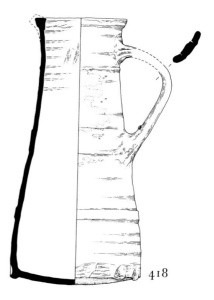

417

418

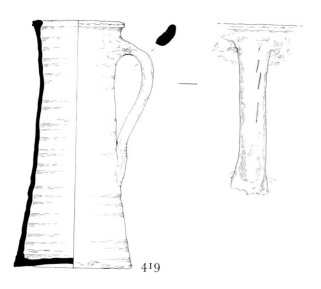
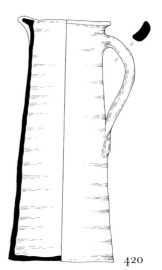

419

420

107. Coarse Border ware : conical jugs. (Scale 1/4)

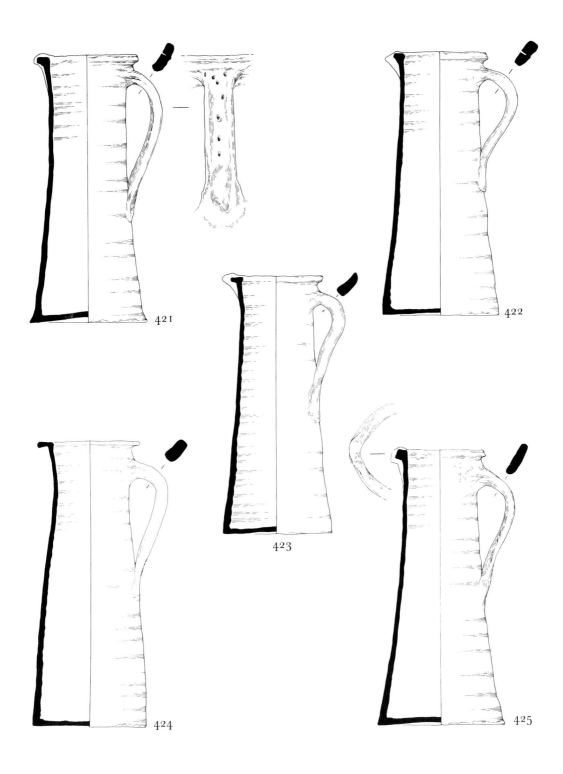

421

422

423

424

425

108. *Coarse Border ware : conical jugs. (Scale 1/4)*

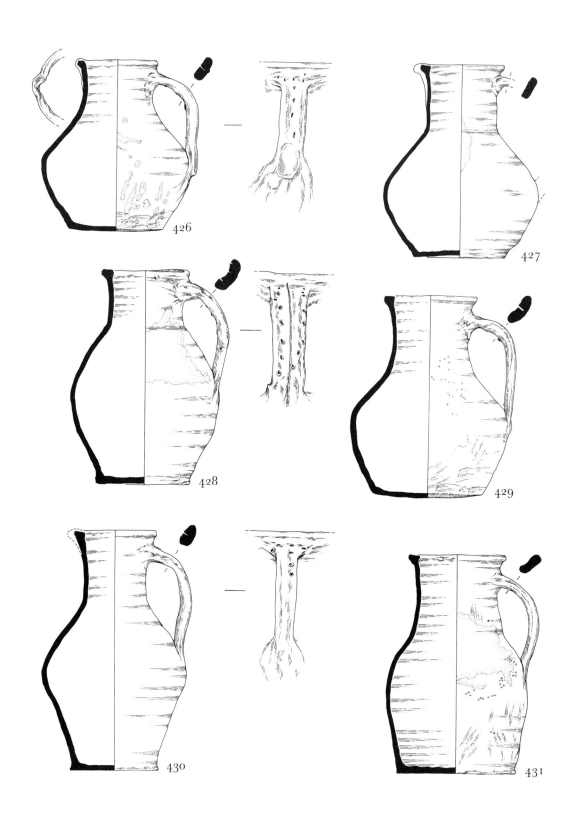

109. Coarse Border ware: rounded jugs. (Scale 1/4)

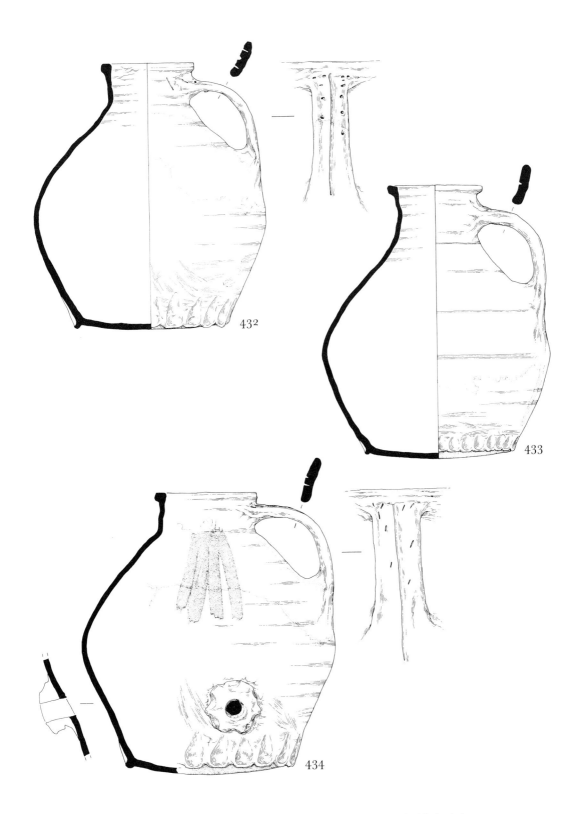

110. *Coarse Border ware : large rounded jugs or cisterns (Nos 432-433) ; cistern (No 434). (Scale 1/4)*

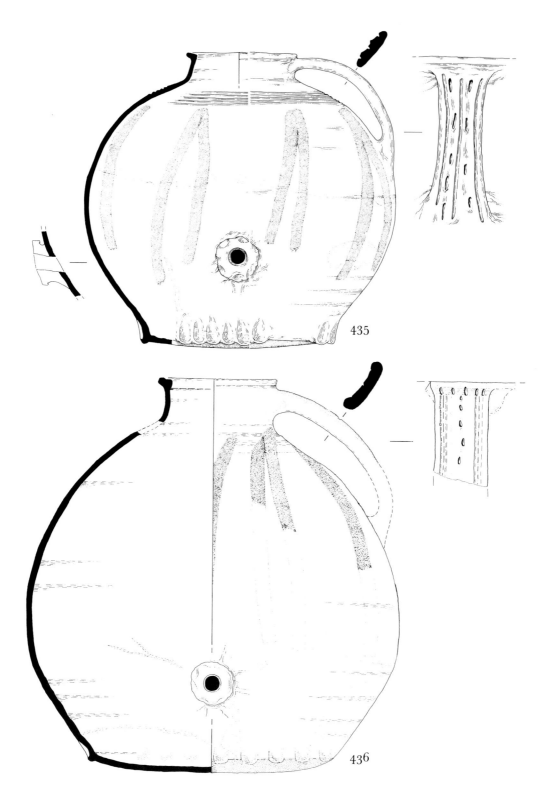

435

436

111. Coarse Border ware : cisterns. (Scale 1/4)

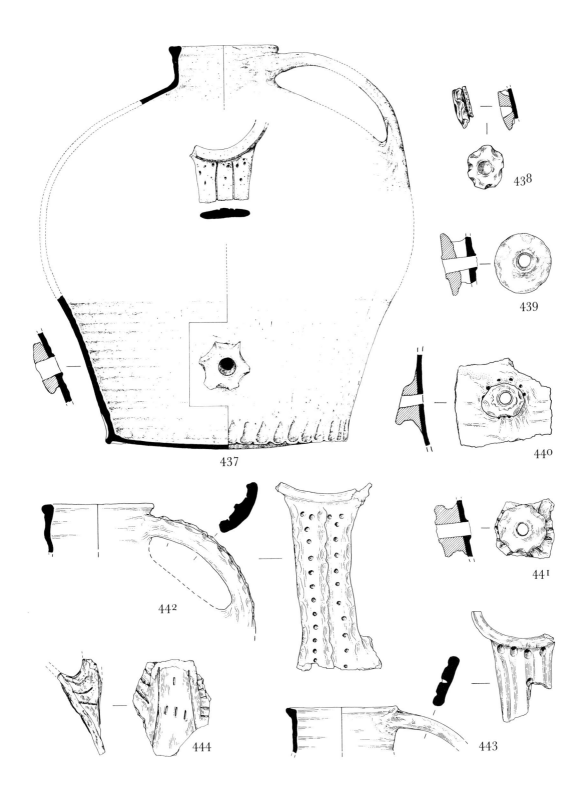

438

439

440

437

441

442

444

443

112. Coarse Border ware: cisterns (Nos 437-441); miscellaneous large rounded jug or cistern fragments (Nos 442-444). (Scale 1/4)

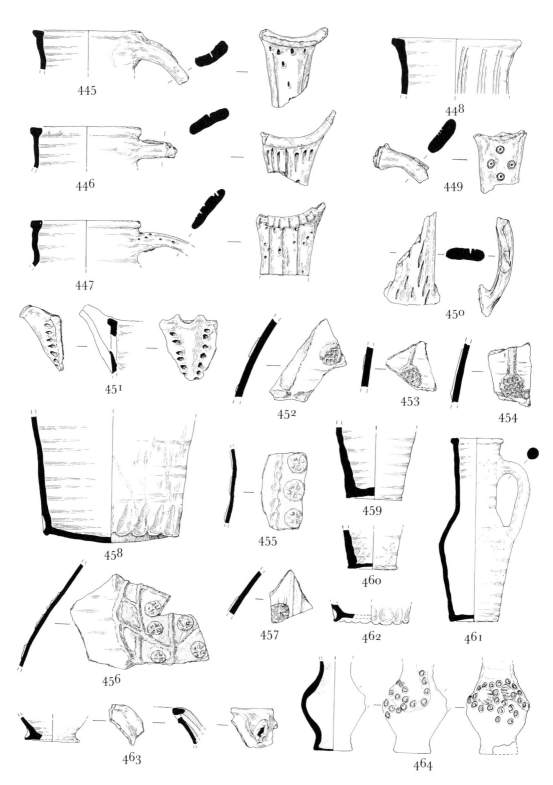

113. *Coarse Border ware: miscellaneous jug fragments (Nos 445-458); biconical jugs (Nos 459-461); miniature jug (No 464); puzzle jug (No 463). (Scale 1/4)*

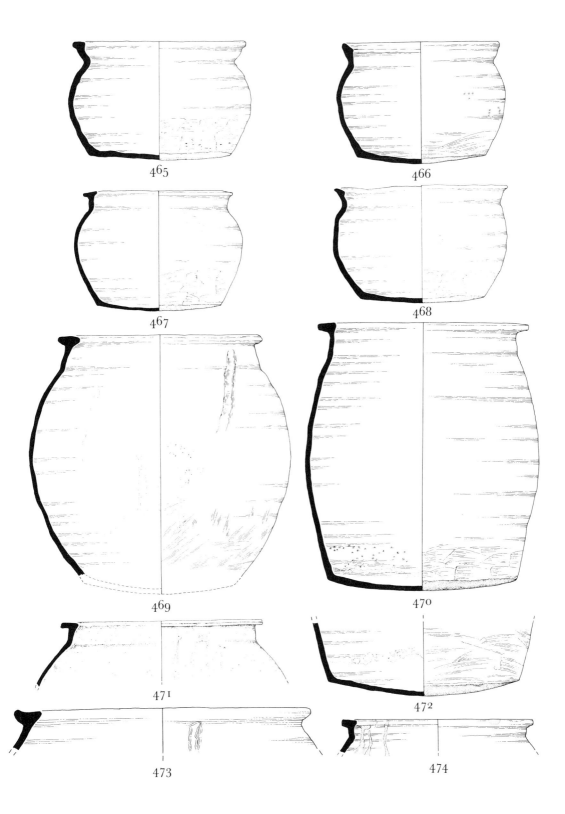

465

466

467

468

469

470

471

472

473

474

114. Coarse Border ware: cooking pots. (Scale 1/4)

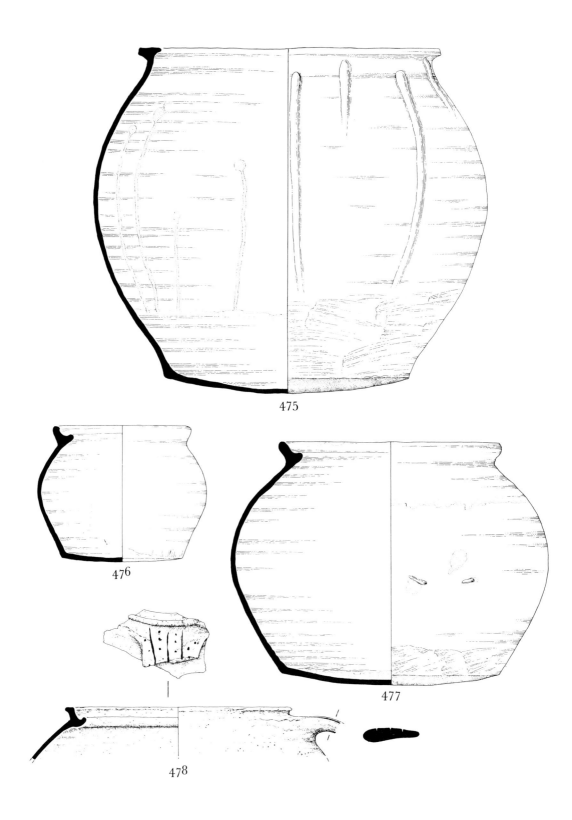

115. Coarse Border ware : large cooking pot or storage jar (No 475) ; lid-seated cooking pots (Nos 476-478). (Scale 1/4)

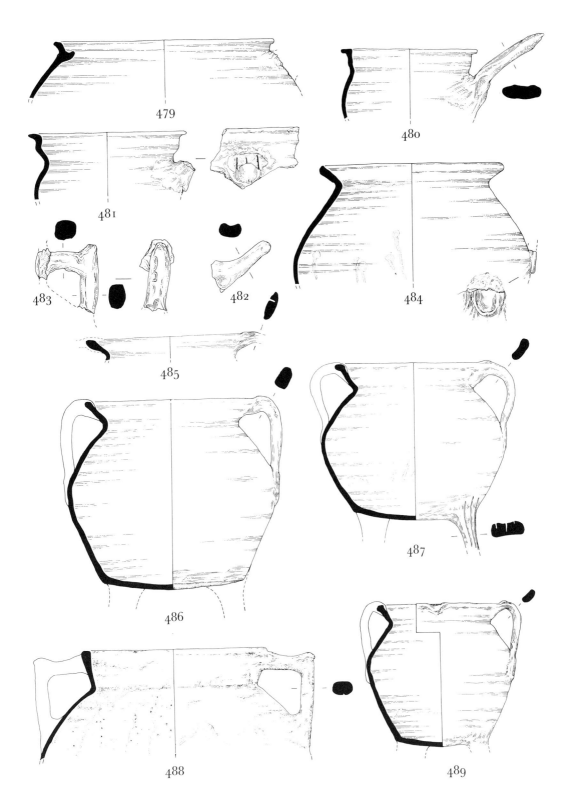

116. *Coarse Border ware : lid-seated cooking pot (No 479) ; pipkins (Nos 480-482) ; cauldrons (Nos 483-489). (Scale 1/4)*

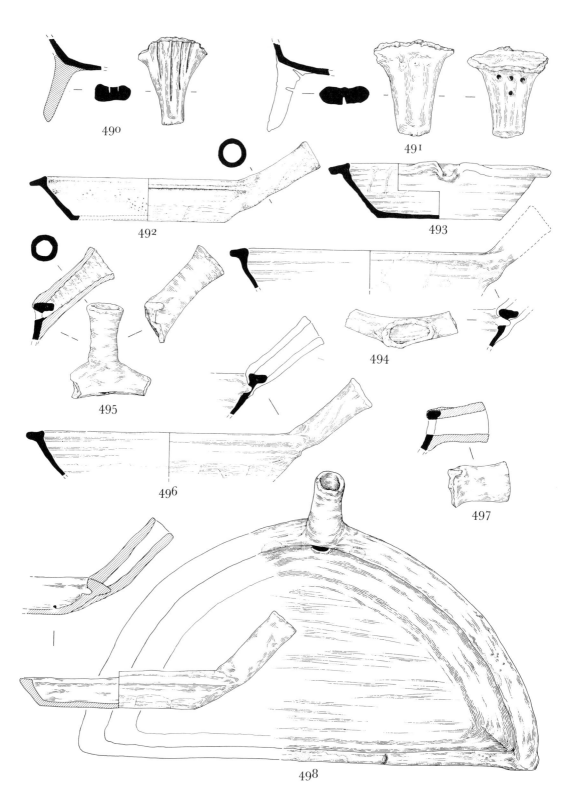

117. Coarse Border ware: cauldrons (Nos 490–491); frying pans (Nos 492–497); dripping dish (No 498). (Scale 1/4)

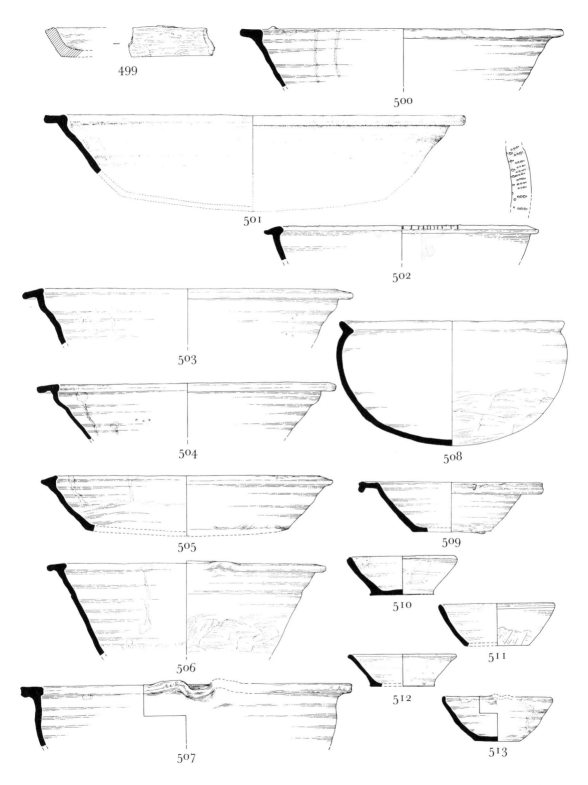

118. *Coarse Border ware: dripping dish (No 499); bowls (Nos 500–509); small dishes or 'saucers' (Nos 510–513). (Scale 1/4).*

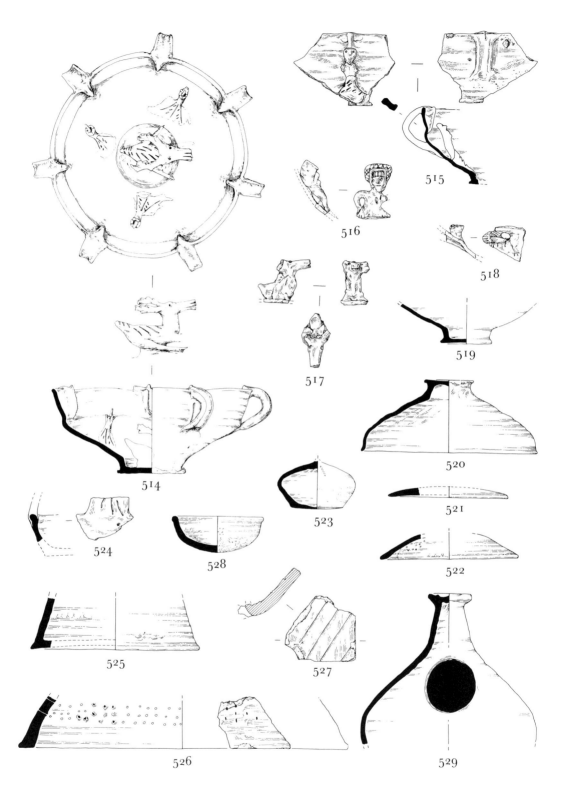

119. *Coarse Border ware: lobed cups (Nos 514-519); lids (Nos 520-522); money-box (No 523); condiment (No 524); chafing dish (No 525); curfew (No 526); louver (No 527); crucible (No 528); urinal (No 529). (Scale 1/4)*

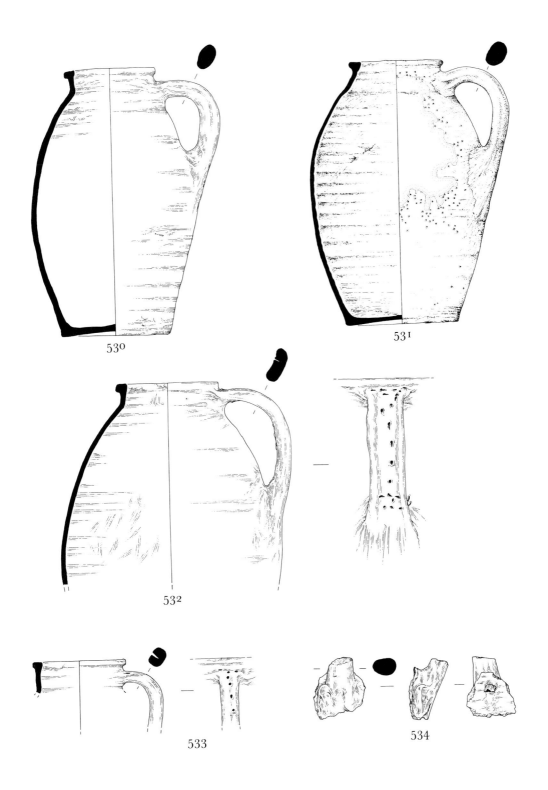

530

531

532

533

534

120. Cheam whiteware : barrel-shaped jugs. (Scale 1/4)

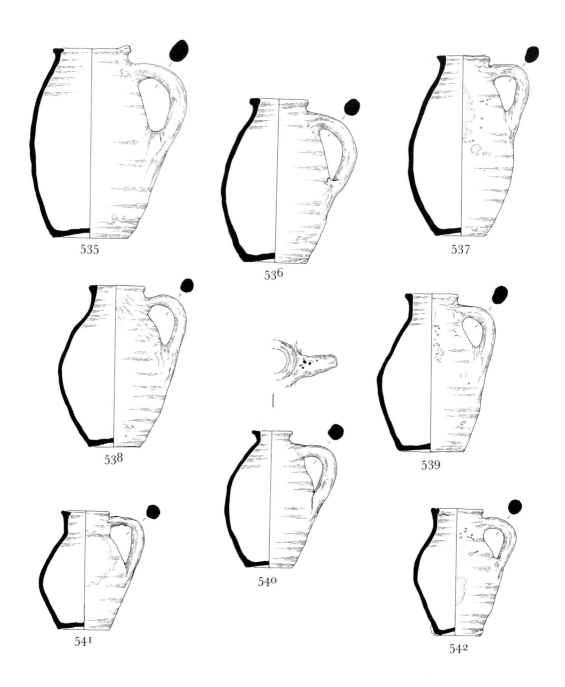

535

536

537

538

539

540

541

542

121. Cheam whiteware : barrel-shaped jugs. (Scale 1/4)

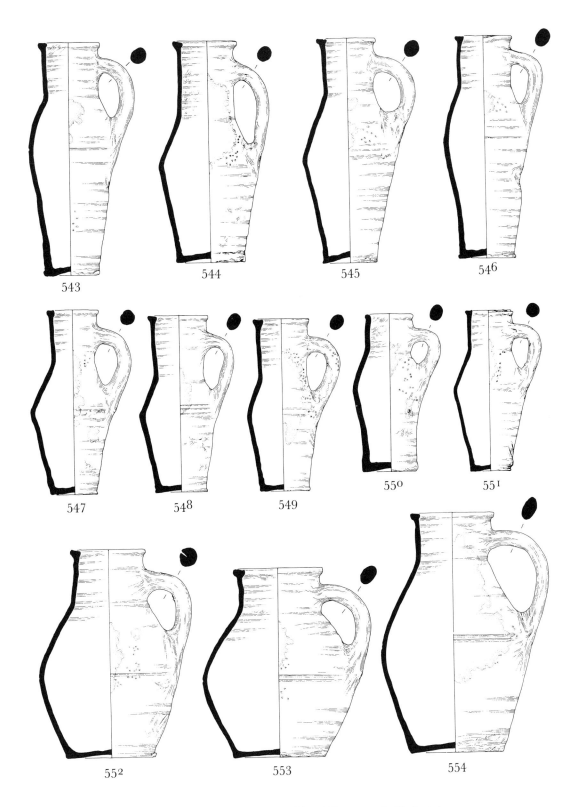

543 544 545 546

547 548 549 550 551

552 553 554

122. Cheam whiteware : biconical jugs (Nos 543-551) ; rounded jugs (Nos 552-554). (Scale 1/4)

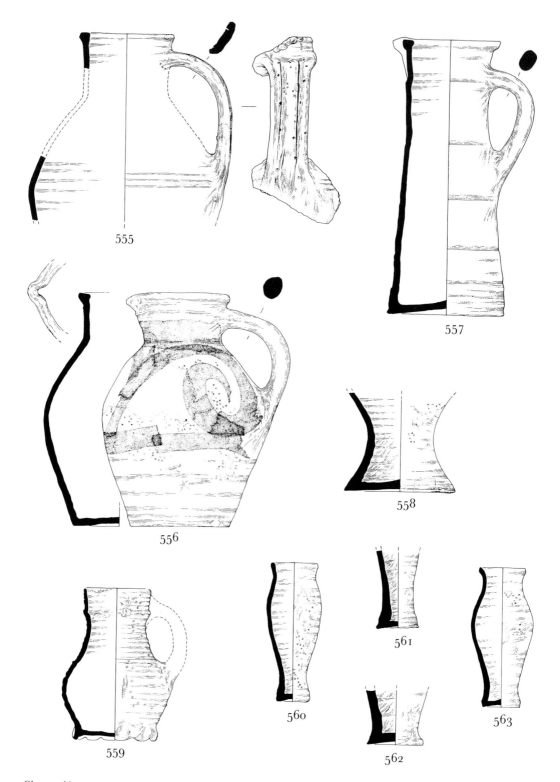

555

557

556

558

559

560

561

562

563

123. *Cheam whiteware: rounded jug (Nos 555-556); conical jug (No 557); baluster jug (No 558); small rounded drinking jug (No 559); measures (Nos 560-563). (Scale 1/4)*

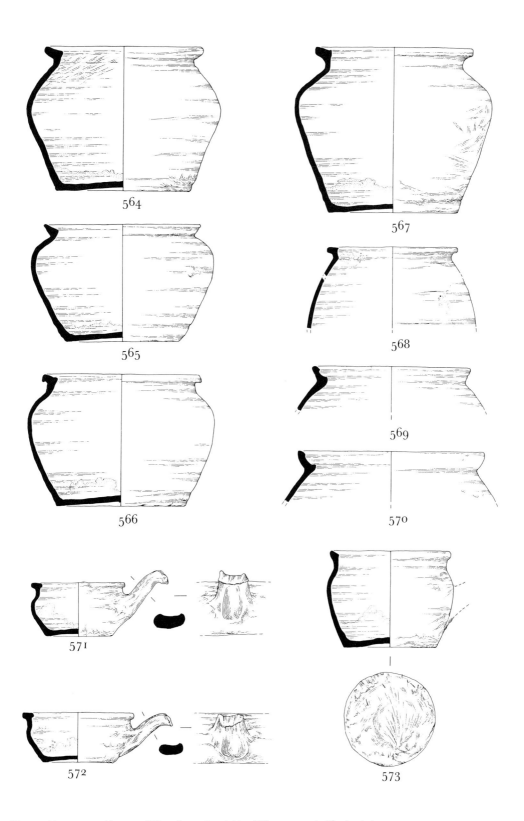

564

567

565

568

566

569

570

571

572

573

124. Cheam whiteware : cooking pots (Nos 564-570) ; pipkins (Nos 571-573). (Scale 1/4)

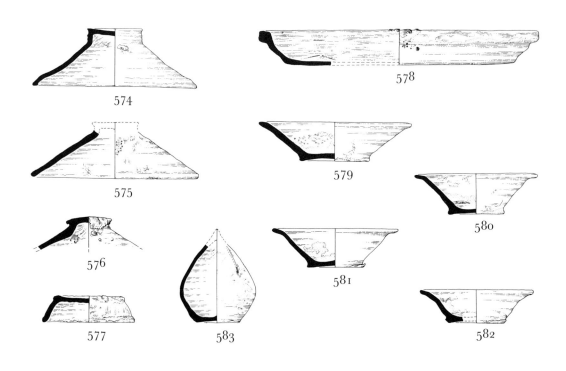

125. *Cheam whiteware: lids (Nos 574-577); frying pan (No 578); small dishes or 'saucers' (Nos 579-582); money-box (No 583). (Scale 1/4)*

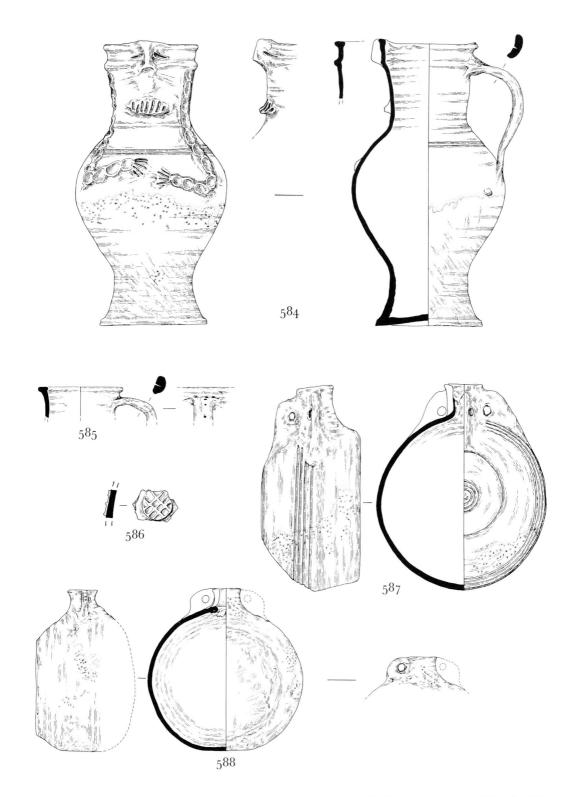

584

585

586

587

588

126. 'Tudor Green' ware: baluster jug with anthropomorphic decoration (No 584); miscellaneous jug fragments (Nos 585-586); costrels (Nos 587-588). (Scale 1/4; No 586 Scale 1/2)

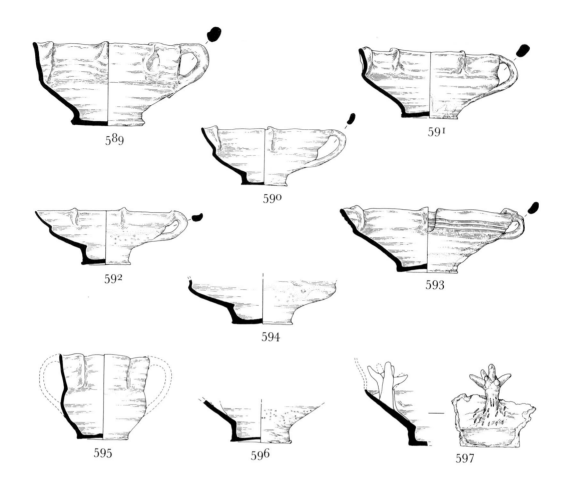

589

590

591

592

593

594

595

596

597

127. 'Tudor Green' ware: lobed cups. (Scale 1/4)

APPENDIX 1: CONCORDANCE LIST FOR FIGURES

Unless otherwise stated, vessels are in the collection of the Museum of London (MOL). Pottery from DUA excavations is referred to by site code and context number (for expansions of site codes, see Appendix 3, Nos 107-57). The provenance of museum finds is illustrated in Figs 5-8, and a full concordance is present in the DUA archive.

Throughout the Museum of London archive records the following abbreviations have been used: Kingston-type ware – KING; Coarse Border ware – CBW; Cheam whiteware – CHEA; and 'Tudor Green' ware – TUDG; Early Surrey coarse ware – ESUR.

Abbreviations:
BoE = Bank of England Collection catalogue number
BM = British Museum Dept. Medieval and Later Antiquities Accession Number

CAA = Cambridge University Museum of Archaeology and Anthropology accession number
CM = Cuming Museum accession number
ER = Guildhall Museum excavation register
FMC = Fitzwilliam Museum Cambridge accession number
GM = Castle Arch Museum, Guildford accession number
MM = Maidstone Museum and Art Gallery accession number
SM = Stevenage Museum accession number
NN = No accession number recorded
VA = Victoria and Albert Museum accession numbers

Fig 10	A2001	
Fig 11	5633	
Fig 12	14562	
Fig 13	5591	
Fig 14	13613	
Fig 15	A10824	
Fig 16	A26449	
Fig 17	5606	
Fig 18	a) 5664	
	b) 18919	
	c) A27865	
Fig 19	a) TL74 191	
	b) A10155	
Fig 20	a) 78.159/102	
	b) 13599	
Fig 21	a) 13007	
	b) 14448	
	c) A27227	
	d) 15943	
	e) A27219	
	f) 16220	
Fig 22	a) 5594	
	b) 11863	
	c) A20233	
	d) 78.159/20	
	e) A22353	
	f) A2001	
Fig 23	a) A2001	
	b) 5662	
	c) ER524B	
	d) ER524A	
	e) A27227	

	f) A24420	
	g) ER799B	
	h) ER524A	
	i) 18919	
Fig 24	a) 11755	
	b) 12817	
	c) A27198	
	d) 83.462/56	
	e) 5617	
	f) 5619	
Fig 25	a) 5746	
	b) 12453	
	c) 5591	
	d) 3912	
	e) 5593	
	f) 5594	
Fig 26	a) 5618	
	b) 5661	
	c) 5675	
Fig 27	a) A3907	
	b) A22570	
	c) A3907	
	d) A22570	
	e) 5675	
	f) A9422	
Fig 28	a) A17200	
	b) 5608	
	c) ER799	
Fig 29	A3914	
Fig 30	10632	
Fig 31	A15285	

Fig 32	a) 15005	
	b) TL74 429	
	c) 10632	
	d) BWB83 147	
	e) TL74 1955	
	f) TL74 431	
Fig 33	a) 68.135	
	b) CAP86 614	
Fig 34	5906	
Fig 35	23756	
Fig 36	5725	
Fig 37	A22817	
Fig 38	24708	
Fig 39	From left to right:	
	A26449	
	A2001	
Fig 40	From left to right, back row:	
	68.133	
	14562	
	A3907	
	LUD82 1048	
	Front row:	
	5940	
	23850 ER762	
Fig 43	From left to right, back row:	
	5653	
	5737	
	A15285	
	Front:	
	18775	

Fig 45   From left to right:
P325
12123

Fig 46   From left to right, back row:
24966
A24924
Front row:
A4933
A19236

Fig 48   1. A20984 and A27175
2. 78.159/104

Fig 49   3. LUD82 1041

Fig 50   4. VA LCC Loan 2
5. 18919
6. 11863
7. LUD82 1041

Fig 51   8. MOL NN

Fig 52   9. 5633
10. A2001
11. A27219
12. 5619

Fig 53   13. BM B114
14. 5613
15. 5675
16. 14444
17. BM B28

Fig 54   18. BM 1915 10-8 94
19. 78.159/24
20. 22713
21. BM B96
22. A11893

Fig 55   23. A23661
24. 18292
25. 5640
26. 22775

Fig 56   27. 5581
28. A22540
29. 5618
30. A10155
31. A20608
32. A10154

Fig 57   33. 5615
34. A22508
35. 14446
36. A22815
37. 5607
38. 78.159/45

Fig 58   39. GM NN
40. 5659
41. 84.13/2
42. 17627
43. 5609

Fig 59   44. 14562
45. BM B98
46. 15139
47. A27544
48. A27865

Fig 60   49. A24134
50. 25781

51. 78.159/16
52. 78.177/1
53. A25086
54. BM B13

Fig 61   55. BM 1939 1-1 1
56. A21791
57. 5622
58. A23583
59. FMC 2-1928
60. 33.296/4
61. A28243

Fig 62   62. 5663
63. FMC 4-1928
64. 10633

Fig 63   65. 5591
66. BoE 421
67. CLE81 875
68. VA 596-1906
69. A3907

Fig 64   70. 74.363
71. OST82 190
72. A22604
73. 5631
74. 5592

Fig 65   75. OST82 190
76. A5231
77. A16918
78. 16754
79. 25823

Fig 66   80. BM B167
81. 13613
82. A17170
83. A20383
84. A10824
85. 13007
86. 5662
87. A26449
88. A5068
89. A2337
90. 5582
91. Z3364

Fig 68   92. 78.159/5
93. LUD82 1078
94. ER799(A)
95. ER799(B)
96. 23333 (ER799)

Fig 69   97. MM NN
98. A5219
99. MM NN

Fig 70   100. 5661
101. 5623
102. A25459
103. BM B34 (51 11-9 1)
104. A14509
105. 17730
106. 11386

Fig 71   107. 5594
108. A3912
109. 19551

110. BM B40

Fig 72   111. BM B41
112. A24316
113. A22570
114. A9422
115. 5620
116. 5608

Fig 73   117. BM B32
118. A13798
119. 5596
120. 13599
121. 20239
122. BM B131
123. 37.222/55

Fig 74   124. 26724
125. 5656
126. BM B54
127. 5672
128. VA C723 1923
129. 13600
130. A13371
131. P338

Fig 75   132. BM B130
133. 20238
134. 78.159/43
135. BoE 424
136. BM B54

Fig 76   137. VA 2077-1901
138. A13370
139. 78.159/21

Fig 77   140. 22711
141. A23238
142. A23553

Fig 78   143. 83.462/37
144. 13007
145. OST82 1041

Fig 79   146. A13773
147. 78.159/30
148. A4649
149. BM B139 (56 7-1 1546)
150. A5064
151. 68.11/5
152. A13393
153. A1628
154. A5217
155. A27478
156. 18910
157. 5699
158. BM B238
159. A5078

Fig 80   160. 22118
161. A11779
162. MOL NN
163. 23879
164. 5611
165. A23357
166. BM B235
167. 25518
168. A5065

345. SWA81 2146
346. TL74 1590
347. 83.487
348. SWA81 2108
349. BM 1946.97 6615   Fig 104
350. P329   Fig 105
351. 16616
352. A16863
353. TL74 2532
354. 20755   Fig 106
355. A9520
356. 16619
357. 78.159/7
358. 16617   Fig 107
359. A27346
360. 5756
361. 16230
362. 78.159/13   Fig 108
363. 10508
364. BM1946-10016618
365. 68.11/22
366. A299
Fig 99   367. A22979   Fig 109
368. TL74 47
369. BM B92
370. 5682
371. BM B260
372. A19230
373. A25710   Fig 110
374. 5767
375. 18397
376. BM B182(962-134)   Fig 111
377. A3855
378. 12453   Fig 112
379. A11223
380. BM B183(962-132)
381. 5684
382. 5683
383. BM 1915 12-8 199
Fig 100   384. A16796
385. 2515
386. BM B87   Fig 113
387. A3914
388. 5686
389. A24191
Fig 101   390. 5769
391. 12453
392. MOL NN
393. 12453
394. BM B106 (65 32 15)
395. LUD82 1041
396. 13185
397. MOL NN
398. A1226
399. 24001
400. CAA RC 23 549
Fig 102   401. LUD82 1041
Fig 103   402. MOL NN
403. TL74 1181

404. TL74 2416
405. MOL NN   Fig 114
406. TL74 787
407. ER517
408. MOL NN
409. C682
410. 10632
411. FMC 12-1925
412. 5628
413. ER165
414. A25120
415. A16910   Fig 115
416. GM 980
417. 5612
418. 33.9/4
419. ER187(2)   Fig 116
420. BM 1938 7-1 1
421. A5067
422. BM B164
423. VA 2012-1901
424. BM 1904 10-25 2
425. 5653
426. 5740
427. A27629
428. P339
429. 5737
430. 22728   Fig 117
431. LWA84 3
432. 5621
433. 78.159/21
434. A15285
435. GM AG150
436. POM79 2048
437. TL74 368
438. 11755
439. TL74 291   Fig 118
440. GDH85 941
441. TL74 2684
442. TL74 2340/1651
443. TL74 415
444. ER188
445. TL74 1743
446. TL74 368
447. SWA81 2107
448. ER146
449. TL74 429
450. TL74 2332
451. TL74 416
452. TL74 1955
453. TL74 431
454. TL74 1955   Fig 119
455. BM 56 7-1 1536
456. 15005
457. BWB83 147
458. TL74 368
459. TL74 453
460. TL74 416
461. 20562
462. TL74 291
463. SWA81 2126

464. Private collection
465. 18775
466. 22750
467. BM B152
468. 23703
469. 18402
470. 22710
471. TL74 323
472. 18403
473. TL74 415
474. BWB83 147
475. TL74 1743
476. 12122
477. 5945
478. TL74 368
479. TL74 368
480. TL74 416
481. TL74 368
482. TL74 452
483. TL74 2670
484. SWA81 2115
485. TL74 368
486. 24970
487. 18?91
488. TL74 786
489. A2328
490. ER187
491. TL74 368
492. TL74 323
493. TL74 323
494. TL74 429
495. BIS82 927
496. TL74 306
497. 14241
498. 16748
499. TL74 1956
500. SWA81 2108
501. TL74 368
502. TL74 2700
503. TL74 453
504. BWB83 147
505. ER186
506. TL74 414
507. BIS82 927
508. BoE 425
509. TL74 323
510. TL74 414
511. TL74 2660
512. TL74 1457
513. TAV82 96
514. 5906
515. CAP86 614
516. 68.135
517. 15956
518. 1942.86
519. BM B216b
520. EST83 9
521. TL74 548
522. TL74 416
523. 1930-172

	524. TL74 368		583. 18481
	525. TL74 368	Fig 126	584. A22817
	526. TL74 415		585. TL74 414
	527. TL74 364		586. PET81 1848
	528. TL74 274		587. 5707
	529. BM B216 (96 2-1		588. ER161B
	30)	Fig 127	589. MOL NN
Fig 120	530. 24966		590. BM B246
	531. TL74 368		591. 24708
	532. TL74 364		592. SWA81
	533. TL74 274		593. A5333
	534. TL74 274		594. SWA81 2112
Fig 121	535. P321		595. BM B245
	536. 5635		596. SWA81 2103
	537. 22117		597. 5907
	538. A5054		
	539. 5732		
	540. 16755		
	541. 5627		
	542. A4933		
Fig 122	543. 78.159/31		
	544. 16637		
	545. A5215		
	546. 26421		
	547. P325		
	548. A5059		
	549. A5060		
	550. A5075		
	551. A5063		
	552. 5648		
	553. 68.11/3		
	554. A24924		
Fig 123	555. 24790		
	556. 5725		
	557. A11535		
	558. TL74 368		
	559. 5701		
	560. 78.159/47		
	561. SWA81 2103		
	562. TL74 368		
	563. A19236		
Fig 124	564. 17894		
	565. 5828		
	566. 24976		
	567. 12123		
	568. TL74 323		
	569. TL74 368		
	570. TL74 368		
	571. TL74 275		
	572. TL74 368		
	573. Tl74 364		
Fig 125	574. ER190A		
	575. TL74 275		
	576. TL74 364		
	577. TL74 275		
	578. TL74 306		
	579. TL74 368		
	580. TL74 452		
	581. TL74 275		
	582. TL74 368		

APPENDIX 2 : KEY TO FIGURES 2-4

List of find-spots of Surrey whitewares, and other contemporaneous kiln sites in south-east England.

Inner London

  1) City (DUA excavations)
  2) London-type ware kilns (Pearce *et al.* 1985)
  3) Aldwych (MOL A22817)
  4) Baker St. (MOL C723-1923)
  5) High Holborn (MOL 68.11/5)
  6) Islington (MOL 5599)
  7) Law Courts, Strand (MOL A5075)
  8) Shoreditch High St. (MOL 74.363)
  9) Tower of London (Redknap 1983)
 10) Westminster Abbey (Platts 1976)

Greater London

 11) Barking Abbey (Passmore Edwards Museum)
 12) Cheam
 13) Greenwich (MOL A5063)
 14) Kennington (Dawson 1976; Cuming Museum)
 15) Kingston upon Thames
 16) Lesnes Abbey (Dunning 1961)
 17) Merton Priory (Turner 1967)
 18) Northolt Manor (Hurst 1961)
 19) Southwark (Celoria and Thorn 1974)
 20) Sutton (Jope 1952)
 21) West Ham (Passmore Edwards Museum)

Essex

 22) Dagenham (Passmore Edwards Museum)
 23) Hadleigh Castle (Drewett 1975)
 24) King John's Hunting Lodge, Writtle (Rahtz 1969)
 25) Mill Green (Pearce *et al.* 1982)

Hertfordshire

 26) Kings Langley (Verulamium Museum, St. Albans)
 27) Manor of the More, Rickmansworth (Biddle *et al.* 1959)
 28) St. Albans (Verulamium Museum, St. Albans)

Kent

 29) Dartford (Mynard 1973)
 30) Joydens Wood (Dunning 1958)
 31) Lullingstone Roman Villa (Dartford Museum unpubl.)
 32) Tyler Hill kilns

Surrey

 33) Ash
 34) Brooklands, Weybridge (Hanworth and Tomalin 1977)
 35) Earlswood (Turner 1974)
 36) Farnborough Hill (Holling 1977)
 37) Godalming Old Minster (Castle Arch Museum, Guildford)
 38) Guildford (Castle Arch Museum, Guildford)
 39) Hookwood, Charlwood (Turner 1977)
 40) Reigate, Church St. (Castle Arch Museum, Guildford; Turner 1975)
 41) Titsey (Castle Arch Museum, Guildford)
 42) Walton Downs (Castle Arch Museum, Guildford)

Other Sites

 43) Abingdon, Oxon. (Vince 1983)
 44) Alton, Hants. (Vince 1983)
 45) Ashmansworth, Hants. (Vince 1983)
 46) Bayham Abbey, Sussex (Orton 1982b)
 47) Bodiam Castle, Sussex (Myres 1935)
 48) Brill, Bucks. (Jope 1953-4)
 49) Eastbourne, Sussex (Orton 1982b)
 50) Ewen, Glos. (Vince 1983)
 51) Highclere, Hants. (Vince 1983)
 52) Huish, Hants. (Vince 1983)
 53) Mapledurwell, Hants. (Vince 1983)
 54) Monks Sherborne, Hants. (Vince 1983)
 55) Rye, Sussex (Barton 1979)

APPENDIX 3: KEY TO FIGURES 5-8

List of find-spots in the City of London of Surrey white-wares from museum collections and from DUA excavations, preceded by their site codes. In the case of museum accessions for which a street name only is recorded, the find-spot has been arbitrarily positioned centrally within that street.

1) Aldermanbury
2) Aldersgate St.
3) 83-6 Aldgate High St./155-7 Minories
4) All Hallows, Lombard St.
5) Angel Court, Walbrook
6) Austin Friars
7) Baltic Exchange, 14-28 St. Mary Axe ER165
8) Bank of England
9) 5-15 Bankside, SE1
10) Bartholomew Lane
11) 40 Basinghall St. ER799
12) Bell Alley
13) Belle Sauvage Yard
14) Billingsgate Bath House, 100 Lower Thames St.
15) Billiter Sq.
16) Billiter St.
17) Bishopsgate
18) Bishopsgate/ Leadenhall St.
19) Blackfriars Improvement Cofferdam
20) Blossoms Inn Yard
21) Bow Lane
22) Bucklersbury
23) 65-6 Cannon St.
24) 116-26 Cannon St.
25) 130-1 Cheapside
26) Child's Bank, 1 Fleet St.
27) Christ's Hospital, Newgate
28) Church Alley ER1220b
29) 5 Clarks Place, Bishopsgate
30) Coleman St.
31) 77 Coleman St.
32) Creed Lane
33) Cripplegate St.
34) Crosby Hall
35) Crutched Friars
36) Drapers Hall
37) 35 Fenchurch St.

38) 112 Fenchurch St.
39) Fenchurch St.
40) Fetter Lane
41) Finch Lane
42) Finsbury Circus
43) Fish St. Hill
44) Fleet St.
45) Furnivals Inn
46) Fore St.
47) Gateway House, 12-16 Watling St. ER187
48) Golden Lane
49) 29-31 Gracechurch St.
50) 36 Gracechurch St.
51) Gracechurch St.
52) Gresham House, Broad St.
53) 20-28 Gresham St. ER471
54) Greyfriars Monastery, Smithfield
55) Guildhall Library, Aldermanbury ER1238
56) Guildhall Yard
57) Hatton Garden
58) Holborn Circus
59) King St. ER375
60) King William St.
61) King William St./Abchurch Lane
62) Leadenhall St.
63) Lime St.
64) 1-3 Little Britain/195-7 Aldersgate St.
65) Little Trinity Lane
66) 54 Lombard St.
67) Lombard St.
68) London Wall
69) Mansion House Place, 13-14 George St.
70) 71-4 Mark Lane
71) Mincing Lane
72) Mitre St., Aldgate

73) Moor Lane
74) Moorfields
75) Moorgate
76) Newgate St.
77) Nicholas Lane
78) Noble St.
79) Northgate House, Copthall Close
80) Old Bailey
81) 36-8 Old Change
82) Palace of the Bishops of Ely, Holborn
83) Phoenix House, King William St.
84) Plantation House, Eastcheap
85) Plough Court
86) Post Office Court, Lombard St.
87) Public Cleansing Depot, Dowgate ER466
88) Queen Victoria St.
89) Salters Hall, Walbrook
90) Seething Lane
91) Smithfield
92) St. Alban's House, 126 Wood St. ER762
93) St. Anthony's Hospital, Threadneedle St.
94) St. Bartholomew's Hospital
95) St. Bartholomew's Priory, Cloth Fair
96) St. Botolph's, Aldgate
97) St. John's Priory, St. John St.
98) St. Martins-le-Grand
99) St. Mary Axe
100) St. Stephen's, Coleman St.
101) St. Stephen's, Walbrook
102) St. Swithins Lane
103) Throgmorton St.
104) Tokenhouse Yard
105) Whitefriars St.

106) Windsor Court
107) ACE83 77-9 Gracechurch St.
108) ADM81 Alderman's House, 34-7 Liverpool St.
109) AL74 62-4 Aldgate High St.
110) ALD82 Rotunda, Aldersgate
111) ALG84 7-12 Aldersgate St.
112) APO81 Apothecaries Hall, Blackfriars Lane
113) BIG82 (and BWB83) Billingsgate Lorry Park, Lower Thames St.
114) BIS82 76-80 Bishopsgate
115) BOP82 28-34 Bishopsgate
116) CLE81 29-32 Clements Lane
117) CLO83 62-7 Long Lane/26-36 Cloth Fair
118) COL81 19-20 College Hill
119) CRC82 22 Creechurch Lane
120) CRE79 33 Creechurch Lane
121) CST85 6-7 The Crescent
122) EST83 27-9 Eastcheap
123) FEN83 5-12 Fenchurch St.
124) FLE82 180-3 Fleet St./140-3 Fetter Lane
125) FNS72 110-114 Fenchurch St.
126) HIL84 7-8 Philpot Lane
127) HOP83 3-5 Bishopsgate
128) IME83 27-30 Lime St.
129) KNG85 36-7 King St.
130) LEA84 71-7 Leadenhall St./32-40 Mitre St.
131) LIM83 25-6 Lime St.
132) LOG82 84-5 Long Lane
133) LOV81 St. Mary at Hill/21-4 Lovat Lane
134) LUD82 42-6 Ludgate Hill/1-6 Old Bailey
135) LWA84 43 London Wall
136) MAN82 29-33 Mansell St.
137) MIL72 10 Milk St.
138) MLK76 1-6 Milk St.
139) NBS84 35-8 New Bridge St.
140) NPY73 New Palace Yard
141) OST82 7-10 Foster Lane
142) PCH85 1-3 St. Paul's Churchyard
143) PDN81 118-127 Lower Thames St.
144) PEN79 Peninsular House, 112-16 Lower Thames St.
145) PET81 St. Peters Hill, Castle Baynard St./Upper Thames St.
146) POM79 GPO Middle Area, Newgate St.
147) QUN85 61 Queen Street
148) QVS85 167-79 Queen Victoria St.
149) RAG82 61-5 Crutched Friars/Rangoon St.
150) SH74 Seal House/106-8 Upper Thames St.
151) SKI83 3 Skinners Lane/36-8 Queen St.
152) SLO82 Beaver House/Sugar Loaf Court
153) SWA81 Swan Lane Car Park, 95-103 Upper Thames St.
154) TAV82 29-31 Knightrider St.
155) TL74 Trig Lane, Upper Thames St.
156) WAY83 10-13 Ludgate Broadway
157) WIT83 18-23 St. Swithins Lane/113-14 Cannon St.

APPENDIX 4: NEUTRON ACTIVATION ANALYSIS

Michael Cowell

Introduction

The late medieval pottery with a distinctive white fabric known as 'Surrey whiteware' is frequently found in the London area and several kiln sites are known which could have supplied material for this market. Suitable raw materials are assumed to have been exploited from the Reading Beds (see p.11). The kiln sites are often in close proximity to outcrops or deposits of this, for example along the eastern end at Cheam and at the western end north of Farnham. Sometimes, such as at Bankside and Kingston upon Thames, the kilns are not sited directly over the beds, hence transportation of clay over moderate distances must have been common practice. The intention of this study was the chemical analysis of products from some of the kilns and a selection of typical pottery mainly from the London area to determine whether or not their sources could be characterised and how this would compare with a stylistic survey.

Material for analysis

Excavated material from three production areas in the London region was analysed: Bankside, Kingston (2 excavations) and Cheam (3 excavations):

Site	Number	Reference
Southwark:		
Bankside	6	Dennis & Hinton 1983
Kingston:		
Knapp-Drewett (KND82)	6	
Eden Street (KND68)	6	Hinton 1980
Cheam:		
Cheam (CA69) 14th C	6	Orton 1979
Cheam (1924) 14th C	10	Marshall 1924
Cheam (CA69 U/S) 15th C	6	Orton, 1979

Data from the two kilns at Kingston were combined, as were those from the 14th-century kilns at Cheam, before statistical analysis. The unsourced pottery which was also analysed, predominantly with London find-spots, is mainly of 'Kingston-type ware' or 'Cheam whiteware' style. However, also included were a few 'Coarse Border ware' style items (Fig 128 numbers 80, 81, 83) which may have manufacturing origins in the Farnham area. All the pottery was obtained from the collections of the British Museum or the Museum of London.

Analytical technique and statistical methods

The method of chemical analysis used was neutron activation (NAA) which is widely applied to pottery for provenance or characterisation purposes (Widemann 1980). Although the analysis itself is non-destructive, a sample is required, ideally 50-100mg, which in this case was removed by drilling with tungsten-carbide or diamond embedded bits. In a few cases only about 30mg of sample was obtainable due to the small size of particular sherds. Generally, samples were taken from fracture surfaces by drilling into the interior of the body, avoiding surface contamination and glaze. On complete pottery the base was usually sampled and surface material discarded.

Full technical details of the NAA technique used would be out of place here but a description of the method used at the British Museum is given by Leese *et al.* 1986. The following fourteen elements were quantified in all the whiteware samples analysed and used in the statistical analysis: potassium (K), scandium (Sc), iron (Fe), caesium (Cs), lanthanum (La), cerium (Ce), samarium (Sm), europium (Eu), terbium (Tb), ytterbium (Yb), lutetium (Lu), hafnium (Hf), tantalum (Ta) and thorium (Th). In fact, several

No.	Mus/Exc Ref	Provenance	Dist	Ce	Tb	Th	Hf	Cs	Sc	Fe	Eu	Ta	La	K	Yb	Lu	Sm
1		BANKSIDE Kiln		60	.58	12.5	6.2	6.6	14.7	1.9	.86	2.0	36	1.35	2.3	.36	4.08
2		BANKSIDE Kiln		73	.70	14.5	6.6	7.5	17.2	2.4	.92	2.3	42	1.55	2.6	.37	4.04
3		BANKSIDE Kiln		62	.58	12.5	6.2	6.7	14.5	2.0	.85	2.1	35	1.65	2.2	.36	3.66
4		BANKSIDE Kiln		74	.72	13.8	6.7	7.9	15.9	2.1	.97	1.5	42	1.94	2.6	.41	4.78
5		BANKSIDE Kiln		73	.56	14.0	6.5	8.6	16.2	2.1	1.01	4.9	36	1.52	2.2	.32	3.81
6		BANKSIDE Kiln		65	.61	12.8	6.6	6.7	15.1	1.8	.85	3.4	36	1.42	2.4	.37	3.86
7	KND 82/1	KINGSTON KND82 Kiln		71	.64	13.5	7.6	6.0	14.5	1.9	1.05	2.7	39	1.56	2.6	.41	4.26
8	KND 82/2	KINGSTON KND82 Kiln		67	.61	13.8	6.9	6.9	15.8	2.2	.95	2.7	38	1.55	2.3	.37	4.15
9	KND 82/3	KINGSTON KND82 Kiln		70	.62	13.8	7.1	6.9	15.7	2.0	.96	3.3	38	1.64	2.6	.41	4.69
10	KND 82/4	KINGSTON KND82 Kiln		70	.69	13.5	6.6	7.5	16.3	2.0	.99	3.1	40	1.62	2.6	.39	4.99
11	KND 82/5	KINGSTON KND82 Kiln		51	.48	10.3	6.0	5.2	11.6	1.3	.69	2.7	29	1.29	1.8	.30	3.43
12	KND 82/6	KINGSTON KND82 Kiln		62	.63	13.1	9.9	6.3	14.2	1.8	.85	2.7	35	1.61	2.4	.39	3.87
13	KD 68/1	KINGSTON KD68 Kiln		61	.56	11.9	6.2	6.1	14.1	1.7	.88	2.0	35	1.49	2.2	.34	3.87
14	KD 68/2	KINGSTON KD68 Kiln		66	.59	13.1	7.2	6.8	15.1	2.0	.86	2.5	39	1.67	2.5	.36	4.23
15	KD 68/3	KINGSTON KD68 Kiln		69	.66	14.0	6.8	6.9	15.5	2.0	.94	2.8	42	1.53	2.7	.39	4.28
16	KD 68/4	KINGSTON KD68 Kiln		70	.70	13.8	7.3	8.0	16.3	2.3	1.10	2.9	40	1.77	2.5	.44	5.59
17	KD 68/5	KINGSTON KD68 Kiln		71	.73	14.0	7.6	7.3	16.4	2.1	1.08	2.1	42	1.73	2.6	.44	4.71
18	KD 68/6	KINGSTON KD68 Kiln		51	.53	11.3	6.9	6.1	12.7	1.5	.71	1.7	30	1.30	2.0	.37	3.47
19	1924,1-23,8	CHEAM (14C) Kiln		58	.50	11.3	7.0	6.6	13.3	1.6	.83	3.5	36	1.82	2.3	.36	4.01
20	1924,1-23,20	CHEAM (14C) Kiln		56	.59	12.0	8.8	6.4	13.6	1.7	.79	2.7	34	1.74	2.3	.40	3.96
21	1924,1-23,5	CHEAM (14C) Kiln		52	.49	10.4	7.5	5.9	12.0	1.5	.79	1.6	30	1.39	2.1	.37	3.24
22	1924,1-23,7	CHEAM (14C) Kiln		58	.56	11.7	7.0	6.0	13.4	1.6	.89	2.2	57	2.37	3.4	.58	6.27
23	1924,1-23,9	CHEAM (14C) Kiln		56	.58	11.6	9.0	6.4	13.3	1.7	.76	2.1	32	1.36	2.3	.38	3.74
24	1924,1-23,21d	CHEAM (14C) Kiln		79	.69	15.3	8.1	8.5	17.7	2.1	1.10	2.4	45	2.10	2.8	.44	4.92
25	1924,1-23,11	CHEAM (14C) Kiln		56	.57	20.4	8.0	6.4	14.6	2.5	.79	1.7	34	1.59	2.5	.46	4.06
26	1924,1-23,12	CHEAM (14C) Kiln		71	.62	12.9	6.1	6.9	14.4	1.8	.93	2.0	44	1.66	2.5	.35	4.34
27	1924,1-23,21b	CHEAM (14C) Kiln		67	.50	12.3	7.0	6.6	13.6	1.7	.88	1.5	36	1.61	2.2	.36	4.28
28	1924,1-23,21d	CHEAM (14C) Kiln		76	.62	14.6	7.5	8.2	17.1	2.0	1.06	2.0	46	1.70	2.9	.47	5.22
29	CA69 14(C)	CHEAM (14C) Kiln		51	.49	10.3	8.2	5.6	12.2	2.1	.73	2.3	28	1.23	2.1	.34	3.10
30	CA69 14(A)	CHEAM (14C) Kiln		56	.57	11.3	8.2	5.8	12.6	1.6	.88	2.2	31	1.59	2.3	.38	3.58
31	CA69 14(B)	CHEAM (14C) Kiln		55	.54	10.8	7.9	5.6	12.1	1.7	.77	3.9	30	1.39	2.1	.34	3.07
32	CA69 14(D)	CHEAM (14C) Kiln		61	.59	11.9	7.7	6.3	14.1	1.8	.90	2.8	37	1.64	2.4	.40	4.04
33	CA69 VII (2)	CHEAM (14C) Kiln		60	.55	12.5	6.9	7.2	14.7	1.9	.78	2.5	35	1.51	2.3	.42	3.98
34	CA69 VII (2)	CHEAM (14C) Kiln		55	.56	13.6	8.4	8.7	16.4	1.9	.81	2.6	32	1.46	2.5	.46	3.63
35	CA69 U/S (A)	CHEAM (15C) Kiln		36	.46	11.8	8.5	6.9	16.9	2.2	.59	3.3	18	.81	2.4	.40	2.26
36	CA69 U/S (B)	CHEAM (15C) Kiln		37	.62	12.0	8.0	6.9	16.0	2.2	.74	3.6	20	1.10	2.4	.40	2.65
37	CA69 U/S (C)	CHEAM (15C) Kiln		38	.51	12.8	8.2	7.2	18.1	2.3	.70	3.5	19	.87	2.6	.41	3.19
38	CA69 U/S (D)	CHEAM (15C) Kiln		46	.55	12.1	9.4	6.2	17.3	2.4	.87	1.7	27	1.36	2.5	.43	3.36
39	CA69 U/S (E)	CHEAM (15C) Kiln		28	.54	12.1	7.8	6.3	16.5	2.2	.64	1.7	15	1.02	2.5	.45	2.67
40	CA69 U/S (F)	CHEAM (15C) Kiln		32	.48	12.3	7.6	7.4	16.8	2.2	.60	1.8	17	.77	2.4	.38	2.61
41	1918,12-8,194	LONDON WALL	14.2	54	.55	10.5	5.9	6.1	12.4	1.6	.85	2.0	32	1.48	1.9	.32	3.73
42	B167:54,11-30,56			66	.70	11.6	8.0	5.9	12.4	1.9	1.03	2.1	34	1.41	2.5	.43	4.60
43	B13:56,5-24,1	FLEET ST.	9.3	67	.59	12.5	5.7	6.9	14.3	1.9	1.00	2.3	38	1.57	2.2	.35	4.26
44	B98			80	.77	11.9	8.3	5.7	12.5	1.7	1.14	2.2	45	1.82	2.7	.44	4.53
45	B32:99,5-8,7	LONDON	32.2	61	.62	11.6	5.6	6.6	13.9	1.9	.92	2.8	35	1.47	2.1	.37	3.39
46	B114	MINCING LANE	26.1	65	.65	11.4	8.0	5.4	12.2	1.4	.98	1.6	36	1.56	2.5	.41	4.46
47	B131		24.5	58	.52	12.0	6.2	5.6	13.8	2.1	.87	2.5	37	1.50	2.2	.33	3.64
48	B238:54,11-30,63	LONDON	14.9	55	.49	10.9	6.4	5.4	12.7	1.6	.76	1.3	33	1.58	2.1	.37	3.38
49	B146	OXFORD	16.5	60	.48	12.1	6.1	6.7	14.7	1.9	.86	3.5	34	1.38	2.0	.34	3.65
50	B219		28.9	55	.48	10.6	5.9	6.2	12.1	1.6	.91	1.3	34	1.55	2.2	.33	3.63
51	B106:65,3-2,15		26.1	59	.61	12.1	8.1	6.9	13.8	1.6	.91	2.5	36	1.62	2.6	.37	4.24
52	B183	BATH ST.	25.6	71	.68	13.4	10.	7.8	16.4	2.1	.99	2.5	45	1.68	2.8	.42	4.30
53	B260:99,5-8,27		30.0	43	.45	9.4	6.3	5.1	12.1	1.7	.69	2.1	25	1.30	1.9	.28	2.95
54	1915,12-18,198	NEWGATE		52	.47	9.9	6.0	5.3	11.3	1.5	.73	2.4	32	1.23	1.8	.37	3.44
55	B180			60	.56	11.4	6.6	6.7	13.6	1.6	.86	2.5	23	1.03	1.5	.25	2.62
56	B262:54,11-30,78	LONDON	15.8	57	.47	11.5	6.8	6.0	13.6	1.6	.87	2.1	34	1.39	2.1	.35	3.75
57	B182:96,2-1,34	LONDON	24.5	74	.55	15.0	9.3	7.3	16.2	2.4	.94	2.2	43	1.76	2.4	.38	4.05
58	B166:55,10-29,10		21.3	57	.52	10.2	5.5	5.6	12.4	1.8	.85	1.6	31	1.27	1.9	.31	3.67
59	B87	LONDON		156	.97	11.7	5.5	5.4	11.9	1.2	2.00	1.6	71	2.90	5.1		8.86
60	B165:64,3-19,44	LONDON		57	.51	10.8	5.8	6.3	13.2	1.8	.92	3.3	35	2.02	2.1	.31	3.45
61	B92:99,5-8,25		24.5	56	.52	10.4	5.6	5.7	11.8	1.6	.79	1.1	32	1.03	2.1	.33	3.59
62	Context 2502	Trig Lane, London	9.1	58	.60	10.5	6.8	6.3	12.6	1.5	.88	2.8	32	1.51	2.3	.38	3.72
63	Context 2503	Trig Lane, London	16.4	61	.63	11.6	7.1	7.2	14.4	1.9	1.02	2.7	35	1.72	2.4	.38	3.93
64	Context 2242	Trig Lane, London		64	.62	10.9	7.1	5.5	14.6	1.9	.87	2.5	33	1.49	2.3	.40	3.79
65	Context 1871	Trig Lane, London		67	.72	9.6	8.2	5.4	10.4	1.9	1.03	1.6	38	1.44	2.3	.38	4.05
66	Context 47B	Trig Lane, London	8.5	62	.65	11.7	6.8	6.9	13.6	1.9	.97	2.2	34	1.67	2.4	.40	4.22
67	Context 47C	Trig Lane, London	29.3	72	.77	12.2	8.0	6.6	14.5	2.1	1.13	2.8	37	1.50	2.8	.42	4.88
68	Context 47	Trig Lane, London	15.9	68	.75	12.8	7.6	7.9	15.7	2.2	1.04	2.9	38	1.50	2.7	.43	4.43

No.	Mus/Exc Ref	Provenance	Dist	Ce	Tb	Th	Hf	Cs	Sc	Fe	Eu	Ta	La	K	Yb	Lu	Sm
69	Context 47A	Trig Lane, London		67	.70	12.2	7.5	6.6	13.5	1.8	.97	2.4	35	1.67	2.7	.41	5.49
70	Cheamware (1)	LONDON	16.5	57	.58	12.4	8.4	6.3	13.6	1.6	.84	2.3	34	1.38	2.3	.44	3.85
71	Cheamware (2)	LONDON	15.6	63	.58	12.9	7.9	7.5	14.6	1.6	.96	1.8	38	1.95	2.4	.41	4.37
72	Cheamware (3)	LONDON	25.2	59	.53	11.4	6.3	5.2	13.3	1.6	.98	1.2	36	1.52	2.3	.38	3.92
73	Cheamware (4)	LONDON	17.1	58	.51	11.4	7.8	5.8	13.8	1.6	.81	1.3	35	1.94	2.4	.42	4.02
74	Cheamware (5)	LONDON	11.3	64	.59	12.6	9.0	7.4	15.2	1.7	.91	2.1	39	1.76	2.8	.47	4.25
75	Cheamware (6)	LONDON	20.1	62	.48	12.1	8.3	6.6	14.3	1.7	.94	1.7	37	1.83	2.3	.39	4.31
76	Cheamware (7)	LONDON		195	1.4	13.9	5.1	6.9	15.1	2.3	3.09	2.2	89	1.98	2.7	.50	14.4
77	Cheamware (8)	LONDON	2.9	58	.57	12.2	7.4	6.9	14.5	1.7	.83	1.6	36	1.62	2.5	.41	4.22
78	Cheamware (9)	LONDON	10.4	62	.67	12.5	7.3	6.5	14.3	2.1	1.00	1.4	37	1.78	2.5	.43	4.29
79	Cheamware (10)	LONDON	7.2	64	.58	12.5	7.7	6.5	14.5	1.8	.89	1.3	38	1.93	2.5	.42	4.30
80	B101	LONDON		180	1.3	14.4	5.9	6.7	16.1	1.9	2.43	2.8	83	1.95	3.0	.45	8.76
81	1958,4-1,158			154	1.0	15.0	6.8	7.6	17.5	2.0	1.94	4.0	81	1.95	3.0	.42	10.5
82	B145			58	.39	11.4	6.1	5.6	14.0	2.1	.79	2.8	30	1.36	1.9	.27	3.14
83	55,7-24,2			107	.61	11.4	4.8	6.9	14.4	2.1	1.02	3.2	55	2.04	2.1	.29	4.62

128. NAA results.

other elements were also measured, but were excluded from the statistical analysis because of possible contamination or interference from the drill material and in some cases low precision through small sample weights.

The analytical data on all the samples, kiln material followed by unsourced pottery, is given in Fig 128 together with museum references and find-spots, where known. The data from the kiln groups is summarised below in the form of means and standard deviations.

Two statistical techniques were used to assist in the interpretation of the analytical data: linear discriminant analysis and cluster analysis.

Discriminant analysis estimates the parameters of items within previously defined groups so that the groups as a whole can be compared. In addition, an individual can then be classified according to its distance from each of the group centroids. The method was used to compare the groups of kiln site material and also to determine the similarity of the unsourced pottery's composition with that of the kiln sources.

Cluster analysis looks for structure in multi-dimensional data by grouping together those items showing some measure of similarity. Unlike discriminant analysis the method makes no *a priori* assumptions about grouping in the data. The cluster analysis package CLUSTAN (Wishart 1978, 1982) was applied using Ward's method with reallocation. Cluster analysis was used primarily to examine the composition of the finished pottery for groupings.

Before commencing any statistical analysis, the data were examined to see if they should be first transformed by scaling to correct for the variations induced in the absolute concentrations as a result of different amounts of added temper and any measurement bias, particularly important if samples are processed in several batches. Scandium is commonly used for this purpose because it is normally present in moderate, precisely measureable quantities and can be shown to be related to the total amount of clay material (Aspinall 1977).

In this case, scandium was found to be particularly highly correlated with iron, and, since the temper used in this pottery is thought from thin-section studies to be a ferruginous sandstone (cf Appendix 5), it is possible that a significant proportion of the scandium is associated with this source rather than with clay. This could be a good reason for not scaling in this instance. In fact, tests revealed that the use of unscaled rather than scaled data made no significant difference to the statistical analysis and hence only scaled data were subsequently used.

After scaling, the data were log-transformed. Log-transformation is often applied to ceramic data because geochemical studies show that trace elements are usually log-normally distributed within any one source and statistical techniques require the data to be as near normally distributed as possible.

Discussion

a) Kiln material

The initial stage of statistical analysis was intended to determine whether or not the kiln material, grouped according to site, could be reliably distinguished chemically. Discriminant analysis was applied to the four kiln groups using the full suite of fourteen elements, but they were incompletely separated except for the 15th-century Cheam whiteware which was clearly differentiated from the other groups. A measure of the success with which the groups can be distinguished was obtained by submitting each group member in turn to classification, as if it was of unknown source. A rather strict, but realistic, criterion was used whereby an individual being classified is not included in the estimation of its group parameters (jack-knife method). As a result, only 35% of the Bankside, Kingston and 14th century Cheam material were correctly classified, which is marginally better than chance. The 15th-century Cheam samples were, on the other hand, classified consistently well. The chief distinguishing elements responsible for separating the Kingston, Bankside and early Cheam groups from the 15th-century Cheam samples are lanthanum and cerium, and to a lesser extent, samarium and potassium. The differences and similarities can be appreciated from the summarised data in Fig 129 and 130.

Possible differences between all the groups were also explored with a restricted suite of elements. As noted above, Surrey whitewares are thought to contain a ferruginous sandstone temper and elements which might be associated with this phase were sought. Those highly correlated with iron, but uncorrelated with typical clay-associated elements (lanthanum and potassium, for example) were looked for and as a result, caesium (alkali metal) and lutetium and ytterbium (heavy lanthanides) were selected. However, it is most unlikely that these elements are restricted solely to the source or quantity of temper added since iron is present in both temper and clay phases.

In fact, using this restricted dataset, none of the groups (including the 15th-century Cheam

examples, which were distinguished easily by the full set of elements) were satisfactorily separated. In isolation, therefore, the elements which may be associated primarily with the temper are not able to distinguish any of the groups. Where differences are found, the kiln products seem to be distinguished by clay rather than temper.

Thus, whereas the later Cheam material forms a chemically distinct group, the other kilns cannot be differentiated. It must be assumed therefore, that either the same sources of raw material were being used at all the other kilns, or, if different sources were used, they are not chemically distinctive. For the purposes of comparison with unsourced pottery, therefore, the material from Bankside, Kingston and the early Cheam kilns were treated as one group and the 15th-century Cheam material as a second.

b) Unsourced pottery
The chemical data from the items of unsourced pottery (unknowns) without kiln site provenances were analysed in two ways: they were compared with the kiln data (controls) using discriminant analysis and were examined for structure using cluster analysis.

As noted above, for the discriminant analysis, the data for all but the 15th-century Cheam material were combined and therefore just two control groups were assumed. After estimating group parameters, the individuals were classified to groups according to the relative magnitudes of the 'distances' (Mahalanobis d-squared) of the individuals from each of the groups. Since, in this method of classification, an individual will always be assigned to a group (the 'nearest'), irrespective of its degree of similarity, some limit is required

129. Means and standard deviations of kiln groups.

Kiln		Ce	Tb	Th	Hf	Cs	Sc	Fe	Eu	Ta	La	K	Yb	Lu	Sm
Bankside	Means	67.7	0.63	13.4	6.5	7.3	15.6	2.1	0.91	2.7	37.7	1.6	2.4	0.37	4.0
	S.D.	6.0	0.07	0.86	0.2	0.8	1.0	0.22	0.07	1.3	3.6	0.21	0.17	0.03	0.4
Kingston	Means	64.8	0.62	13.0	7.2	6.7	14.9	1.9	0.92	2.6	37.2	1.6	2.4	0.39	4.3
	S.D.	7.4	0.07	1.2	1.0	0.8	1.5	0.28	0.13	0.5	4.4	0.15	0.28	0.04	0.6
Cheam 14C	Means	60.5	0.56	12.7	7.7	6.7	14.1	1.8	0.85	2.4	36.7	1.6	2.4	0.41	4.1
	S.D.	8.4	0.05	2.5	0.8	1.0	1.7	0.25	0.1	0.6	7.7	0.29	0.34	0.06	0.8
Cheam 15C	Means	36.0	0.52	12.2	8.3	6.8	16.9	2.2	0.69	2.6	19.5	0.99	2.5	0.41	2.8
	S.D.	6.0	0.06	0.34	0.6	0.5	0.7	0.09	0.1	0.9	4.3	0.2	0.09	0.02	0.4

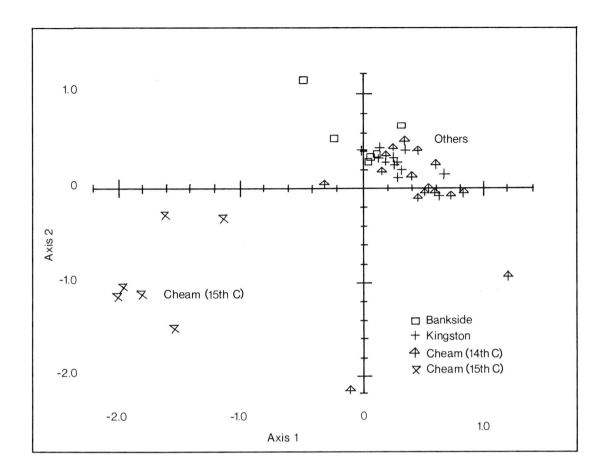

130. Multidimensional scaling (MDS) plot of the production site data showing the separation achieved for the 15th century Cheam material and incomplete differentiation of the other sites.

with which individuals can be rejected as being unlike any of the control groups. This was established by applying the 'jack-knife' method to a proportion of the control samples and determining the distance at which, arbitarily, 90% of these individuals were correctly assigned. This distance (33) was then applied in the classification of the unknowns as a limit with which to reject unlikely assignments. Using this criterion, 29 of the 43 unknowns showed strong similarities with the combined Bankside, Kingston, early Cheam group but none were like the later Cheam material. Those items which are similar to the combined group are identified in Fig 128 by a value in the 'distance' column. A smaller value indicates greater similarity.

The cluster analysis of the 43 unknowns resulted in the formation of several groups. A particularly extreme separation was obtained for four samples, two of which are of Coarse Border ware (80, 81), one apparently of 'Kingston-type ware' (41) and one of 'Cheam whiteware' (59). They are rather easily identified since all contain con-

siderably enriched amounts of the lighter lanthanide series of elements (La, Eu, Ce, Sm). None of the kiln samples has a composition remotely comparable with them. Clearly they have been manufactured using a raw material source quite unlike that typically exploited for the Kingston, Bankside or Cheam wasters, assuming that the kiln products examined are representative. The similarity of the two, apparently, London-type wares (41 and 59) to the Coarse Border ware suggests that they were manufactured outside the London area.

A further group of six items consisted of numbers 42, 44, 46, 64, 65, 69 (Fig 128). From their appearance, these may be slightly earlier in date than the majority of the pottery analysed. However, although all members of this group share common features which indicate early manufacture, there are a number of other items, of similar early style, which do not fall within this cluster. A possible explanation is that some of the early pieces were manufactured from a wider variety of raw materials which were not available for the later material.

The remaining items broadly split into two poorly separated groups, the first of which includes many of those identified by discriminant analysis as most similar to the combined Kingston, Bankside and early Cheam products. However, there seems to be no consistent difference in typology between the two groups. The remaining Coarse Border ware item was included with the second of these groups and hence is unlike the London kiln products.

Summary

In general, it has been found impossible using either discriminant analysis or cluster analysis to distinguish between most of the groups of kiln products, except those of 15th-century Cheam. Evidently, raw materials of the same range of composition were being used at all the London area 14th-century kiln sites examined, although not necessarily from the same source. Provenancing the pottery to individual manufacturing sites operating contemporaneously in London is therefore not possible, although it seems that a significant proportion are similar to the material from Cheam, Kingston and Bankside. Although the analysis did not find groups corresponding precisely with the London kilns, some early pottery was separately grouped, as was the Coarse Border ware. The latter is quite different in composition from the products of the Kingston and Cheam kilns, implying that the composition of the clay at the western end of the Reading beds is markedly different from that to the east.

APPENDIX 5: PETROLOGICAL ANALYSIS

Seventy-five samples of Surrey whitewares have been examined under the binocular microscope, described on record cards and deposited in the DUA pottery fabric reference collection. Of these, 56 have been thin-sectioned and their inclusions identified and described. There is a clear textural difference between the three groups: Kingston-type ware, Cheam whiteware and Coarse Border ware, but there proved to be no clear-cut division between the three groups and a wide textural range within the groups. The largest number of samples, 23, were of Kingston-type ware and included material from the Knapp-Drewett kiln site, the Bankside waste and material from Trig Lane, which from its typology and context could be dated to the late 13th to early 14th century and the late 14th century. There was no apparent link between fabric and kiln site, nor between fabric and date of manufacture.

Petrology

For each thin-section, the presence/absence of inclusion types was noted and for common types their frequency was classified into sparse, moderate or abundant. As a check on this method a sub-sample was examined using an image analysis system at the British Museum Research Laboratory. All inclusions over 0.1mm in their largest dimension were examined within selected areas of the section until a minimum of 50 inclusions had been recorded. The system then calculated the maximum diameter and the diameter of the circle with the same circumference as that of the inclusion (abreviated to Dmax and Dcircle). This data was then examined in several ways in an attempt to differentiate samples, but with the same general results as were obtained by binocular microscope study and qualitative thin-section analysis.

All the samples shared the same basic clay and sand characteristics - sparse white mica, up to 0.1mm long; sparse rounded opaque, iron-rich inclusions up to 0.2mm across; sparse angular opaque, iron-rich inclusions less than 0.1mm across and moderate to abundant angular quartz up to 0.1mm across.

Chert, flint?, glauconite and haematite were present in small quantities and, although not present in every section, do not appear to correlate with known source or chronological groups.

The most diagnostic characteristic of the Surrey whitewares examined in thin-section, also clear visually, is the variation in quartz grains over 0.1mm across. Cheam whiteware contains few such inclusions. Coarse Border ware contains sparse to abundant quartz inclusions, the largest of which are rounded fragments between 1.0 and 2.0 mm across. Kingston-type ware contains abundant quartz inclusions, mainly less than 1.0mm across. Despite this apparently simple division there are many examples of sherds from Kingston-type ware production sites with coarser inclusions than normal and some which have a much finer texture, akin to that found in Cheam whiteware.

The following list of thin-sectioned Surrey whiteware sherds in the DUA fabric collection gives fabric codes, indentification and provenance.

Note: the fabric codes are explained in the DUA pottery archive handbook which may be obtained on application to the Museum of London. The common name codes are those used in the Museum of London computerised record (for expansions see p. 173).

Number	Fabric	Code	Site	Context	Comment
140	TUDC	Sgw 1475			
311	CBW	Sgw 2478			
312	CBW	Sgw 2478			
384	CBW		TL74	274	
385	CBW		TL74	274i	
386	CBW		TL74	29i	
387	CBW		TL74	29li	
388	CBW		TL74	306	
389	CBW		TL74	306i	
563	KING	Sgw 1214	SM75	91	
600	CBW	Sgw 595	ACW74	2	
601	KING	Sgw 1209	SM75	62	
602	KING	Sgw 613	ACW74	2	
603	CBW	Sgw 599	ACW74	2	
610	CHEA	ISgw 1196	NFW74	8	
611	KING	ISgw 2094	AL74	1352	
615	CHEA	Sgw 1655	CA69	4	CHEAM KILN
617	KING	Sw 1227	SM75	62	
623	KING	ISw 1207	NFW74	47	
624	KING	Sgtw 1136	SM75	62	
625	KING	Sgw 1231	SM75	65	
626	CBW	Sgw 1213	NFW74	73	
627	CBW	Sgw 1198	NFW74	44	
628	CBW	Skw 597	ACW74	2	
629	KING	Sgw 2055	AL74	1357	CAUL
667	KING	Sgw 601	ACW74	2	
668	KING	SH 74		435	JUG
669	KING	MSgw 2358	SH74	386	
670	KING		SH74	301	JUG POLY
671	KING		SH74	301	JUG
672	KING		SH74	386	JUG POLY
673	KING		SH74	303	JUG
674	KING		SH74	386	JUG
675	KING		TL74	548	JUG
676	KING		TL74	548	JUG PLAIN
677	KING		TL74	548	JUG PLAIN
678	KING		TL74	548	JUG PLAIN
679	KING		TL74	548	JUG PLAIN
680	KING		TL74	548	JUG
681	KING		TL74	47	JUG BOSS
682	KING		TL74	47	JUG BOSS
683	KING		TL74	47	JUG BOSS
684	KING		TL74	47	JUG BOSS
685	KING		TL74	47	JUG BOSS
686	KING		TL74	306	JUG BOSS WH SL
732	KING				BANKSIDE KILN I

Number	Fabric	Code	Site	Context	Comment
733	KING				BANKSIDE KILN 2
734	KING				BANKSIDE KILN 3
735	KING				BANKSIDE KILN 4
736	KING				BANKSIDE KILN 5
737	KING				BANKSIDE KILN 6
738	KING	MOL 78.159/16			RIM
739	KING	MOL 78.159/16			HANDLE
740	KING	MOL 78.159/16			BODY
741	KING	Sgw 607	ACW74	2	CBW?
743	KING	Sgw 612	ACW74	2	
744	CBW	Sgw 593	ACW74	2	
745	CBW	Sgw 615			
746	CHEA	Sgw 1292			
748	CBW	Sgw 603			
749	KING	Sgw 608			
750		Sgw 2125			
751	KING	Sgw 2265			
752	CBW	Sgw 604			
753	KING	Sgw 609			
754	CBW	Sgw 594			
755	CBW	Sgw 619			
756	CBW	Sgw 602			
757	KING	Sgw 605			
758	KING	Sgw 616			
759	CBW	Sgw 2015			
760	KING	Sgw 1493			
761	KING	Sgw 1212			
762	CBW	Sgw 596			
763	KING	Sgw 601			
764	KING	Sgw 618			
766	KING	Sgw 614			
767	KING	Sgw 614			
797	KING				KINGSTON
798	KING				KINGSTON
799	KING				KINGSTON
800	KING				KINGSTON
801	KING				KINGSTON
1042	KING?	Sgw 123			
1292	CHEA?	ISgw 358			

131. Thin-sectioned Surrey whitewares in the Museum of London.

APPENDIX 6: QUANTIFIED DATA

The study of the Surrey whitewares from London has gone through several stages. At first only material stratified within the medieval revetment dumps at Trig Lane and Seal House was studied and a rough split into Kingston-type ware, Coarse Border ware and Cheam whiteware was made. The quantity of pottery by both eves and weight was recorded and the results used to construct an overall picture of London's medieval pottery from the 12th to the 15th centuries (see Pearce *et al* 1985, Fig. 7). Similar figures were later obtained for revetment dumps excavated at Billingsgate Lorry Park and Swan Lane (see Vince, 1985). These data confirm the overall pattern of the growth of the Surrey whiteware industry and the replacement of Kingston-type ware by, first, Coarse Border ware and, subsequently, Cheam whiteware during the 14th century. It was not possible to use them to study the progression of forms and decorative styles since, unlike London-type ware, it was not possible to identify many types of jug from rim sherds nor can the majority of body sherds be assigned correctly to a type.

The Kingston-type wares were then re-examined and a small number of sherds re-identified and re-recorded. A qualitative impression of the amount of jug sherds of each major type was obtained and has been used as the basis of the present work.

After studying material from the Knapp-Drewett kiln it was realised that there was a considerable amount of standardisation within the products of a kiln and subtle differences between the products of the Knapp-Drewett kiln and those from other groups of waste but that it would not be possible to demonstrate this without very large samples and much more detailed recording than was then being carried out in the Museum of London. Consequently, when the Coarse Border ware and Cheam whiteware from Trig Lane and Swan Lane was being re-examined measurements of rim and base diameters, rim and base eves,

handle types, spout types, base and body decoration were made. The total size of the assemblages was too small to make worthwhile conclusions but once the material from 'Baynards Castle dock (BC72)', and more recent excavations has been studied in the same way it should be possible to identify individual kiln products, or at least to split contemporary Surrey whitewares into sub-groups based on manufacturing and decorative methods.

The data described above is held on the Museum of London computer where it can be consulted. Further details of the data structure can also be found in the Museum of London archive. It has been used to produce two diagrams, which supercede previously published data concerning London's Surrey whitewares. Fig 132a shows the overall composition of the wares by form. With the exception of the very small sample of 'Tudor Green' ware, all the groups are dominated by jugs of various shapes and sizes but a clear difference can be seen between Coarse Border ware, where cooking pots and other kitchen wares from a sizeable element and Kingston-type and Cheam whitewares, where the only products other than jugs are a range of 'fine wares' of which dishes are the most important numerically. The diagram amalgamates material from a number of sites ranging in date from the mid-13th century to the mid-15th century. There were no noticeable trends visible when the data were analysed by site or period and it therefore seems that the overall output of the industries remained stable.

Fig 132b shows Surrey whitewares as a proportion of all pottery from selected deposits and differs from previously published data in showing that there is a small but definite amount of Coarse Border ware from *c.*1250 to *c.*1320 (mostly combed jugs and unglazed cooking pots) but confirms the sudden increase in the proportion of this ware in the mid-14th century.

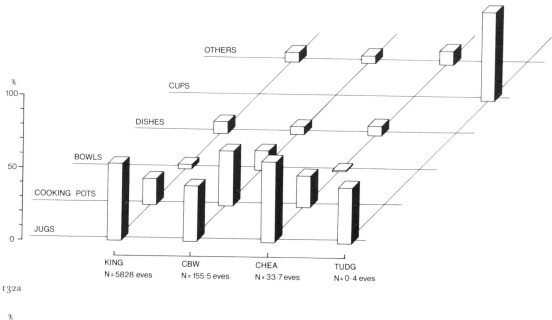

132a

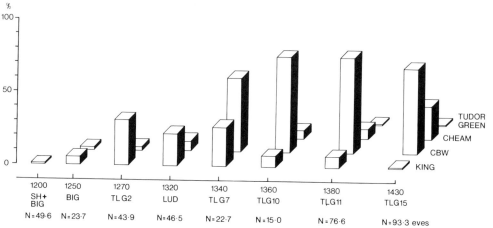

132b

132. *Quantified data. a) the overall composition of Surrey whitewares by form; b) the proportion of Surrey whitewares from selected excavated deposits.*

BIBLIOGRAPHY

Aspinall, R, 1977 Neutron activation of medieval ceramics, *Medieval Ceramics*, **1**, 5-16

Barton, K J, 1979 *Sussex medieval pottery*

Beckmann, B B, 1974 The main types of the first four production periods of Siegburg pottery, in *Medieval pottery from excavations: studies presented to Gerald Clough Dunning* (eds V I Evison, H Hodges & J G Hurst), 183-220

Biddle, M, Barfield, L, & Millard, A, 1959 Excavation of the Manor of the More, Rickmansworth, *Archaeol J*, **106**, 136-79

Brears, P C D, 1971 *The English country pottery, its history and techniques*

Celoria, F S C, & Thorn, J C, 1974 A medieval deposit from 244-246 Borough High Street, Southwark (TQ 3234-7967), *Trans London Middlesex Archaeol Soc*, **25**, 264-272

Cherry, J, 1985 Sex, magic and Dr. Gerald Dunning, *Medieval Ceramics*, **9**, 5-20

Cunnington, C W, & Cunnington, P, 1952 *Handbook of English medieval costume*

Dawson, G J, 1976 *The Black Prince's Palace at Kennington, Surrey*, Brit Archaeol Rep, **26**

Dennis, G, & Hinton, P, 1983 A medieval kiln group from Bankside, S.E.1., *London Archaeol*, **4**, 283-7

Drewett, P L, 1975 Excavations at Hadleigh Castle, Essex 1971-2, *J Brit Archaeol Assoc*, 3rd ser **38**, 90-154

Dunning, G C, 1958 Report on the medieval pottery from Joydens Wood, near Bexley, in Medieval buildings in the Joydens Wood square earthwork (P J Tester & J E L Caiger), *Archaeol Cantiana*, **72**, 31-39

——, 1961 A group of English and imported medieval pottery from Lesnes, Kent; and the trade in early Hispano-Moresque pottery to England, *Antiq J*, **41**, 1-2

——, 1975 Roof Fittings, in Platt & Coleman-Smith 1975, 186-197

——, 1976 Aardenburg ware from Manningtree, Essex and finds of Aardenburg ware and other pottery imported from the Low Countries found in England and Wales, *Essex Archaeol Hist*, **8**, 184-199

Dyson, T, unpubl *Ludgate Hill – historical survey*, Museum of London Documentary Survey

Eames, E S, 1980 *Catalogue of medieval lead-glazed earthenware tiles in the Department of Medieval and Later Antiquities, British Museum*

Guiseppi, M S, 1937 Medieval pottery in Kingston upon Thames, *Surrey Archaeol Collect*, **45**, 151-2

Hanworth, R, & Tomalin, D J, 1977 *Brooklands, Weybridge: the excavation of an iron age and medieval site 1964-5 and 1970-1*, Res Vol Surrey Archaeol Soc, **4**

Hinton, M, 1980 Medieval pottery from a kiln site at Kingston upon Thames, *London Archaeol*, **3**, 377-83

Holling, F W, 1971 A preliminary note on the pottery industry of the Surrey-Hampshire borders, *Surrey Archaeol Collect*, **68**, 57-88

——, 1977 Reflections on Tudor green, *Post-medieval Archaeol*, **11**, 61-6

Hurst, J G, 1961 The kitchen area of Northolt Manor, Middlesex, *Medieval Archaeol*, **5**, 211-299

Jenner, M A, & Vince, A G, 1983 A dated type-series of London medieval pottery, part 3: a late medieval Hertfordshire glazed ware, *Trans London Middlesex Archaeol Soc*, **34**, 151-70

Jope, E M, 1952 A medieval jug from Sutton, Surrey, *Surrey Archaeol Collect*, **52**, 83-5

——, 1953-4 Medieval pottery kilns at Brill, Bucks., *Records Bucks*, **16**, 39-42

Ketteringham, L L, 1976 *Alsted: excavation of a thirteenth-fourteenth-century sub-manor house with its ironworks in Netherne Wood, Merstham, Surrey*, Res Vol Surrey Archaeol Soc **2**

Leese, M N, Hughes, M J H, & Cherry, J, 1986 A scientific study of north Midlands tile production, *Oxford J Archaeol*, **5**, 355-70

Lewis, J M, 1978 *Medieval pottery and metal-ware in Wales* Nat Mus Wales guidebook.

Marshall, C J, 1924 A medieval pottery kiln discovered at Cheam, *Surrey Archaeol Collect*, **35**, 79-94

——, 1941 The sites of two more thirteenth-century pottery kilns at Cheam, *ibid*, **47**, 99-100

Matthews, L G, & Green, J M, 1969 Post-medieval pottery from the Inns of Court, *Post-medieval Archaeol*, **3**, 1-17

McCracken, S, Nenk, B, & Vince, A G, forthcoming The excavation of a late fourteenth-century pottery kiln at the Knapp-Drewett site, 22-34 Union Street, Kingston upon Thames, 1982

Milne, C, & Milne, G, 1982 *Medieval waterfront development at Trig Lane, London*, London Middlesex Archaeol Soc Special Paper, **5**

Moorhouse, S, 1979 Tudor green: some further thoughts, *Medieval Ceramics*, **3**, 53-61

Morgan, R, & Schofield, J, 1978 Tree-rings and the archaeology of the Thames waterfront in the City of London, in *Dendrochronology in Europe* (ed J Fletcher), British Archaeol Rep International Ser, **51**, 223-38

Musty, J, Algar, D J, & Ewence, P F, 1969 The medieval pottery kilns at Laverstock, near Salisbury, Wiltshire, *Archaeologia*, **102**, 83-150

Mynard, D C, 1973 Medieval pottery from Dartford, *Archaeol Cantiana*, **88**, 187-99

Myres, J N L, 1935 The medieval pottery at Bodiam Castle, *Sussex Archaeol Collect*, **76**, 222-30

Nelson, S, 1981 A group of pottery waster material from Kingston, *London Archaeol*, **4**, 96-102

Orton, C R, 1977 Medieval pottery, in Excavations at Angel Court, Walbrook 1974 (T Richard Blurton), *Trans London Middlesex Archaeol Soc*, **28**, 14-100

——, 1979 Medieval pottery from a kiln site at Cheam: part 1, *London Archaeol*, **3**, 300-4

——, 1982a Pottery evidence for the dating of the revetments, in Milne & Milne 1982, 92-9

——, 1982b The excavation of a late medieval/transitional pottery kiln at Cheam, Surrey, *Surrey Archaeol Collect*, **73**, 49-92

Orton, C R, & Pearce, J E, 1984 The pottery, in Excavations at Aldgate, 1974 (A Thompson, F Grew & J Schofield), *Post-Medieval Archaeol*, **18**, 34-68

Pearce, J E, 1984 Getting a handle on medieval pottery, *London Archaeol*, **5**, 17-23

Pearce, J E, Vince, A G, & White, R, with Cunningham, C M, 1982 A dated type-series of London medieval pottery part 1: Mill Green ware, *Trans London Middlesex Archaeol Soc*, **33**, 266-98

Pearce, J E, Vince, A G, & Jenner M A, 1985 *Medieval pottery London-type ware: a dated type-series of London medieval pottery part 2: London-type ware*, London Middlesex Archaeol Soc Special Paper, **6**

Platt, C, & Coleman-Smith, R, 1975 *Excavations in medieval Southampton 1953-1969, vol 2, the finds*

Platts, E, 1976 The pottery, in Excavations in the subvault of the misericorde of Westminster Abbey (G Black), *Trans London Middlesex Archaeol Soc*, **27**, 135-78

Rackham, B, 1972 *English medieval pottery*, rev ed by J G Hurst

Rahtz, P A, 1969 *Excavations at King John's Hunting Lodge, Writtle, Essex 1955-57*, Medieval Archaeol Monograph, **3**

Randall, L M C, 1966 *Images in the margins of Gothic manuscripts*

Redknap, M, 1983 The pottery, in The western defences of the inmost ward, Tower of London (G Parnell), *Trans London Middlesex Archaeol Soc*, **34**, 120-35

Richardson, B, 1983 Excavation round-up, 1982, part 2, *London Archaeol*, **4**, 288-291

Spencer, B, 1969 A face jug from the site of the Old Bailey, London, *Antiq J*, **49**, 388-90

Streeten, A D F, 1981 Craft and industry: medieval and later pottery in south-east England, in *Production*

and distribution: ceramic viewpoint (ed H Howard & E L Morris), British Archaeol Rep International Ser, **120**

——, 1982 Medieval ceramics in south-east England: a regional research strategy, *Medieval Ceramics*, **6**, 21-32

Thorn, J C, 1975 Medieval pottery, in Excavations at the Custom House site, City of London, 1973, part 2 (T Tatton-Brown), *Trans London Middlesex Archaeol Soc*, **26**, 118-151

——, 1978 Medieval and later pottery, in [Excavations at] 201-211 Borough High Street (E Ferretti & A H Graham), in *Southwark Excavations 1972-4* **1** (ed J Bird, A H Graham, H Sheldon & P Townend), London Middlesex Archaeol Soc/Surrey Archaeol Soc Joint Publ, **1**, 128-40

Thorn, J, & Thorn, D, 1972a Heraldic jug, *London Archaeol*, **2**, 23

——, 1972b Heraldic jugs of forgotten potters, *ibid*, **1**, 372-7

Turner, D J, 1967 Excavations near Merton Priory, 1962-63, *Surrey Archaeol Collect*, **64**, 35-70

——, 1974 A medieval pottery kiln at Bushfield Shaw, Earlswood: interim report, *ibid*, **70**, 47-55

——, 1975 Report on the medieval pottery, in Excavations in Reigate 1974 (H Woods), *ibid*, **70**, 88-94

——, 1977 A moated site near Moat Farm, Hookwood, Charlwood, *ibid*, **71**, 57-87

Vince, A G, 1977 The medieval and post-medieval ceramic industry of the Malvern region: the study of a ware and its distribution, in *Pottery and early commerce* (ed D P S Peacock), 257-305

——, 1983 The medieval ceramic industry of the Severn Valley, unpubl thesis, Southampton University

——, 1985 Saxon and medieval pottery in London: a review, *Medieval Archaeol*, **29**, 25-93

Vince, A G, & Jenner, M A, forthcoming *Aspects of Saxon and Norman London*, II: Finds and Environmental Evidence, London & Middlesex Archaeol. Soc. Special Paper

Ward Perkins, J B, 1940 *London Museum medieval catalogue*

Widemann, F, 1980 Neutron activation analysis for provenance studies, *J Radioanalytical Chemistry*, **55**, 271-81

Williams, D M, 1983 16 Bell Street, Reigate. Excavation of a medieval and post-medieval site 1974-6, *Surrey Archaeol Collect*, **74**, 47-89

Wishart, D, 1978 *Clustan user manual*, 3rd ed

——, 1982 *Clustan user manual*, supplement to 3rd ed

Youngs, S M, & Clark, J, 1982 Medieval Britain and Ireland in 1981, *Medieval Archaeol*, **26**, 164-227

Youngs, S M, Clark, J, & Barry, T B, 1983 Medieval Britain and Ireland in 1982, *Medieval Archaeol*, **27**, 161-229